WHAT IS TRUTH?

By the same Author:

The Concept of Reality
Change and Selves

What is Truth?

EDO PIVCEVIC
University of Bristol

Routledge
Taylor & Francis Group
LONDON AND NEW YORK

First published 1997 by Ashgate Publishing

Reissued 2018 by Routledge
2 Park Square, Milton Park, Abingdon, Oxon, OX14 4RN
52 Vanderbilt Avenue, New York, NY 10017

Routledge is an imprint of the Taylor & Francis Group, an informa business

A Library of Congress record exists under LC control number: 97071971

ISBN 13: 978-1-138-35904-8 (hbk)
ISBN 13: 978-1-138-35912-3 (pbk)
ISBN 13: 978-0-429-43390-0 (ebk)

Contents

Preface

This book grew out of the lectures I gave in China at the University of Baoding, Hebei, and Renmin University in Beijing during September/October 1991. I am grateful to Professors Bao Xun Wu and Liu Dachun for inviting me to their respective departments, and providing me with an opportunity of airing some of my ideas before a mixed and intensely alert and lively audience of students and professors, whose searching questions have helped me to knock many a hazy thought into shape. Subsequently I have presented papers on some of the topics dealt with in the book at a Philosophy Colloquium held at the College of the Holy Cross in Worcester, Mass. in October 1994, and at an international conference on the 'Nature of Truth' organised by the Institute of Philosophy of the Czech Academy of Sciences in Prague in September 1996.

Some of the key propositions that I shall be advancing derive their tortuous lineage from the arguments on truth presented in an earlier book (*The Concept of Reality*, 1986), but my discussion there was much too sketchy and inadequate, and it is hoped that the present treatise provides a more precise and cogent as well as more detailed working out of the approach adumbrated in that earlier work.

I wish to thank the colleagues and friends who have read various portions of the text and have given me the benefit of their views. I am particularly grateful to Peter Strawson for his comments on an earlier version of chapter 2, even though our views on the desirability of a 'strategy of austerity' remain far apart. I have also greatly profited from the comments on this and other matters dealt with in the book by John

Cleave, Stephan Körner, Ross Harrison, John Mayberry, Jacques Bouveresse and John Shand. Last but not least, I wish to thank my pupils at Bristol, whose unflagging interest has sustained me in my work and from whom, as always, I have learned more than any book could teach me.

Department of Philosophy
University of Bristol

Edo Pivcevic

Outline of argument

The nature of truth, in so far as truth has a 'nature', lies in the manner of its occurrence. This is the view that I shall be advancing: that truth is an event, i.e. it does not exist until it occurs, and survives only as long as the requisite conditions for its occurrence are in place.

In ordinary discourse we use 'true' and 'false' in a way that seems to suggest that truth is a kind of property. But what kind of property it is, and under what conditions it can be significantly ascribed to what items, are open to dispute. In what way, for example, does the possession of the property of truth modify its bearer? And in particular: If x is a bearer of truth, what *makes* x true? It is questions such as these that have animated traditional arguments about truth, and the answers given range from a) if x is true, it must 'correspond with the facts', b) it must fit into the jigsaw of similar mutually supporting items which together form a coherent system, c) it must be conducive to a successful action; and so on.

Then there is another view, which has gained prevalence in recent times and according to which truth does not represent a 'genuine' property at all. To call a proposition 'true', it is maintained, is not like calling an apple 'red'. The word 'true' does not add anything to the *content* of the proposition thus qualified. There are natural and logical properties, and if truth can be classified as a property at all, then it belongs in the latter category, i.e. it is a *meta*linguistic property whose sole function is to highlight what a specific item of language is ordinarily meant to convey, viz. that things are such and such. Even 'non-predicative' expressions such as 'It is true that . . .', in the final analysis, are employed merely for 'emphasis or for stylistic reasons', and do not add to the content of the proposition in question one whit. But if so, then there is nothing much that can — or need — be said about truth. There is no 'problem of truth'; or, more accurately, there is no problem of the *meaning* of truth. Truth is a logically simple notion, which does not lend itself to an explicit definition. There is only a problem of the criteria under which in given circumstances it is appropriate to regard something as true, and such criteria in the nature of things can only be specified in pragmatic terms.

The view that I shall be advancing deviates sharply from both these types of approach. To begin with, it is necessary to draw a distinction between the concept of truth and ascriptions of truth predicates. In a broad sense, every predication is a form of property ascription, and this applies equally to the use of 'true'; nevertheless it does not necessarily follow that because 'true' is used predicatively truth must be a kind of property that typically requires, and 'inheres in', a bearer, although it is easy enough to be misled into drawing such an inference. Language here sets traps for the unwary. In so far as calling an x — a proposition, or belief, say — 'true' involves a property ascription, then it does so, I shall argue, only in this sense: that such an x *enters into* truth; that it is *part* of a 'truth event'.

The predicate 'true', that is, flags out a claim as to the *occurrence* of truth; and the same applies to phrases such as 'It is true that . . .'. However, to provide an explanation of what is involved in such an occurrence is a complex and arduous task. Truth is not, as the second approach above implies, so simple and transparent a concept that it does not require any underpinning explanatory 'theory'. On the contrary, it is a fascicular notion consisting of several inter-braiding strands, and in order to highlight its inner fabric it is necessary to begin by asking not 'What *makes* x true?' but rather 'How does truth come into being', or, more clearly, 'What conditions must be fulfilled for such a phenomenon to come into existence?' This means that we shall have to focus primarily on acts of assertion, or *truth claims* (which, incidentally, may or may not involve the use of truth predicates) and explore their structure.

For truth claims, I shall argue, are essential to truth, even though they, alone, cannot guarantee its occurrence. There can be no truth in abstraction, or independently of the possibility of any truth claims.

However, once we focus on truth claims (which are 'intentional acts') the immediate task that confronts us is one of clarifying the relationship between the *meaning content* of such claims and the relevant *states of affairs*. The reason for this is self-evident: if, as is normally accepted, the same state of affairs can be targeted via different contents, then the inevitable question is, exactly which aspects of the content are *truth-relevant*?

A great deal hinges on this question. One possibility is to approach it from a 'reductionist' point of view, and argue that the differences in meaning, such as they are, ultimately do not matter, provided the asserted propositions are *extensionally isomorphic*. Thus if two propositions convey the same state of affairs, they will always be both true if either of them is, no matter how different they happen to be; and if so, it might be argued, then surely they can to all intents and purposes be treated as expressing the *same* truth.

Yet this clearly is unsatisfactory. It is one thing to say that 'Jones is a teetotaller' and quite another that 'The philosopher with a squint does not drink alcohol' even if Jones does happens to be the philosopher with a squint who is being talked about. Similarly the semantic differences between 'Socrates loves Alcibiades' and 'Alcibiades is loved by Socrates' may be contextually significant, even though the same extralinguistic state of affairs seems to underlie both reports. And of course we all know that a bottle can be 'half full' as well as 'half empty'. Such differences indicate how things appear to the *judging subject*, and the manner of their appearance is a constitutive part of what is claimed to be the case. How, then, can they be irrelevant to truth?

But if they are *not* irrelevant, then certain important consequences follow. Thus truth can no longer be said to consist in the 'mapping' of, or the 'correspondence' with, certain extralinguistic states of affairs. A truth claim plainly presupposes the existence of an extrapropositional world, and hence involves a tacit acceptance of a form of realism. But truth does not hold a mirror to such a world. The claim that the sun rises in the East addresses itself to an extralinguistic state of affairs, but it is true only in virtue of the manner in which such a state of affairs is refracted in an observer's perception.

In short, there are no facts existing 'in themselves'. Things are such and such only from a specific point of view, viz. such as is evinced by the meaning content of a truth claim. But, then, clearly if the meaning content changes, truth can hardly fail to follow suit. In other words, if two truth claims differ in meaning, they will *not express the same truth, even if they happen to be extensionally isomorphic.*

This is a natural corollary of a rejection of the 'reductionist' approach, and it has considerable implications. Expressed in terms of belief, it can be phrased in the following way. Truth does not exist independently of whether something is held or believed to be true. Unless certain beliefs are entertained by someone, truth cannot come into being. Moreover, if two different beliefs should turn out to be extensionally isomorphic, i.e. target the same state of affairs, it does not follow that they 'express' the same truth. Truth takes on the colour of belief in all its nuances. At the same time, truth is not a 'property' of belief, or constellation of beliefs. Without an act of believing or holding things to be such and such truth cannot come about, but the 'correctness' of a belief presupposes, does not explain, the occurrence of truth. Nor is truth a property that attaches to propositions as potential objects of belief. Rather a proposition *enters* into truth together with the relevant act of belief under certain conditions of appropriateness and coherence, which confer upon it a degree of objectivity. The criteria of appropriateness and coherence, however, can only be defined with respect to certain institutionalised standards within the relevant socio-historical context.

The key to what truth 'means', then, lies in the way truth comes about. Truth is not an entity or a property, including a relational property, of anything. Nor is it some sort of atemporal state, or set of states, conveyed by propositions suitably cleansed of tense and other indexical features. Rather it resides in the peculiar pattern in which it occurs within a concrete historical context. It is a complex event, and a fragile thing. It survives only as long as there are minds who entertain certain beliefs under given objectivity conditions, and without all of its constituent elements present it just ceases to be.

1 The problem of truth, or how does thought hook onto the world?

To make a truth claim, either by asserting a proposition or indirectly by characterising a proposition as 'true', is to say that things are as they are said to be. It is to signal or affirm that a certain situation or constellation of circumstances obtains in reality. This surely is as plain as day — what more might there be to add? Yet on closer inspection this produces more bafflement than light, and in particular it does nothing to explain why the concept of truth has such a powerful hold on our imagination.

What we need to know is not just that an assertion, if true, conveys what obtains in actual fact. This comes uncomfortably close to trading synonyms for synonyms. For how do we explain what facts are except by saying that certain propositions are true? We need to know just what such conveying involves and under what conditions it is effected, or can be effected. Without an account of such conditions to give substance to our claims, the search for truth reduces to a mere groping in the void.

Consider what it is to explain a concept. To explain a concept is to set out how that concept may be legitimately applied, and in so doing circumscribe its extension; it is to specify the criteria for sorting out the items that fall under it from those that fall outside it. It follows that part of an explanation of truth will have to be an account of the conditions under which a proposition might legitimately qualify as true. Not all truth claims can be validly made. Sometimes what is said or written will fail as a vehicle for conveying facts as a matter of principle on account of some semantic incongruities or bad syntax. The random anagrammatic sequence 'Book in sentence this false is every' does not add up to an English sentence, whereas its unscrambled version 'Every sentence in this book is false', though syntactically impeccable, fails a consistency test: if it is true, then it is false. It has no unequivocally specifiable content, and by definition cannot qualify as a truth candidate.

Again, in other cases what looks like a semantically as well as syntactically sound declarative sentence will produce an inconsistency merely by virtue of being asserted. Thus I cannot assert 'I am not now uttering a sound' without contradicting, by my act of utterance, what I claim to be the case. Nevertheless the sentence itself is both syntactically and semantically unimpeachable, and if it were to be written down by me rather than uttered, or if it should be transposed into a third person idiom and asserted by any old onlooker, that would cause no difficulty, and might well be true.

Nor is this a rare occurrence. It is well known that the thought a sentence carries, or what is sometimes called its 'propositional content', can fluctuate and change depending upon the circumstances of utterance; with verbally and syntactically identical sentences, as a result, transmitting different messages. Conversely, it is sometimes possible deliberately to alter the sentence, and moreover alter it extensively in respect both of meaning and syntax, without thereby necessarily altering the state of affairs conveyed in the given instance. But if so, then the inevitable question is, exactly what elements or aspects of the meaning content have a bearing upon the truth or falsity of what is said? And above all, what factors are instrumental in determining such a content?

Truth-relevant content and *extensional isomorphism*

At first glance, the answer to this may not seem difficult. The clue, surely, lies in the *extensional* properties of what is said or claimed to be true. After all, we all have a good intuitive grasp of what it is for two different declarative sentences to carry the same factual freight; for example, when two non-synonymous but co-referential singular expressions, i.e. expressions sharing the same designation, are substituted for each other; or, perhaps, when a general term appearing in a subject position in a general proposition is replaced with another of the same extension. Thus if 'The Morning Star' designates the same object as 'The Evening Star', then the *truth-relevant* content of 'The Morning Star moves around the sun' and 'The Evening Star moves around the sun' is surely the same. And so is that of 'Whales are not fish' and 'The largest marine animals are not fish'. There is nothing arcane or startling about that. It is common practice to make use of different but contextually co-extensive expressions, either in order to help the message on its way, or deliberately to highlight things from a different angle, or simply to avoid repetition or relieve tedium. If I *fly* to Boston, I go there *by aeroplane*. These are not synonyms. Nevertheless contextually they amount to a description of the same event. What matters in such and similar cases is that the contextual isomorphism of the terms used ensures that the two sentences, for all their differences, are both true if either of them is. Provided the extensional properties of their terms do not change, their truth-relevant content will remain the same.[1]

Yet how do we decide that two sentences are 'extensionally isomorphic' in the sense just described — i.e. convey the same state of affairs — except by considering their respective meaning contents? It is only through their meaning that we can access their 'extensional properties'. But if it is necessary first to sort out those aspects of the meaning content which account for their extensional isomorphism, then how can we appeal to their extensional isomorphism in order to account for their joint truth-relevant content? Surely a different approach is required if we are to keep well clear of any vicious circularity. In point of fact, I shall argue that whilst it is possible for non-synonymous sentences to target, and convey, the same state of affairs, conveying the same state of affairs is not the same as expressing literally the same *truth*. Truth, as we shall see, is a much more complex phenomenon than that. It follows that any radically 'reductionist' treatment of truth-relevant content will have to be rejected as inappropriate. The reductionist policy is propelled by the belief that *only some*, not all features of the content are relevant to a consideration of truth or falsity. Sentences, it is argued, may differ in meaning as well as

[1] What I here call 'extensional isomorphism' should not be confused with other forms of extensional equivalence. There is a sense of equivalence in which every true sentence 'materially' implies, and is implied by, any other true sentence. Again it is possible for two non-synonymous sentences to be 'extensionally equivalent' such that if either of them is true, then *necessarily* both are, without being isomorphic in the above sense, and hence *without* carrying the same truth-relevant content. But I am not concerned with such cases here.

'surface' syntax while nevertheless sharing the same *truth-relevant core*, and this common core, which represents their 'propositional substance' — or quite simply the relevant *proposition* — can be isolated from the surrounding frippery and rendered explicit by a suitable method of logical paraphrase. There is always a quantity of meaning which can safely be axed without altering the substance of the message, or detracting from its truth.

But the problem is that we need a criterion for deciding which aspects of the content are essential, and which are not essential, and can therefore be safely left to one side; and any such criterion is likely to be susceptible to critical challenge. Above all, before we can begin a process of selective pruning we need to understand the meaning of a sentence in its entirety. Nothing can be dismissed a priori as irrelevant. But if the meaning in its entirety is thus instrumental in determining the truth-relevant content, then that is what the truth-relevant content *is*. And if that is the case, i.e. if the truth-relevant content embraces all the aspects of the meaning content (of that which can be self-consistently uttered, at any rate), then how can it be justifiably claimed that two non-synonymous sentences, even if they do happen to convey the 'same' state of affairs, have exactly the same *truth-conditions*? And if they don't have the same truth-conditions, how can they 'express' the same truth?

Access to truth-relevant content via predicates and variables of quantification

These questions cannot be shirked. Nevertheless the temptation to adopt a 'reductionist' approach with regard to the truth-relevant content remains strong and persistent, for obvious reasons. It has to do with the natural desire to eliminate any fuzziness or ambiguity from truth claims, and make their content precise. We saw that such claims cannot always be taken at their face value; that they sometimes carry a different message to what appears on the surface, or are simply muddled. It might seem, therefore, that the best — perhaps the only — way to bring out with sufficient clarity what truth-relevant content they may carry in a given instance is to transpose what is said into a more rigorous albeit more austere language of *predicates and variables*; and, having accomplished this task, carry the whole process a step further, perhaps, by undertaking a thoroughgoing analysis of predicates and their logical relationships in the light of their extensional properties.

In order to illustrate what is at stake here, consider sentences about fictional entities. What, for example, might be the *truth-relevant* content of 'The philosophers' stone is brittle'? As it stands, the sentence cannot significantly be characterised as either true or false, for the philosophers' stone does *not* exist. Should we then say that the sentence in reality does *not* have a truth-relevant content? This seems much too extreme, for the sentence, on the face of it at least, is semantically sound as well as syntactically well formed. Perhaps all that is needed is to spell out more clearly its underlying essentials. It might accordingly be felt that the appropriate way to proceed is to rephrase the whole sentence into an existentially quantified form, signalling in a general way that the relevant predicate (or concept) does indeed apply to something, or that there is something answering the given description. The idea, in short, is to show that the sentence at root says something about a *predicate*, not about any specific entity. On this interpretation, our example above will unfold into: *There is something which uniquely has the properties of the philosophers' stone, and is brittle*; in which form it evidently can be asserted or denied without any problems. That, at any rate, is how things seemed to Russell.[2]

This method of paraphrase, as I have already indicated, can be applied, and indeed has on occasion been applied, universally, with far-reaching implications. Thus some philosophers (e.g. W.V. Quine) have taken the view, in effect, that *all* significant assertions without exception can be expressed in terms of predicates and variables along these lines. Moreover the tendency often has been to use this kind of logical manipulation, designed with the explicit purpose of highlighting the truth-relevant content and making it precise, as a starting-off point for some sweeping reductionist epistemological operations on predicates, by subjecting them to rigorous phenomenalist or physicalist tests.

But just how necessary, one might wonder, is it to go to such lengths in order to extract the truth-relevant content from any old significant sentence, and ensure that it can be asserted free from any ambiguity?

[2] Russell, incidentally, defined the uniqueness condition along the lines of Leibniz's *principle of indiscernibles*, viz. by stipulating that two entities are numerically indistinguishable if they have the same predicates. See chapter 4.

One — the most familiar — objection to the above method of logical paraphrase comes from Russell's critics, like P.F. Strawson, who claim that the attempt to make all significant sentences without exception accessible to truth value in the way described suggests a confusion of existential *presuppositions* with existential *assertions*. Thus, to take our example again, 'The philosophers' stone is brittle' *presupposes* rather than asserts the existence of the relevant entity, and since the presupposition is incorrect, the question of truth or falsity does not arise. Given that the vital existential prerequisite is not fulfilled, the sentence is automatically disqualified as a legitimate vehicle of a truth claim. At the same time, this manifestly does not render the sentence meaningless. The sentence, as it stands, may fail to satisfy the conditions of 'assertibility', but it does not cease to be intelligible on that account. And this, it is argued, only goes to prove that if a sentence makes good sense, this has nothing to do with its capability, or otherwise, of having a truth value; rather the sources of its meaningfulness should be sought elsewhere — more specifically, in the customs and practices that govern our use of language.

What is more, the problem of 'assertibility', it is pointed out, is not confined solely to sentences about fictional entities. There are countless other sentences which cannot legitimately be asserted or denied, although they are not only syntactically and semantically sound but target actually existing entities; the simple reason being that certain other vital truth conditions are not fulfilled. Thus given that Kant never wrote poetry, the sentence to the effect that he was a dismal poet clearly cannot be appropriately asserted. At the same time, any attempt to make such a sentence accessible to truth value by translating it into an existentially quantified sentence, saying that there was 'someone or other' answering Kant's description who wrote bad verse, in accordance with the method of paraphrase suggested by Russell[3], is surely absurd, for the sentence is intrinsically *singular*, not existential.

The substance of the above criticism of the reductionist paraphrase in terms of predicates and variables à la Russell is thus: a) that a declarative sentence may have a meaning without necessarily satisfying the conditions needed for it to have a truth-value; and b) that in such a case the sentence cannot properly be said to possess the kind of truth-

[3] Although Russell himself reserved his method of paraphrase only for 'definite descriptions', some of his followers (e.g. Quine) had no qualms applying it to names as well.

relevant content conveyed by the paraphrase in question (which, therefore, becomes superfluous). In short, the question of meaningfulness of declarative sentences and the question of their truth-value are not necessarily linked, and have to be treated separately. A declarative sentence may have a meaning without qualifying for truth value, and it is only those that do so qualify that can legitimately be asserted.

Conditions of assertibility

But plausible though this solution may seem at first sight, it creates serious problems of its own. What is suggested, basically, is that the subject 'talked about' in the given instance must exist, and in some cases, moreover, has to have certain specified attributes (such as Kant writing poetry, in our example above), before the relevant truth claim, or claims, can validly be made. But does this mean that we should suspend our truth claims until we are quite sure that the required truth conditions are satisfied? On the above view, a decision as to whether a given truth claim should be allowed to stand or be dismissed as invalid presupposes an *agreed ontology*. More than that: there must be an agreed decision procedure, enabling us to establish whether such conditions are fulfilled in the given case. But there might be no such agreement. It is conceivable that — with the exception, possibly, of some simple sentences such as e.g. 'It is cold here', or some first person statements — we may never be in a position to know with certainty if the required assertibility conditions are fulfilled. And if so, how then are we to decide what can and what cannot be appropriately claimed to be *true*?

In a sense, it was this very difficulty that the 'predicates and variables' theory referred to earlier was, in part at least, designed to meet. Its underlying motive was to pre-empt any disagreements over which significant sentences can, and which cannot, appropriately be asserted, or said to be true or false, by suggesting a way of paraphrasing their truth-relevant content in such a way that they *automatically* become accessible to truth value. There was thus no need to wait for an agreement as to whether the entity, or entities, 'talked about' in a given instance did actually exist. The paraphrase in terms of predicates and (bound) variables guaranteed instant assertibility. This greatly simplified things, and moreover offered palpable advantages in terms of enhanced clarity and precision. But — as always — there was a price to pay. For such a paraphrase inevitably entailed a loss of certain important features of sentential meaning. Indeed the more assiduously such a paraphrase was pursued the more its reductionist consequences became apparent. Thus it entailed dispensing not only with singular expressions (such as 'The philosophers' stone'), but also with proper names, personal pronouns, indeed with most 'indexical' expressions, which pervade ordinary speech in such glorious profusion, and which, I shall argue, so far from simply adding charm and episodic colour to our utterances represent important constituent elements of their *truth-relevant content*.

There is, however, a third option, which avoids such undesirable consequences, without at the same time tying us in advance to any specific choice of entities. This is to accept that sentences like 'The philosophers' stone is brittle' and 'Kant was a dismal poet' *can* act as vehicles of genuine truth claims, although not (as Russell would have it) because they reduce to existentially quantified sentences whereby a property is attributed to certain predicates or concepts (viz. that such predicates apply to something, or that the concepts in question are not empty), but because they may be taken as saying that an irreducibly unique individual with certain attributes is part of the actual world. If anything is 'presupposed', then, it is the existence of a world as a totality of what is the case. The problem of assertibility can thus be solved without engaging in doubtful reductionist manoeuvres to which the 'predicates and variables' theory seems to be irrevocably committed, and, at the same time, without waiting for an agreement about ontology.

On this view, 'The philosophers' stone is brittle' effectively unfolds into: 'The philosophers' stone is part of the actual world, and is brittle'. Similarly the sentence 'Kant was a dismal poet' spells out as: 'The world contained the individual *Kant* who wrote bad verse'. The underlying assumption, that is, is that there is a world in which such states of affairs are *embedded*. This interpretation may seem strange at first sight, but it isn't really. We don't make assertions about things in a vacuum. Rather it is part of what a truth claim means that there is a world in which we ourselves and everything else have a place. This is the 'neighbourhood' where things are to be found, where they are identified as being such and such, and are 'present' or 'missing', just as furniture is 'present' or 'missing' within a room or house.

Notice, by the way, that the above interpretation allows us to preserve all the aspects of meaning of the relevant sentences. Indeed the main difference between this way of dealing with sentences which appear to lack the relevant truth conditions, and the method of existentially quantified paraphrase advocated by Russell, is that here no paraphrase is involved or required in terms of 'predicates and variables'. The idea is simply that in seriously asserting a sentence (not just 'declaiming' it from a stage) one is de facto saying that the actual world has the *specified feature*; no more and no less. This method thus not only makes room for a broader concept of truth-relevant content but it allows of a vast variety of sentences to act as vehicles of meaningful truth claims — even though what is claimed in a given instance may turn out to be an error. (See chapter 8.)

These, then, are some of the issues before us, and it is clear that they demand a substantive account of the *conditions of truth*. To say that a truth claim conveys or expresses a fact is to say nothing much unless an explanation is given of how such conveying or expressing does or can take place. What we have to ask ourselves, is: If there is a phenomenon such as truth, how does such a phenomenon come into being, and what is the manner of its occurrence? What are the minimal conditions that must be satisfied, and what conditions are sufficient? What role do truth claims play in relation to truth, and what kind of utterances, and under what conditions, qualify as valid instruments of such claims? The intuitive notion that we have of truth as consisting in things being as it is said or thought they are, does not help to throw light on any of these questions, and yet they are all relevant and have to be addressed if justice is to be done to the complexity of the task in hand. In order to clarify the concept of truth, it is necessary to investigate the conditions under which truth comes into existence, or, expressed differently, the conditions under which thought hooks onto the world.

Thought and language

What I here mean by 'thought', as ought to be obvious by now, is the *propositional* thought as expressed in an indicative sentence.

Nevertheless thoughts are not the same as sentences, and thinking is not, as some philosophers have suggested, a kind of silent speaking, even though the process of thinking in a given instance may involve a 'silent' use of varying amounts of publicly available lexical material in grammatically recognisable sequences.

Let us pause and consider this for a moment. We generally take it for granted that the same thought, or rather the same type of thought, can in principle be expressed in different sentences any number of times in any number of different languages, and hence that there is no strict one-to-one correspondence between thinking and public speaking. There are no logical as distinct from sheer physical limits to the number of different linguistic skills that one might acquire, or to the variety of techniques and symbolisms that one might invent to express and transmit one's thoughts. What is more — as those in particular who have laboriously tried to teach themselves a foreign language know full well — the process of thought, in so far as it involves a 'silent' use of words or sequences of words, may on occasion include borrowings from a variety of linguistic sources, often in highly irregular and idiosyncratic syntactical combinations. Such lexical props can be very useful, especially as mnemonic devices, but they are no more than that, and their choice is often purely arbitrary or just fortuitous. Whilst it is demonstrably true that the acquisition of a linguistic skill plays a vitally important role in the development of thought, it does not follow that the process of thinking is necessarily analogous to the use of words, let alone that it must obey the syntax of a specific public (or potentially public) language.

Nevertheless if thought is to be successfully transmitted in a public medium, there must exist a certain isomorphism between what is thought and what is expressed. This isomorphism can be traced to certain logical structures which remain unchanged despite the variations of surface syntax. That, at any rate, is the stock-in-trade supposition of any logical analysis of language. But while some logicians have been content to study the morphology of the logical syntax supposedly shared by all languages whose expressive power generally equals our own, others have gone considerably beyond this, arguing that there exists, in addition, an internal and wholly inborn *language of thought*, with rules entirely of its own, and a stock of elementary concepts in terms of which all other concepts can be specified. The thesis put forward, in short, is that there exists a self-contained internal code whose expressive power not only matches that of any given public language, however complex or rich such languages might be, but what is more represents an indispensable instrument through which public linguistic skills are acquired in the first place. Thinking, it turns out, is a kind of silent speaking after all, even though it isn't strictly comparable to speaking in any specific 'public' language.

Fanciful as this idea might seem, it nevertheless has a respectable metaphysical ancestry, and can in fact be traced to the difficulties — which notably exercised Plato, among others — of accounting for the possibility of *learning*, or acquisition of new knowledge (including linguistic knowledge). For how is it possible, Plato wondered, to acquire new knowledge without possessing the resources that enable one to decode and understand new information in terms of what one knows *already*? His own answer to this is well known. All acquisition of genuine knowledge, he claimed, was merely a form of remembering of that which the soul in its pre-embodied existence had known with undimmed clarity all along, but which had become blurred, or had fallen into oblivion, as a result of the soul's entry into the 'shadowy' world of appearance.

The rationalist epistemology and metaphysics have traditionally followed Plato in emphasising the innate roots of knowledge, whilst at the same time largely rejecting what Leibniz called the Platonist 'error of pre-existence'. Leibniz's own position on this is of special interest, and is best summed up in his own words. 'We have in our mind' — he writes — 'all forms, and, indeed, we have them from all time; for the mind always expresses all its future thoughts and already thinks confusedly of all that it will ever think distinctly. We could never be informed of anything whose idea we do not already have in the mind — an idea which is like the matter from which this thought forms itself. Plato had an excellent appreciation of this when he put forward his theory of "reminiscence", a theory which has much solidity provided that one takes it in the right way, that one rids it of the error of pre-existence, and does not imagine that the soul must at some previous time have known and thought distinctly what it learns and thinks now.'[4]

---

[4] See: 'Discourse on Metaphysics'; in '*Leibniz: Philosophical Writings*', ed. G.H.R. Parkinson, 1988, pp. 35-6.

In other words, the innate knowledge is inscribed in our mind in an inchoate form, and it only gradually evolves to full clarity and distinctness. Nevertheless all the basic seeds of what we know, or are ever likely to know, are already there from the beginning.

The more recent arguments specifically relating to the problem of language acquisition owe a great deal to the innateness hypothesis as outlined and argued for by Leibniz. The basic idea put forward is that it is strictly impossible to learn a language which is richer and generally more powerful than the language (or languages) with which one is already familiar, since one needs to have prior resources sufficient to define the truth conditions involved in the application of the concepts which one is in the process of acquiring. In order to be able to understand what one is trying to learn, it is necessary that one's own language (i.e. the language used in the process of learning) and the language that one is trying to acquire should be evenly matched in terms of their expressiveness and logical range. From this general premise the conclusion is derived that if learning is to be possible at all, there must exist a sufficiently rich *internal* code which one knows — in a sense of 'know' which is left deliberately vague; Leibniz would say 'confusedly knows' — *without*, and *prior* to learning, and which represents the primitive 'language of thought'.[5]

The difficulty, however, is that such an 'internal' code, if it exists, almost by definition cannot be clearly specified. In order to articulate its rules and vocabulary we would have to make use of the resources of a given *public* language, and yet it is the possibility of acquisition of just such a public language that the internal code in question is supposed to help explain. But even assuming it were possible to specify such an internal code with sufficient precision, there is no conceivable way in which it might be proved that any process of thinking whatever would have to conform to its rules. Indeed an attempt to provide such a proof would only lead to an infinite regress. And without such a proof, and especially in the absence of any clear specification of the rules and the vocabulary, any hypothesis concerning the existence of such an innate language must remain vacuous. Fortunately in the context of our present discussion there is no need to concern ourselves with such ideas in any further detail.

[5] See Jerry A. Fodor: *The Language of Thought*, 1975; especially chapter 2. Also his *The Modularity of Mind*, 1983.

Truth and the modes of presentation

Let us now return to the question of truth-relevant content. As I indicated earlier, an 'extensionalist' interpretation of the content causes severe problems, sensible though such an interpretation might appear at first sight. Thus the first reaction when confronted with the pair of propositions 'The Morning Star moves around the sun' and 'The Evening Star moves around the sun' is to say that surely they must have the same truth-relevant content because they are 'extensionally isomorphic'. If 'The Evening Star' and 'The Morning Star' designate the same entity, then the relevant truth claims are necessarily both true if either of them is. Unfortunately this overlooks the centrality of the 'mode of presentation' in establishing the truth-value of either.[6] The Evening Star, after all, is the star that comes on brightest in the early evening sky, whereas the Morning Star shines brightest in the morning. The conditions, therefore, which determine the truth or falsity of the two claims cannot be the same; and if so, how can their truth-relevant content be the same?

Now conceivably at this point one might resort to the familiar method of 'predicates and variables', and try to articulate the supposedly joint truth-relevant content of the two claims by paraphrasing the propositions concerned, thus: 'Something has the property of shining brightest in the evening sky and whatever shines brightest in the evening sky also shines brightest in the morning sky, and there is no more than one such entity; and that entity moves around the sun.' But it would be foolish to pretend that this settles the issue. To begin with, there are obvious logical difficulties involved in individuating an entity in terms of its predicates (or properties). The point is that whilst the possession of a specific predicate, or a set of predicates, may very well make the relevant entity unique as a matter of fact, it does not do so

[6] The term 'mode of presentation' is intended here to be evocative of what Frege called *Die Art des Gegebenseins*, although I should emphasise that I propose to use this term in a more embracing sense, to include whole sentences as well as singular terms. I might also add the following qualification. Frege, as is well known, distinguished between an objective and a subjective aspect of the mode of presentation, i.e. between the 'objective sense' of what is actually uttered and the 'associated ideas' which might accompany the utterance, and are peculiar to the individual language user. But the distinction objective/subjective should not blind us to the fact that the 'mode of presentation' in any of its aspects is an expression of a *point of view* — either individual, or collective and institutionalised in various degrees — and is therefore *intentional* in origin. See chapters 3 and 4.

necessarily. However unlikely, it is not logically impossible that there should be duplicate entities and duplicate worlds, all of which are qualitatively indistinguishable from each other; and consequently that no description in terms of predicates, however exhaustive, would mark out unequivocally a single target. But if, therefore, a unique reference is not necessarily assured, then a paraphrase in terms of predicates cannot do full justice to what either of the singular propositions above is intended to convey.

Secondly, it should be borne in mind that the two truth claims concerned each involve a different act of reference, and that the supposition underlying the above paraphrase, viz. that the entity talked about in the two cases is numerically the same is a *separate hypothesis*, which so far from being explicable in terms of predicates, defines the condition under which attributions of different predicates to the same entity might take place. It is always possible that 'The Morning Star moves around the sun' and 'The Evening Star moves around the sun' could be true or false independently of each other. That they are not does not mean that their truth-relevant content must literally be the same. The assumption that it is demands that they both be paraphrased in such a way that their semantic differences be set aside as far as truth is concerned. But this, as we have seen, is not a defensible option.

In short, the truth-relevant content, so far from reducing to certain 'extensional' features of truth claims, comprises the semantic load of the sentences featuring in such claims in its entirety. The extensional properties, after all, can be accessed only via specific 'modes of presentation'. But quite apart from this, it surely is nonsensical to suppose that sentences which happen to be 'extensionally isomorphic' (in the sense in which I have been using the term) but differ as to meaning all 'hook' onto the world in the same manner, and hence have identical truth conditions. They express different beliefs, and in so far as they reveal a fragment of reality, they do so through the *totality of what they express*.

If this is granted, however, then it follows that the concept of truth requires a much broader approach than is sometimes thought necessary, or appropriate. In particular, truth does not consist literally in the 'correspondence with', or the 'mapping' of, certain extra-linguistic states of affairs. Unquestionably a truth claim as an intentional act presupposes the existence of an extralinguistic reality, and hence involves a tacit acceptance of a form of realism. But it does not follow from this that truth consists simply in the existence of the 'targeted' extra-linguistic states of affairs, or in the 'mapping' of a reality external to thought. Different, non-synonymous truth claims can convey the same extralinguistic state of affairs, most certainly; but if they do, they do so from different points of view, and hence do not literally 'express' the same truth. Rather, I shall argue, they form part of different truth events.

The complexity of truth

This, briefly, is the view which will be defended: that truth is not separable from the *acts* of thinking or believing something to be true.[7] Truth is an event of which the propositional contents of truth claims and the relevant states of affairs form two distinct constituent features — with 'propositional content' to be taken here in the widest sense, viz. as encompassing the 'mode of presentation' in its entirety. Moreover if the mode of presentation changes, even if the state of affairs conveyed does not, truth will change too. In addition, a truth claim has to comply with certain criteria of coherence and appropriateness, which confer upon it a degree of objectivity, and which can only be defined with respect to certain institutionalised standards within the relevant socio-historical context.

Truth, then, so far from being atemporal inhabits the historical time. It comes into being when a given state of affairs, under certain conditions of objectivity, presents itself to a judging agent in such and such a manner, and no sooner. Only when all these conditions are fulfilled does truth emerge into existence. It *literally* is not there until it occurs, and it survives only as long as such conditions are in place.[8]

It follows that truth has a complex structure, and that its analytical account, accordingly, will have to be complex. No simple formula can

[7] In *Grundgesetze der Arithmetik* Frege makes much of the distinction between *Wahrheit* (truth) and *Fürwahrhalten* (holding something to be true), arguing that the latter has nothing to do with truth properly so called, but it is part of my thesis that in abstraction from *Fürwahrhalten* truth ceases to have any meaning.

[8] William James in his *Pragmatism* spoke of truth as an 'event, a process', but, as will become apparent, my own view of what constitutes such an event differs from his. I shall comment on James's position in chapter 6.

fully capture its meaning. In particular, truth does not reduce *tout court* to 'true propositions'. Propositions, or rather propositional contents, enter into truth as its constitutive components; they cannot, in abstraction from the conditions under which truth takes place, be characterised as 'true' or 'false'.

It follows further that the use of truth predicates cannot be compared with property ascriptions in an ordinary sense. Truth is as little a property of propositions as existence is a property of objects. However, this is not due, as is sometimes supposed, to the fact that locutions such as 'p is true' or even 'It is true that p', which we find so handy and often use with reckless abandon, can in general be dispensed with, and the relevant message conveyed in other ways. Whether the predicate 'true' can in principle be dispensed with, or replaced by other expressions, in every instance of its use is not the main issue. The main issue concerns the structure of truth claims, not the necessity or otherwise of truth predicates; and, on the view that I am propounding, a truth claim in respect of p, *no matter how it is expressed*, should be interpreted in the sense of p being *part of*, or *entering into*, truth as an event. It is because truth is an event that it does not require a 'bearer', and that, therefore, any theory based on the idea of truth as a property, or a relational property, of an x (which, incidentally, includes most versions of the so-called 'correspondence theory') is misconceived, and should be rejected.

It is important that both these points, viz. the complexity aspect and the 'no bearer' aspect, should be clearly brought out at the outset, if only because they are sometimes thought (wrongly, as we shall see) to exclude each other. The fact that truth does not have a bearer does not mean that it therefore must be a simple concept. Quite the opposite: truth is made up of several components, with propositions, or rather the propositional contents of sentences employed as vehicles of truth claims, entering into it, under certain specific conditions, alongside the respective states of affairs they are meant to convey (provided the latter do exist).

Some doubts and objections

Inevitably, all this invites numerous questions, and moreover may be found to be at such odds with normal susceptibilities, that it is likely to attract a great deal of hostile criticism. Two objections in particular are likely to be immediately raised.

The first objection concerns the relation between account of truth and account of truth conditions. The stated aim is to provide an account of truth through an explanation of the conditions under which truth claims can be meaningfully made. But, it might be said, to provide an explanation of truth conditions is not necessarily the same as providing an account of truth. To begin with, although some explanations undoubtedly consist of statements of truth conditions, or might be interpreted in terms of such, not all explanations fall into this category. Some semantic definitions in particular do not lend themselves easily to such a classification. To say that 'the number *pi*' stands for the ratio of the circumference of a circle to its diameter is to explain the symbol without saying anything about truth conditions. Conversely, there are accounts of truth conditions which strictly do not qualify as 'explanations'. The most conspicuous example of this is provided by the classical 'simple' definition of truth itself. Thus to say that p is true if, and only if, things are as stated is to supply a necessary and a sufficient condition of p being true *without* providing an explanation.

Secondly, any search for an 'explanation' as far as truth is concerned is bound to degenerate into circularity anyway. For consider what is being claimed. It is claimed that in order to explain the concept of truth we should strive for a (non-tautologous) account of the conditions that make it possible for truth to 'occur'. But how can we embark on an analysis of such conditions without already possessing a basic grasp of the concept? Such an 'explanation', if we are lucky, might provide some clue as to the extension of the concept, but does it help explain its meaning? A theory of truth conditions can be as complex as we like, but without the initial insight into the meaning of truth it is as nothing. And just such an insight is captured by the familiar statement that to predicate the truth of a proposition is to declare that what the proposition says is a fact. To try to provide an 'explanation' of truth beyond and above such trivialities is to involve oneself in an infinite regress. In a sense it is not unlike trying to explain the meaning of 'good'. If 'good' were to be defined in terms of some other property — pleasure, say, or wisdom, or justice, or whatever — it would still be possible to ask 'Why is the possession of such a property good?', and the definition, in consequence, would not have achieved its purpose. The point is (so the argument is likely to be continued) that like 'good', 'truth' is a logically primitive notion. But, then, apart from laying down certain formal conditions for the application of the predicate 'true', for example in order to avoid the paradoxes of self-reference, and such like, there is very little that, in addition, can be said about the concept. Whilst there may be some merit in the general policy of trying to explicate the meaning of factual statements in terms of the latter's truth conditions, any attempt to provide an account of *truth* in terms of truth conditions is self-stultifying.

Truth and the conditions of its occurrence

These objections are misplaced, and part of my aim in the following pages will be to show why they are misplaced. I shall specifically discuss the view that truth is a logically simple notion in the next chapter, and as for other critical objections that might be brought against the approach outlined above, they will be dealt with later on, when the general argument that I shall be presenting has established the position from which they can be successfully addressed. For the present, suffice it to highlight the following points.

If 'true' is defined in terms of 'things being as stated', then this is question-begging, and tells us little. It is entirely correct to say that this represents no explanation. But, then, what is meant by the conditions of truth in the context of the present discussion is not what such a definition conveys anyhow. For what we are looking for is not simply a definitional articulation of what it is for an x to possess the quality of 'truth in itself', so to speak, but rather the conditions of the *occurrence of truth*; i.e. the conditions that explain the possibility and the manner in which truth takes place. These conditions are manifold and they all enter into the definition of the concept. The idea, in essence, is to try to specify the extension of 'truth', whilst showing at the same time that the manifold conditions which determine its extension are a constitutive part of its *meaning*.

The fundamental initial premise is that the topic of truth should be addressed through an analysis of *truth claims*. Truth claims can be made either directly, viz. by asserting a proposition, or indirectly, by, for example, describing a proposition as 'true'. The use of truth predicates is often convenient, and contextually may even be unavoidable, but nothing of any great philosophical consequence turns upon it. Truth is not a kind of property which 'attaches' to, or 'inheres' in certain items, which are its natural 'bearers'. Indeed what an analysis of truth claims shows is precisely that there are no 'bearers' of truth, only vehicles of truth claims.

It follows that the question 'Is p true?' should be read as meaning: 'Is there an actual state of affairs such that it forms part of a truth event in the way in which it is represented by p?' The issue, that is, is about what is, or could be, part of a truth event, and under what conditions. And to be *part* of F evidently is not the same as having the *property* F.

An account of truth, in other words, must include a comprehensive account of the *conditions* under which truth 'comes about', and by implication an account of the conditions under which thought displays what actually is the case, or else it is at best incomplete or at worst vacuous. If the idea of things being as it is said they are means anything, then it is only that the world is such that there exists a state of affairs which, within the relevant categorial system of reference, enters into, or forms part of truth just as it is represented by p. Now, admittedly, this, alone, may not seem to be much of an explanation — indeed the word 'truth' appears in the explanans; nevertheless it helps to steer us in the general direction, where, hopefully, an explanation might be found.

The method of inquiry

In the following, I propose to pursue my goal through a discussion of three basic types of approach to an analysis of truth conditions, which in varying degrees of approximation and consistency have been employed by philosophers, and which I shall call the *naturalistic*, the *phenomenological* and the *socio-historical* approach, respectively. I should emphasise at the outset that my objective is not to attempt a classification or exegesis of any existing theory, and that my use of these terms is merely a convenient device for flagging out certain ideal theoretical positions or *models of reasoning about truth*, irrespective of whether, or to what extent, they happen to coincide with any theory or theories that have actually been put forward. Nevertheless these theoretical positions help highlight the principal guiding notions that have shaped thinking about truth conditions as well as providing vital insights into the different methods of philosophical explanation.

What I call 'naturalism' draws its root in large measure from ordinary common sense, and embodies the metaphysical realist thesis, according to which there exists a world antecedent to, and independent of, thought. This view, essentially, underlies the classical correspondence theory of truth. I use the term 'phenomenological' as a convenient label for the kind of epistemological approach to truth conditions that involves linking truth with the decidability of truth claims, and ultimately with the idea of *certainty*. In so far as this approach looks for evidence in what is in principle accessible to direct experience, it is related to the verificationist epistemology. However, the verificationist epistemology, in its most familiar — i.e. the *Positivist* — version takes much too narrow a view of evidence, and typically excludes everything other than the most simple sense phenomena from the domain of what can be directly known, and thereby from what qualifies as basic; which the more liberal verificationist approach which I term 'phenomenological' does not do. Finally, what I call the 'socio-historical' approach to truth conditions places the main emphasis on the socio-historical conditions of *objectivity*.

I shall presently, as a preliminary exercise, sketch out the main principles of these three different types of theoretical approach by way of prefacing a more detailed discussion in chapters 3-5. The most frequent cause of confusion in philosophical debates about truth can be traced to the failure clearly to distinguish between the different aspects that these three different types of approach bring to bear on the problem of truth, and to appreciate that although mutually incompatible in certain respects, and, if viewed separately, variously defective and limited in scope, they nevertheless contain all the ingredients needed for a *unified theory* of truth.

The core issue from all three standpoints concerns the criteria to be followed in deciding what determines the specifically 'truth-relevant content' of an indicative sentence featuring in a truth claim. This issue, however, generally tends to be debated in the context of what I shall argue is the mistaken common sense belief that different truth claims, involving the use of nonsynonymous expressions as well as different syntax, can nevertheless express the 'same truths'. Accordingly we are urged to accept that the truth-relevant content in the given case may but need not necessarily wholly coincide — although obviously it must to a large extent overlap — with the meaning content of the sentence taken as a whole. Taking their clue from this common sense belief, many philosophers have therefore undertaken to separate out the specifically truth-relevant content from what they saw as the subject-related, 'egocentric' features of the 'mode of presentation', which supposedly had no influence on the truth-value of the sentence in question, i.e. its truth or falsehood. This has resulted in a variety of reductionist strategies, some more radical than others, and has largely set the framework for much of the modern philosophical debate about truth.

As is clear from my earlier remarks, I reject this approach. The idea that nonsynonymous propositions can 'express' the same truth arises from a fundamental misconception about what truth really means. However, it will not be possible to avoid altogether speaking in terms of the distinction between the truth-relevant and the general meaning content for a while, especially when discussing the three types of approach referred to earlier, before outlining my own views on the subject.

Another terminological point that must be cleared up before I proceed, is this. Some logicians, in drawing a distinction between truth-relevant and general meaning content, tend to identify 'truth-relevant content' with 'proposition', and to regard propositions, accordingly, as automatically having a truth-value, i.e. as being by definition true or false. As against this, I shall find it convenient to use the term 'proposition' in a broader sense, and — subject to certain formal restrictions — treat the propositional content as indistinguishable from the meaning content taken in its entirety, while at the same time repudiating the view that truth reduces to a 'property' of propositions.

The full implications of this will become apparent later on. In the meantime, the key preliminary issue that needs to be addressed is, how should an analysis of the truth-relevant content of what is claimed to be true be approached? It is in virtue of such a content that what is asserted captures, or, for that matter, fails to capture a fact. But exactly what does go into making up such a content? If the veil of obscurity that envelops the relationship between thought and reality is to be lifted, then clearly it is necessary to investigate the factors that are instrumental in determining such a content. But how should such an investigation be pursued?

One possibility is to take the view that the truth-relevant content of an indicative sentence depends upon, and can only be explained in terms of, its logical structure and the referential properties of its constituent terms; and concentrate accordingly on an exploration of the general characteristics of *structure* and *reference*. This is largely the strategy of what I have called the 'naturalistic' approach. The 'phenomenological' approach reverses this position in as much as it involves an attempt to explain structure and reference through an analysis of the truth-relevant content, whilst at the same time looking for clues to such a content through an analysis of what is in principle *evidentially accessible* in perceptual and other mental acts. Finally, what I have dubbed the 'socio-historical' approach gives the inquiry into the truth-relevant content a new twist and emphasis by in particular bringing to bear upon it the social-historical considerations, with a view to clarifying the intersubjective conditions of the objectivity of content.

Truth and the external world

The emphasis placed by the naturalistic approach upon structure and reference as a key to truth-relevant content is coupled with the thesis that such a content is independent of the intentions of the language user. The supporting argument runs as follows. The speaker's intended meaning in any given circumstances may but need not coincide with what he actually *succeeds* in conveying. This is partly due to the fact that the objective sense is often contaminated with the 'associated' subjective ideas which accompany individual acts of thought, and partly to the fact that what the speaker purports to refer to by the words he uses — his 'intentional object' — need not necessarily coincide with what his words actually designate in the context in which they are used. In other words, the 'intentional object' in the given case may but need not coincide with the 'real' (or 'external') object; and it is the latter, i.e. 'real' object which is instrumental in determining the objective, and hence the truth-relevant, content of utterance.

Consider an example. If under the false impression that the seat of the European Commission is in Paris, I say 'Europe is now governed from France', it is obvious that the objective content of my utterance, being dependent, as it must be, upon external factors, will deviate from its 'intentional' content, and it is the former and not the latter that will decide the truth-value (truth or falsehood) of what I say. On the other hand, my — as it turns out, false — belief that the seat of the European Commission is in France might well be instrumental in determining my *behaviour*; for example by prompting me to travel to Paris rather than to Brussels.

The naturalistic position is thus that what matters as far as truth-value is concerned is not what I intend to say but what I objectively *succeed* in expressing; and what I succeed in expressing on a particular occasion will depend entirely upon the circumstances *outside my control*. The beliefs and intentions of the speaker, or speakers, whilst providing useful pointers to the latter's likely *behaviour*, are immaterial to, and need not be taken into account in considerations of the objective sense, or the objective content — and hence the truth-value — of what is said or claimed to be true. What is more, what the speaker succeeds in expressing will be true or false in virtue of external facts, *independently* of the actual availability of the verifying evidence.

There are snags, however. One problem that immediately crops up is, how should the criteria be defined for distinguishing between the 'real' and the 'intended' objects — and no sooner is such a question posed than it becomes clear that on naturalistic premises it is difficult, indeed impossible, to devise a satisfactory theory of reference to go together with the notion of what is called 'objective sense' (i.e. the objective truth-relevant content of utterance). For if the reference is not fixed via someone's intentions, *how is it fixed*? What criteria should one apply in deciding what really is being 'talked about' in the given instance? And if it turns out, as seems likely, that it is impossible to devise satisfactory 'non-intentional' criteria for reference fixing, independent, that is, of beliefs and intentions of language users, how can we decide with sufficient confidence what constitutes the objective sense of what is said or asserted on a particular occasion?

The point is that in ignoring or suppressing all considerations of the typically speaker-related intentional features of utterances, we end up, in effect, with what is little more than an empty propositional shell wrenched from its natural moorings. Radical naturalism involves the thesis that all the ostensibly irreducible self-referential features of mental and speech acts, if closely inspected, will be seen to be eliminable after all; viz. that often with the help of only a moderate amount of paraphrasing they can be safely excised out of the propositional content with no harm done to truth. This of course is just another way of saying that an account of truth-relevant content in the final analysis can be provided in an entirely impersonal language; without resorting, that is, to the use of personal and demonstrative pronouns, reflexive spatial and temporal adverbs such as 'here', 'there', 'now', 'tomorrow', and even singular descriptions and proper names; in short, without any *indexical* expressions whose intelligibility depends upon their reflexive reference to the language user, or time of utterance. Unfortunately once the 'truth-relevant' content is cleansed of all such indexical and episodic features, it is no longer clear how it can succeed in achieving an anchorage in extra-propositional reality. The fact is that an attempt to reduce the sentential meaning to what is regarded as an 'objective' truth-relevant content brings about a massive problem of reference, which the naturalistic approach seems ill-equipped to handle. All that it can do, it seems, is to appeal to our common sense causal intuitions, and assume that the truth-relevant content finds its reference in the actual world as a result of a — yet to be explained — causal interaction at the perceptual level between the agent and the 'external' object. I shall have to say more about this in chapter *three*.

Decidability and certainty

Consider next what I have called the *phenomenological* approach. The central idea now is that the truth-relevant content of utterances needs to be assessed in the light of what can be decided to be true or false on the basis of what is ultimately accessible to direct knowledge. Whereas the naturalistic position is that the truth-relevant content, and with it the truth value, in any given instance, depend upon external circumstances, irrespective of the availability, even in principle, of the verifying evidence, now it is on the contrary the very possibility of such evidence that becomes an overriding consideration. Whereas the naturalistic approach involves an attempt to explain how thought engages with reality through a causal theory of reference (involving the metaphysical thesis of external things 'impinging' upon our cognitive mechanism), now an explanation of the same phenomenon is sought in what is in principle accessible to direct experience and can be known with *certainty*.

Admittedly (as we saw earlier) sometimes what is asserted, or claimed to be true, in the form in which it is phrased, may prove to be 'undecidable' because what is ostensibly talked about happens to be fictional, or because some other conditions that are relevant to deciding the truth or falsity of what is said are not fulfilled. In such a case, the truth claim will have to be disallowed as inappropriate, or else a paraphrase will have to be substituted which, at least in principle, is decidably true or false. I shall discuss the implications of this in chapter *four*.

One characteristic feature of the phenomenological approach is that all the specifically indexical features of acts of thought and utterance which the naturalistic approach tends to exclude from consideration on the grounds that they are irrelevant to truth and ultimately dispensable, are now in large measure taken back on board and acknowledged as important constituents of the content. The guiding principle is that instead of looking to what is supposed to be a mind-independent reality for the content-determining information, the source of such information should be sought primarily in the language user. The truth-relevant content is forged, and can accomplish its role as a vehicle of reference, only within the context of historical mental and speech acts by thinking and judging agents who address themselves to the world of objects from the horizon of their beliefs, and their general interests and needs.

It follows that all such objects now come under the general umbrella of *intentional* objects. Indeed from a phenomenological point of view, any assumptions about 'unconditionally external' objects (i.e. objects that are logically independent of acts of meaning or judging) are inadmissible and should be discarded as strictly void of significance. 'Externality' is now treated as a modality of thought, and any suppositions about external matters of fact are judged in the context in which such matters of facts are posited, or might be posited, by thinking and judging agents. In short, the idea is that there are not two species of object, intentional and real, with the latter being logically independent of the former. Rather the so-called 'real' objects, it is argued, represent a *sub-class* of intentional objects, namely those which acquire the status of 'real' objects within the context of a theory, or a particular constellation of beliefs.

Given the fact that the factors responsible for determining the truth-relevant content of utterance are now sought in the modes of intending and not in any metaphysically external circumstance, it is of course hardly surprising that truth should be linked with certainty. Phenomenologically there is no other benchmark of truth available. Once the metaphysical realist thesis is discarded[9], the demand for a grounding of truth in certainty seems a necessary consequence; with certainty, it should be noted, being defined here essentially in terms of what, in any given case, cannot be coherently disbelieved.

The conditions of objectivity

Finally, it remains to say a few words about what I have called the *socio-historical* approach. This approach gives priority to the social conditions of objective meaning and reference, and generally tends to treat what passes for 'reality' as a social construct. The issue of objectivity which plagues phenomenological epistemology, and which naturalistic metaphysics seems equally ill-equipped to handle, now becomes item one on the philosophical agenda. The phenomenological epistemology embarks on an exploration of the truth-relevant content with an eye to certainty, but has no explanation to offer as to what makes a truth claim objectively valid. The naturalistic strategy, on the other hand, is to try to show that the task of clarifying such a content could be accomplished only through an analysis of the truth conditions of the relevant proposition (i.e. the conditions under which that proposition becomes capable of capturing a fact) in terms of its structure and the referential properties of its terms. But again the question presents itself, what confers *objectivity* upon such an analysis? What assurance do we have that, in the absence of any clear definition of the conditions of objectivity, such an analysis will yield reliable results? It is all very well to speak about the 'objective' truth-relevant content; the problem is that without providing an account of the condition of objectivity

[9] Note that a rejection of metaphysical realism does not necessarily entail relativism in the theory of truth (although e.g. in Pragmatism the two normally go together; see chapter 6).

there is no way of deciding in the given instance just what such an objective content consists in.

The 'socio-historical' approach addresses itself squarely to this issue, with the key thesis being that the question of objective content can be settled only by exploring the social-historical context in which utterances are made and hypotheses advanced. What determines the truth-relevant content of what is said or asserted, and hence the conditions under which a proposition can capture a fact, it is argued, can only be decided by exploring the forms and conditions of *social life*. This topic will be addressed in more detail in chapter *five*.

Structural approach v. austere account

These, then, are the main types of strategies deployed in an exploration of truth conditions. The principal difficulty with all of them, as we shall see, is that each of them focuses on one specific facet of truth claims, respectively, and invests it with superior philosophical importance, which invariably leads to artifice and bad argument, and produces a distorted view of truth. By contrast, my objective will be to try to show that all such facets, at root, are connected with each other, and should be treated as logically on a par. They all necessarily enter into an account of truth. It follows that truth is a complex concept, and that any reductionist treatment of truth conditions is misconceived and should be rejected.

Reductionism, dressed up as an explanatory enterprise designed to make sense of what is complex in terms of what is simple, has been a favourite philosophical pastime; and not only in the theory of truth. And yet it is a philosophically unsustainable strategy in the long run. It invariably tends to bulldoze through problems instead of resolving them, leaving a great mass of debris in its wake, only to run out of steam eventually and expose its enfeebled flanks to sceptical attacks. In the matter of truth-relevant content it is a particularly inappropriate strategy. For the complexity of such a content is profound and ineradicable, and, as I have suggested above, represents a structure of several different and interconnected strands. Yet the difficulties which stand in the way of demonstrating this should not be underestimated. In fact, they are often so unyielding, and the effort required to overcome them so arduous, that it is perhaps not surprising why some philosophers have tended to take the view that a search for a 'substantial' theory of truth is due to a misunderstanding, and to dismiss the difficulties besetting such an enterprise as windmills of muddled thought. The 'substantial' theories, they argue, invariably involve attempts to answer the wrong questions, and end up by misrepresenting the nature of truth. Truth is a simple logical notion, which does not require any 'substantial' explanatory theory. I have already briefly commented critically on this view in passing, but before launching into a systematic discussion of the more 'substantial' theoretical accounts, it is necessary to look at it more closely in order to show just why it won't work.

2 The strategy of austerity

In what follows, I shall draw freely on the so-called 'deflationary' arguments about truth.[1] The focus in such arguments is on truth predicates, and the general aim is to show that such predicates are inessential either because they do not supply any information that cannot be conveyed by simply asserting the proposition, or propositions, concerned, or because the function they perform in the context in which they are actually used can be performed more effectively by other predicates, or by expressions which strictly are not 'predicative' at all; or else, if such predicates are not altogether dispensable, that their function nevertheless does not go beyond signalling the existence of certain purely inferential relationships between the proposition, or propositions, in question, and some other propositions; and so forth. Views and subtly crafted theories proliferate, but I do not propose to engage in exegetic discussion of their finer points. Nor is this necessary for my purpose. Rather I shall make free use of their arguments to sketch out what I shall call the 'strategy of austerity' in the theory of truth, my aim being merely to present a readily identifiable contrasting position against which my own approach might be shown in clearer relief.

Basically, the 'strategy of austerity' unfolds in three main steps and its overall aim is to establish that an account of truth does *not* require a consideration of issues that transcend the boundaries of logic. (The

[1] In modern writings on truth the term 'deflationary' has come to denote a family of arguments ('redundancy', 'disquotational', 'minimalist', etc.) all of which are advanced in a more or less deliberate opposition to the metaphysical, or indeed any kind of 'substantive', and implicitly dismissed as 'inflationary', accounts of truth.

problem of what I called the structure of *truth claims* is considered to be strictly irrelevant to a discussion of the 'nature' of truth.) The first step involves an attempt to show that truth predicates are used mainly for reasons of emphasis and can normally be dispensed with, although contextually they may have a useful metalinguistic function (to be explained presently). The second step is to argue that even if truth predicates stood for genuine properties, such properties are *sui generis*, and could not be compared with 'natural' properties like 'red', 'brittle', 'magnetic', and such like, which under specifiable conditions can be significantly ascribed to certain independently identifiable objects or substances. Finally, the third stage involves the claim that truth is an essentially *simple notion*, and that any attempt to provide an account of it in other than purely formal logical terms rests on a misunderstanding.

The strategy of austerity and the so-called *equivalence schema*

The philosophical implications of this, as might be expected, are far-reaching. Thus it follows that an account of truth does not demand that we engage with topics such as justification of belief, verification, theory of reference, the conditions of objectivity, and generally the question which I have argued sums up the central issue about truth, viz. how does thought 'hook up' with reality? Or, to phrase the question differently, under what conditions does thought show up what actually is the case? Such topics, it is claimed, whilst important in their own right, do not themselves contribute anything to a definition of truth. All the essential information about truth can be derived from the axiomatic 'equivalence schema', viz.

The proposition that p is true ***if, and only if***, *p*

In this schema, the predicate 'is true' has one role, and one role only, viz. to effect a switch from the proposition as *mentioned* to the proposition as *used*, in such a way that the equivalence of the expressions flanking the logical operator (i.e. the biconditional 'if, and only if') remains preserved. There is then no question of ascribing the 'property' of truth in the way in which properties are usually ascribed to ontological items. The assertion of equivalence alone belies any suggestion to the contrary. If truth predicates could be said to convey properties, then it is only in a strictly technical intra-linguistic sense, i.e. in so far as they may be used to signal the possibility of certain *inferences* from one level of discourse to another. This happens in particular when we ascribe truth obliquely to a proposition, or a set of propositions, which have been advanced by others, but which we are often unable to reproduce accurately ourselves, or even not at all. For example, we might say, without necessarily being familiar with the theoretical detail, 'The gravitational theory of the tides is true', or, making a similar global claim about a report which we have reason to think is accurate but are unable to reproduce ourselves in more than bare outline, 'There is nothing in this report that isn't true'; thereby licensing the inferences 'If p&q&r . . . represent the gravitational theory of the tides, then p&q&r . . .' and 'If the report contains p (whatever that might be), then p'.

With the 'problem of truth' being thus reduced to a clarification of the logical grammar of truth predicates along the above lines, it is not surprising that the exponents of the 'austerity' view generally tend to be dismissive about the aura of mystery and glamour that has traditionally surrounded the philosophical debate about truth. As they see it, truth is a far less interesting concept than it is often made out to be. It is a trivial and monochrome notion, in fact, which raises no issues that could not be sorted out with a modicum of logical analysis. Such problems as arise concerning truth have to do more with form than with content. A consideration of content is important, but it does not contribute to the insight into the 'essence' of truth; rather it *presupposes* such an insight. Consequently, there is no reason why we should begin by concerning ourselves with questions such as, What goes into making up the 'truth-relevant content'?, or: What factors are responsible for determining such a content in the given instance? The account provided by the 'equivalence schema', it is claimed, speaks for itself. It is perspicuous and instantly graspable by any rational being, and provides an accurate and complete insight into what truth means.

It does not, of course. Nevertheless in recent times elaborate and forceful arguments have been mounted in support of the above view, in an avowed aim to expose and cut through the layers of misconception, the bogus conundrum and metaphysical artifice that have accumulated around the concept of truth, like so much seaweed.

The analogy with existence

The first thing to note is the similarity between the 'austerity' view of truth and the arguments that are often advanced about *existence*. The 'redundancy theory' of truth predicates has a close counterpart in the 'redundancy theory' of existence predicates. The central premise underlying these theories is that both truth and existence are logically primitive concepts, and cannot, therefore, be 'explained' in terms of any extra-logical conditions of their meaningful application, for such conditions could not even be intelligibly stated without presupposing what they are supposed to explain. Hence neither concept can be said to be typically 'predicative'. Hence neither of them can be said to be typically property-like. Hence the message they convey is not one that requires an elaborate extra-logical theory.

With regard specifically to existence, it has become part of the modern logical canon to emphasise, usually by invoking Kant's famous strictures on the ontological proof of the existence of God, that existence cannot be predicated of objects; or, to employ the usual technical term, that existence is not a 'first-level' predicate. If existence qualified as a property of objects, so would non-existence, but evidently there is nothing of which non-existence could be predicated. To say that 'Africa exists', at best, is to say that 'Africa' is a proper name; but if 'Africa' is a proper name, then existence of what it names is presupposed, and 'Africa exists' is a tautology, while 'Africa does not exist' is referentially inconsistent. Existence, if it can be characterised as a predicate at all, is a sort of 'second-level' predicate; viz. it says something about concepts — or, as logicians generally prefer to put it 'open sentences' — not objects; and what it says about concepts can be expressed without actually using the verb 'exist'. More precisely (so the argument goes) existence predicates can be replaced by 'quantifiers', i.e. phrases such as 'For some (at least one) x . . .', 'There is something or other, such that . . .', etc., and thereby shown to be essentially dispensable. Thus that 'quarks exist' can only mean that something or other is, or has the properties of, a quark; with the predicate 'exist' being thereby exposed as a pseudo-predicate, a mere quirk of syntax. But then there is no special philosophical 'problem of existence', and hence no need for any metaphysical theory of 'being *qua* being'. Existence is a simple logical notion which does not require a 'metaphysical explication'. All that we need to worry about are the kind of *inferences* that may be drawn from the propositions expressing or incorporating existence claims.

The 'reductionist' reasoning in respect of existence as predicate thus neatly dovetails with the 'reductionist' reasoning concerning truth. The overall conclusion seems obvious. Just as there is no special problem of existence, there is no special problem of truth; and consequently no need for a metaphysical theory setting out the 'nature' of either concept. There are no mysteries to explore. Neither truth nor existence hides unfathomable depths. The entire business of 'elucidation' of the two concepts, in the final analysis, reduces to a clarification of the kind of inferences that can be derived from the propositions which act as vehicles of existence — or truth-claims; and that is a task which falls within the province of logic rather than metaphysics. The so-called problem of truth and the problem of being *qua* being can thus both be demystified and disposed of as philosophical issues.

It follows that although I shall be concerned mainly with truth, my comments will inevitably have a bearing upon existence as well.[2] As far as the austerity view of truth is concerned, in particular as represented by the *equivalence schema*, I shall argue that whilst it is entirely correct to say that truth cannot be compared with 'natural' properties, the schema does not provide a basis for a plausible alternative theory, and in so far as it can be made sense of at all, it reduces to a *statement of identity*. Rather than offering an explanation of truth, it declares in effect that none is needed. As against this, I shall argue that there is indeed a need for an explanatory theory. Moreover such an explanatory theory will have to cast its nets wider than is normally thought to be necessary by those who — whether from a naturalistic, phenomenological, or a socio-historical viewpoint — seek to construct a more 'substantial' definition of the concept.

What do true propositions have in common?

Let us now look at some of the key ideas from which the so-called 'redundancy theory' of truth predicates draws its roots. (I should

[2] For a more detailed discussion of the Kantian objections to existence being employed as a first-level predicate, see my book *The Concept of Reality* (chapter 15), London 1986; reprinted 1993.

emphasise that I am concerned here with the 'redundancy theory' only in so far as such a theory forms part of what I have called the 'strategy of austerity', and is intended, accordingly, to help demonstrate that truth is a logically simple notion.)

The 'redundancy' thesis, as is well known, goes back to Frege who, taking a leaf out of Kant's own trenchant criticism of existence as predicate, argued along the following lines. Truth could not be a real predicate, for if it were, then an attribution of truth would modify the content of the relevant sentence; but clearly such an attribution does not add to or take anything away from what the sentence actually expresses. The thought that 5 is a prime number is true contains no more than is expressed by the sentence '5 is a prime number'. Or in Frege's own words: "The truth claim arises in each case from the form of the declarative sentence, and when the latter lacks its usual force, e.g. in the mouth of an actor upon the stage, even the sentence 'The thought that 5 is a prime number is true' contains only a thought, and indeed the same thought as the simple '5 is a prime number'."[3]

In short, all that can or needs to be communicated about the truth of a sentence can, in *normal circumstances* (Frege's qualification as to 'force' is relevant here) be communicated by a straightforward assertion. The conclusion to which Frege is led by his own reasoning is that the truth-value of a sentence can only be its *reference*, and hence that the relation of the sentence to its truth-value is analogous to that between a name and a thing named. In other words, truth and falsehood are not property-like, but are rather a kind of object; and he calls them accordingly *the true* and *the false*, respectively.

Having previously implicitly committed himself to a categorial division of reality into *objects* and *properties*, Frege indeed had little choice but to take the above view. If truth and falsehood are not properties, what else might they conceivably be but objects? There are no other possibilities available. However such an interpretation raises serious problems, and is hardly one that readily commends itself. Thus a corollary of Frege's theory is that all true sentences should be uniformly regarded as having the *same reference*, and similarly for false

[3] G. Frege: 'On Sense and Reference', in *Translations From the Philosophical Writings of Gottlob Frege* by Peter Geach and Max Black, Oxford, p.64.

ones; and hence that all sentences with the same truth value, without exception, can be treated as extensionally equivalent, *irrespective* of their contents.

The problcm is that this tends to throw into confusion the notion of reference. Consider what is at stake here. The idea put forward is that all sentences with the same truth value are extensionally equivalent. But clearly not all such sentences are 'extensionally equivalent' in the same way. Some are entirely unrelated to each other, some are logically linked and inter-dependent, and some are as a matter of fact targeted at the same states of affairs in virtue of the co-referentiality of their terms. Take the last of these, i.e. what I called earlier (chapter 1) 'extensionally isomorphic' sentences. Are we to say that they have *two* kinds of reference, viz. the relevant truth value and the state of affairs concerned, and hence that they are doubly co-extensional? Now of course there is a familiar 'weak' sense of implication in which all sentences with the same truth value might be said to imply each other. But the question is, why should this commit us to the view of truth as an object? How can two sentences which report logically independent facts nevertheless have the same 'reference'? They can both be true, of course. But if they are true, one might argue, then it is simply because they convey certain existing states of affairs, not because they 'refer' to the same truth value.

But while Frege's reification of the two truth-values has found few adherents, his criticism of truth predicates — very much like Kant's criticism of existence predicates — has inspired a large following. Nevertheless the main problem that this criticism raised, namely what to put in place of the discredited property theory of truth, remains unresolved. For once the idea of truth as an (ontological) property has been set aside, the question immediately arises, how do we decide what true propositions *have in common*? There is no way in which this question could be brushed aside; but, as we shall see, it is futile to expect those who pursue the strategy of austerity (whilst at the same time rejecting the Fregean 'solution', involving the treatment of truth values as objects) to provide anything approaching a satisfactory answer.

The redundancy view and the equivalence schema

Consider again the equivalence schema referred to above, viz. 'The proposition that p is true *if, and only if*, p'; or, in an abbreviated form, using angled brackets as a nominalizing device, and taking '<p>' accordingly as a shorthand for the singular term 'The proposition that p' (i.e. a metalinguistic name of p):

<p> is true *iff* (= if, and only if) p

There are at least two problems about this schema that cast doubts about its usefulness as a vehicle of a 'redundancy' argument. The first has to do with its possible generalisation, the other with the meaning of the biconditional. Taken as it stands, the schema represents just an empty matrix with variables, and strictly it is not unless and until it is *generalised* that it amounts to something of a *theory*. But an attempt to generalise it by binding its variables in a universally quantified proposition, viz.

(p) <p> is true *iff* p

immediately gives rise to difficulties. The reason for this is quite simple: whereas on the left hand side of the biconditional the proposition is *named*, on the right hand side it is *used* to assert a fact. In other words, the topic talked about in the former case is the proposition itself, whereas in the latter case what is being talked about is a fragment of the world, and it is not altogether clear what kind of item is being 'quantified over', i.e. what the generalisation is supposed to be *about*.

But let us for the sake of the argument assume that the generalisation is about propositions. This clearly will not remove the difficulty, for we shall still have to settle the problem of the criteria for deciding, in any given instance, what kind of substitutions may be appropriately made for the respective occurrences of 'p' in the schema, given that propositions (represented by p) and *names* of propositions (represented by <p>) may involve very different kinds of expressions. I shall return to this in a moment.

Alternatively, we might abandon any attempt to use the schema as a vehicle for a general 'redundancy argument', and rather than forging out of it a general theoretical proposition about truth by making use of the device of quantification, accept it for what it is: an empty schema — not so much a theory as a syntactical matrix, allowing of a construction of an infinite number of *individual axioms*, each of which provides an account (as well as 'justifying' the use) of the truth predicate for *just the proposition concerned, and no other*.[4] This seems much the most liberal solution, as well as being the least troublesome. In fact, it is vacuous and unhelpful, for in consequence we would end up with an infinite number of instances of the equivalence schema, and no general theory to explain what such instances have *in common*; apart, of course, from the fact that all of them are the result of substitutions into the *same* schema; which is precisely what cries out for a clarification.

The difficulty with the schema is that it is not immediately clear how its biconditional (i.e. 'if, and only if') should be interpreted. At first blush, the schema seems perfectly transparent, almost trite. But on closer inspection it can be seen that it is in fact highly ambiguous, in as much as it is susceptible to two different readings, depending upon whether it is taken in what I shall call the 'extensional' or the 'intensional' sense; with considerable implications for the concept of truth.

Extensional and intensional equivalence

On the 'extensional' reading, the biconditional expresses a material equivalence of the two sides in the schema, meaning that the expression '<p> is true' is as a matter of contingent fact true whenever 'p' is, and vice versa; or (since the same applies if they are false) that the left hand side and the right hand side of the biconditional always agree in respect of their truth value, though not as a matter of semantic necessity; and hence — to employ that much overworked but handy term of modal logic — not necessarily 'in all possible worlds'. This reading of the schema may seem strange, but it is not strange if the substitution for the variable 'p' is confined to sentences of a specific language, or a specific

[4] For an approach along these lines see Paul Horwich: *Truth* (1990).

type of language, for what applies to a particular language, or a type of language, need not apply universally.

But quite apart from this, as we saw earlier, the two expressions flanking the equivalence sign are about two different things: the expression on the left hand side says something about the proposition in question, whereas the expression on the right hand side says something about the world. How, then, can the two sides mean the same? And if they do not mean the same, then the question is, why should they be *necessarily* rather than merely *coincidentally* coextensive? It thus appears, on the face of it at least, that the equivalence that the schema conveys can only be a 'material' or contingent equivalence.

However, from the point of view of the 'redundancy theory', this clearly is insufficient. Indeed the 'extensional' reading of the schema seems to make nonsense of the whole idea of 'redundancy' of truth predicates, for given such a reading we would have to continue employing such predicates, if only in order to make clear just what the equivalence is about in any given instance. So this interpretation manifestly won't do, and must be rejected.

Consider now what I have called the 'intensional' (intensional with 's') reading of the schema. The 'intensional' reading presupposes a much closer relationship between the two sides of the biconditional, in that the expressions '<p> is true' and 'p' are now treated not just as materially but *semantically* equivalent, i.e. as literally meaning the same.

The situation is now radically different. Semantic equivalence entails material equivalence, but not vice versa. Most importantly, on the 'intensional' reading it follows automatically that the predicate 'is true' is dispensable. For if the predicate contributes nothing of substance to what is expressed by 'p' itself, then there is no need for the predicate. If all the facts about the world can be expressed without employing the word 'true', then clearly there is no rational basis for holding on to the view that truth represents some kind of irreducible metaphysical property. All of which goes to show (or so it would appear) that the equivalence schema, on the present reading at least, says all there is to be said about truth, and hence that there is no need for any elaborate exploration of the conditions of the applicability of the predicate in order to elucidate its 'meaning'. The concept of truth is essentially a simple, non-puzzling, trivially transparent concept that requires no 'theory'.

Incidentally, it seems fairly obvious that an interpretation of truth as a 'natural' property is disallowed by either reading of the schema. Nevertheless the difference between the two readings is that whereas the 'intensional' reading rules out all interpretations of truth as an irreducible property of certain (linguistic) entities, the 'extensional' reading, as we saw earlier, seems to leave room for the view that there might be some useful work to do for the predicate 'true'; or, at the very least, it leaves the question of its ultimate eliminability open. It follows that the redundancy thesis, if it is going to work at all, requires an *intensional* reading of the equivalence schema.

Two interpretations of semantic equivalence

Yet what justification is there for supposing that the two sides of the biconditional are not just coextensional but are semantically equivalent, i.e. *mean the same*?

There are two ways in which one might try to provide such a justification: one involves a specific interpretation of propositions, which I shall outline presently, and the other involves appealing to the concept of assertion. As we shall see, it is only in the latter case, viz. by appealing to assertions, that the equivalence in question might conceivably be shown to hold.

Consider the first approach. One might take the view that propositions are such as *automatically* carry a determinate truth value; i.e. that they are intrinsically true or intrinsically false, or else don't qualify as propositions. If this is granted, then evidently to say of a given proposition that it is 'true', if it is true, does not involve ascribing to it a property that it conceivably might not possess. 'P is true' is equivalent with 'p', and 'p is false' with 'not-p'. Moreover the truth value is intrinsic to the proposition in such a way that the proposition cannot forfeit it, or acquire a different truth value without in effect becoming a different proposition. It follows that the predicate 'true' does not convey anything about the proposition which is not present in its content. If the predicate 'true' carries any new or useful information, then this has to do entirely with our own *opinion* as to how the proposition in question should be classified in respect of its truth value — or, as Frege might have put it, with our views as to which of the two truth values the proposition 'names' or 'refers' to — not at all with the nature of the proposition itself. Our own opinion or belief, however, makes not the slightest difference to the facts of the matter. If 'Socrates is bald at t' is true, it is always true; and if 'The French Revolution took place in 1689' is false, it is always false, whatever anyone might think. Truth is the totality of 'eternally' true propositions, and falsehood is the totality of 'eternally' false ones.

The difficulty here lies in the two key assumptions, viz. that every proposition is necessarily true or false, i.e. that it is necessarily subject to the law of the excluded middle; and, secondly, that a proposition cannot change its truth value without ceasing to be the proposition it is. On these criteria, clearly a very large number of sentences, in particular all those containing indexical expressions (i.e. demonstrative pronouns and related adverbs, tensed verbs, etc.), will fail to qualify as vehicles of genuine propositions, for their truth value will depend upon the circumstances of utterance, and consequently may, and indeed often does, change. So either we shall have to find a way of assimilating such sentences to propositions, for example by accepting that if they were to be made sufficiently explicit and supplied with relevant spatio-temporal indices, their truth value might be fixed on a more permanent basis; or, alternatively, we shall have to accept that genuine propositions are to be found only in a fairly limited area, such as mathematics for example, where the truth value of theorems is fixed for all time.

But leaving the issue of 'indexical' sentences to one side for the moment, the main problem that we encounter here surely is this: that if the two assumptions above are accepted, it becomes impossible to make clear sense of the distinction between *necessary* and *contingent* propositions. Thus, to take one of the above examples, we would have to say that given that 'The French Revolution took place in 1689' is false, it is *necessarily* not just contingently false; what is more, if it were possible for this proposition to have a different truth value — if, that is, it could be *true*, e.g. in some world different from our own — then either it would not qualify as a genuine proposition, or else it would have to be treated as a *different* proposition entirely.

So an attempt to defend the 'redundancy thesis' by invoking the supposed truth value determinacy of 'eternal' propositions clearly won't work. But perhaps a consideration of assertions might provide a better way of achieving the desired objective. After all, what truth-relevant semantic difference might there be between claiming that p is *true* and merely *asserting p*? The truth predicate here surely does not supply any information about the proposition that its assertion alone does not provide. Rather than conveying a 'property' of p, the truth predicate, if it serves any purpose at all, then it is simply to add emphasis to what has already been said. It is like saying 'really' or 'honestly' p.

What does the phrase 'The proposition that p' refer to?

This latter approach certainly looks the more convincing of the two; nevertheless it is not going to satisfy the orthodox 'austerity strategist', for he is likely to argue that what matters is not the assertion but the *proposition* asserted. An assertion or a truth claim may or may not be correct in the given instance, but if it is correct, then it is only because the relevant proposition is true. And if 'p is true' means anything, then it is no more and no less than that as a matter of fact p.

In order to settle the issue, let us look again at the constituent elements of the equivalence schema '<p> is true *iff* p'.

The angled brackets around p, as we saw, serve as a nominalizing device, indicating that the reference is made to the proposition, and should be read accordingly 'The proposition that p'. As for the predicate 'true', this predicate is said to act as a 'de-nominalizor'; its function being, as it were, to peel off the nominalizing envelope around p. The idea, in short, is that the predicate's role is to 'cancel' the purely intra-linguistic reference to the proposition, and restore the latter's 'objective' reference, i.e. its reference to reality.

But since we are talking here in terms of *propositions* rather than *sentences*, the question is, how can we be sure that a particular substitution for p on the right hand side of the biconditional is in fact what <p> is meant to name?

The symbol <p> purportedly mentions the proposition which p expresses. But of course there are different ways of 'mentioning' a proposition, viz. by using any one out of a vast variety of possible descriptive expressions, and the problem that immediately presents itself is one of deciding the appropriate criteria of substitution for such expressions. How should such criteria be defined?

Consider the following example.

<The cat is on the mat> is true *iff*
the cat is on the mat

The bracketed symbol on the left-hand side of the biconditional purports to name the proposition expressed on the right-hand side. Since the same English sentence is used in both cases, viz. both within and outside the nominalizing brackets, this may seem evident enough. But suppose we change the referential symbol by replacing the English sentence with a German sentence, thus:

<Die Katze ist auf der Matte> is true *iff*
the cat is on the mat

What is the guarantee now that the referential symbol occurring on the left-hand side does indeed refer to the proposition expressed on the right-hand side? Unless we can be sure that it does, we cannot be sure that the equivalence does indeed hold. But in order to come to a decision about this, we shall need some criteria, if not necessarily of synonymy, then certainly of extensional equivalence; and such criteria cannot be defined without presupposing the notion of truth.

So it appears that we shall have to confine ourselves to talking about *sentences* (of a specific language) after all, rather than talking about elusive translinguistic entities such as 'propositions'. Yet even if we confine ourselves to the idiom of sentences, the equivalence schema is not necessarily thereby made much clearer. For how do we decide whether the two occurrences of p in the equivalence schema signify sentences or sentence-*tokens*? If they signify (admittedly similar, but none the less numerically different) sentence-*tokens*, then equivalence between the left-hand side and the right-hand side of the biconditional is no longer assured, for it is not inconceivable that the two sentence-*tokens* might express different things. I shall return to this presently.

Truth ascriptions in referentially opaque contexts

Consider now a different possibility of interpreting the schema. What are propositions? One way of answering this might be to say that propositions are the sort of thing people assert, suppose, believe, etc. Now suppose that A asserts at *t* that the cat is on the mat. Is it possible on the strength of this fact to substitute the expression 'What A asserts at t' into the schema, and claim the following equivalence:

What A asserts at *t* is true *iff* the cat
is on the mat

Not easily, and the reasons for this are plain to see. For what A asserts need not necessarily be what the sentence on the right hand side of the bicondional expresses. We need a *separate rule* to ensure this. For all we know, A may associate meanings with 'cat' or 'mat' which have nothing to do with the meanings that normally attach to these words. But even if he did employ these words in their customary meanings, such inferences as may legitimately be drawn from the cat being on the mat will not necessarily coincide with those that may be derived from his *assertion* to that effect. Thus if the cat happens to be my cat Sultan, it follows that Sultan is on the mat; but the same conclusion does not necessarily follow from what A wishes to assert, for he may not be aware that the cat is in fact Sultan; or he may positively wish to dispute that Sultan is on the mat. In other words, 'The cat is on the mat' — if true — may with regard to possible inferences that may legitimately be derived from it, comprise more than A is willing to concede.

But let us suppose for the sake of the argument that propositions are literally identical with what people actually assert, suppose, believe, etc.; i.e. that they do not exist *except as* what is asserted, supposed, believed by someone. If this were the case, then the only appropriate way of talking of propositions would be 'What A, B, C . . . (i.e. any specific individual) asserts, supposes, believes, etc.'. But in such a case there would be no clue as to what the variable p occurring freely on the right hand side of the biconditional stood for, and the equivalence schema would no longer make any clear sense. The only way of salvaging some meaning from the schema, in fact, would be to turn it into a straightforward tautology by repeating the same expression on the right hand side of the biconditional, viz. 'What A asserts is true if, and only if, what A asserts is true'. And of course that would not be of much use to anyone. The truth predicate would not have been explained, let alone shown to be 'dispensable'. In short, the strategy of austerity fails in this case too.

Equivalence schema and the infinity of substitution rules

In point of fact, the austerity strategy fails *no matter* how the schema is interpreted. Consider again the status of the variables employed in the schema, and, in connection with this, the problem of substitution. The schema asserts equivalence, but what exactly is supposed to be equivalent with what? If we are talking about the truth of propositions rather than 'sentences', one would expect the schema to work with any coextensive sentence being substituted for p on the right hand side of the biconditional. Thus we might write '<The cat is on the mat> is true *iff* A's only domestic pet is on the mat', assuming of course that 'the cat' and 'A's only domestic pet' have the same reference. The sentences need not be synonymous, only coextensive.

In fact, it is not only that the same sentence need not be repeated on the right hand side of the biconditional for the equivalence to hold: given the 'propositional' reading of the 'p' within the angled brackets it must in principle be possible to effect a substitution with an infinite number of different — albeit coextensive — sentences. Indeed one might even go further and claim that the meaning of the schema is unclear *unless* p is understood as representing an infinite set of such sentences.

If this is accepted, however, then, as we saw earlier, it will be necessary to assume, as a condition of the intelligibility of the schema, the possibility of an infinite number of corresponding substitution rules in each case, allowing for a replacement of p with appropriately coextensive sentences. And since such rules cannot be arbitrary and have to be based on certain objective criteria, we shall soon find that in order to clarify the schema it will be necessary to address the issue of truth on a much broader front, if only because such criteria cannot be specified without involving oneself in extra-logical considerations of truth conditions.

There is one further point that might be added here. It follows from what was said above that whereas 'p' within the nominalizing angled brackets has to be taken as representing a specific *proposition*, the 'p' on the right-hand side of the biconditional, i.e. outside the angled brackets, will have to be treated as a *sentential variable*, viz. as being replaceable by any old sentence that is coextensive with p (and, of course, there is an indefinite number of such sentences). But then the schema becomes intelligible only provided the predicate 'true' appears on *both* sides of the bicondional, viz. '<p> is true *iff* any sentence coextensive with p is true'; and the result is that once again we end up with a tautology, without succeeding in throwing any light upon the concept of truth.

Does the schema work with identical sentences?

So the conclusion must be that in non-trivial — and hence the most interesting — cases, i.e. when we are dealing with coextensive but non-synonymous sentences on the opposing sides of the biconditional, the equivalence schema so far from providing an adequate account of truth merely underlines the need for one.

In fact, it turns out that even in trivial cases the schema proves useless. Let us consider an extreme example. Let us stipulate that the expression '<p>' names a sentence not a proposition, and that the two occurrences of the variable p in the schema should be replaced only by identical sentences, viz. that in both cases one should always use identical strings of symbols; expressly excluding, that is, all substitutions on grounds of coextensiveness, or even synonymy, in order not to get bogged down in the problems of the criteria of substitution. The schema, in short, would be confined strictly to individual sentences of a specific object language, whatever such a language happened to be. This is a familiar metalinguistic stratagem, but, as is easily seen, it is unlikely to absolve us from the need to concern ourselves with extra-logical truth conditions, or render any tautologous repetition of the truth predicate on both sides of the biconditional unnecessary.

To begin with, as we noted earlier, it is necessary to make a distinction between sentences and sentence-*tokens*. We are using admittedly similar but none the less *numerically different* strings of symbols on the two sides of the biconditional. What guarantee is there that the sentence *named* on the left hand side of the biconditional, when its nominalizing envelope is peeled off, conveys what the sentence-token on the right hand side *expresses*? There clearly can be *no* such guarantee; unless, that is, it is possible to devise a plausible theory of reference, and the attendant criteria of extensional equivalence, for sentence-*tokens*. And that of course is just the kind of issue that the strategy of austerity was supposed to be able to bypass. For, as we recall, the intention was to show in particular that an adequate account of truth could be provided *independently* of any theory of reference.

But even assuming that the substitution of the same symbol for the variable p on both sides of the biconditional raised no problems regarding the grounds of the distinction between the sentence and sentence-*tokens*, there would still be a problem about deciding what exactly the schema did say; indeed whether it was about truth at all! The point is that with identical symbols substituted for 'p' on both sides, the predicate 'true' in the schema could be interpreted in any number of different ways which had nothing to do with truth or extra-linguistic reality. All that might be claimed about the schema is that it said something about sentences, but what exactly is unclear. 'True' might even be read to mean 'rhymes with', or 'is a mirror image of itself', or anything one liked, except that the predicate in such a case — whatever that predicate happened to be — would have to be repeated on both sides of the biconditional; yielding an unilluminating tautology. Thus one might end up with equivalencies like "'Socrates is bald' rhymes with 'old' if, and only if 'Socrates is bald' rhymes with 'old'"; '<p> is a mirror image of itself *iff* <p> is a mirror image of itself', etc.

An attempt, then, to restrict the substitutions into the equivalence schema to identical sentences would only help to underscore its uselessness as an account of truth. In particular it would destroy the credibility of any suggestion that the function of the truth predicate is to 'restore' the reference of the sentence to an extra-linguistic reality. In particular, it would provide no clue as to how it is possible, for example, to swap singular terms with the same reference to form co-extensive sentences with identical truth values; something that is normally taken for granted. But above all, as I have pointed out, it would give no indication as to why the schema should be understood as conveying something about truth at all.

And so we come to the final verdict. If the equivalence schema, on any reading, fails to give an adequate account of truth, then the conclusion must be that truth cannot be treated as a purely 'logical' notion, and the strategy of austerity fails. *Which was to be proved.*

Looking beyond the equivalence schema

This, I think, was clear to Frege, who in search of a solution went beyond the boundaries of the 'equivalence schema', although the proposal he came up with, viz. that truth and falsehood should be treated as objects, as we saw, created formidable problems of its own, for it entailed that all true propositions had the same reference, and similarly for false propositions; with the extensional equivalence based on the sameness of truth value obscuring any content-based criteria of equivalence. What Frege was anxious to put across was that truth is not susceptible to a 'definition'. If an account of truth in terms of the 'equivalence schema' fails to yield an adequate insight into the concept, he was in effect saying, then it is because *no* attempt at defining truth is likely to succeed. The only alternative was to accept that *the true* and *the false* were logically unanalysable entities, and that was all that could be sensibly said about them. Frege was wrong of course, but at least there was an implicit admission that truth was not an issue that could be handled by formal logic alone.

But consider now a different possibility of looking at the equivalence schema, viz. by treating it not as an account of truth pure and simple, but rather as an *illustration* of the metalinguistic function of the truth predicate. The purpose of the schema, it might be argued, is to make explicit the basic structure of truth claims rather than to provide a 'definition' of truth. Indeed so far from providing a 'definition' of truth, the schema literally cries out for one. It says nothing about the *conditions* under which whatever it is that the sentence named on the left-hand side of the biconditional stands for coincides with what the sentence on the right hand side expresses. A separate definition, therefore, is a necessity. Nevertheless a definition, if it is going to be adequate, has to be such as to ensure that every well-formed sentence of a given language can be meaningfully substituted into the schema.

This line of approach essentially reflects the view of A. Tarski, and in what follows I shall comment briefly on some of Tarski's ideas, without however going into the details of his theory. An important motivating factor behind his ideas was the need to eliminate certain fundamental ambiguities that surround the concept of truth in the context of ordinary discourse, in particular as exemplified by the *Liar Paradox*. In order to eliminate such ambiguities, it seemed, it was necessary, to begin with, to draw a distinction between 'object language' and 'meta-language', and rather than speaking in terms of truth *simpliciter* treat truth as a metalinguistic predicate applicable to a specified object language. Accordingly Tarski aims at providing an account of 'true in (a formally specified language) L'; the main objective being to establish the necessary and sufficient conditions of the meaningful application of the truth predicate to the sentences of the object language in question. In other words, he is concerned with truth exclusively as a language-relative *not* as a 'translinguistic' concept. This being so, he quite understandably insists upon using the idiom of 'sentences' rather than that of 'propositions'.

At the same time, his theory is based on a clear recognition of the fact that the equivalence schema, alone, so far from providing a complete account of truth, requires a 'more substantial' explanation of the concept, and this is the point that I am anxious to stress in the present context. The 'equivalence schema', I argued earlier, does not give any precise clue as to how the predicate 'true' should be understood, and demands an explanatory account if one is to understand just what a given exemplifying instance of the schema is meant to convey. Now, following in Tarski's footsteps, we might look for such an account by considering predicates or 'open sentences', and trying to establish what conditions, within a given universe of discourse, must be fulfilled for such an open sentence to yield a truth. Take, for example, the open sentence 'x is a dog'. Clearly this will yield us a true closed sentence for every value of x (from the relevant universe of discourse) that satisfies the condition of being a dog. Similarly 'x is taller than y' will come out as true for all ordered pairs that satisfy the condition 'taller than'. Items that satisfy such conditions (or predicates) can be clearly identified and distinguished from each other only if they form part of ordered sets, or *sequences*. A sequence of items from the given universe of discourse that satisfy a particular predicate may or may not be finite. However, it is always possible to construct sequences, i.e. ordered sets, that theoretically extend into infinity; for example, by either 'manufacturing', and stringing up, different coextensive terms, or by endlessly reiterating the last term, or terms, in the sequence (always, of course, subject to a suitable numerical ordering).

'Open sentences', taken by themselves, are of course neither true nor false; they are true or false only with respect to an assignment of values to the free variables. Thus if within a given universe of discourse the variable x in the open sentence 'x is F' is replaced by an individual constant, we obtain a 'closed' singular sentence, viz. 'a is F', which has a truth value. But an 'open sentence' can also be closed in a more general sense by binding its variables to quantifiers, e.g. '(∃x) x is F'; and it is these generalised closed sentences that logicians are particularly interested in. With regard specifically to singular sentences, they are of interest only in so far as they can be treated under the general aspect of operations on predicates.

Yet, as we shall see presently, it is precisely these last sentences that help highlight an important weakness in the suggested definition of truth. Consider what is being claimed. It is claimed that a given predicate, as represented by an 'open sentence', can generate a *true* sentence if there is a sequence of (one or more) things from the relevant universe of discourse that satisfies it. Thus '(∃x) x is F' is true provided there is at least one F-thing such that it satisfies the open sentence 'x is F'. Moreover, according to Tarski's definition, if 'x is F' is satisfied by some sequence from the given universe of discourse *U*, then the existential closure of it is satisfied by *all sequences* of items of *U*, in this sense. The items of *U* are subject to different arrangements, i.e. they can be ordered in different sequences, with all the sequences containing all the items; so we stipulate that if *U*, in a particular instance, satisfies a given open sentence, say 'x_3 is F', for a given assignment of values (i.e. a sequence-generating function) α, then it will also satisfy it under a different assignment α', where α and α' are similar except that α' will have a different item in the third place. Tarski's definition of truth, accordingly, is 'satisfiability by all sequences'.

Notice, however, that the notion of existential quantification is *presupposed*, and indeed plays a key role in the definition of satisfaction, and by implication of truth. This inevitably gives rise to problems when it comes to explaining closed existentially quantified sentences, for we shall not be able to avoid circularity. Thus if the formal sentence 'There is something or other which is a dog' is true, then it is because there is something or other which satisfies the predicate 'dog'; and the fact that the predicate 'dog' is satisfied will have to be explained, in turn, by saying of a universe of discourse that it contains dogs. So nothing much will have been accomplished. For at the end of it all, we seem to be left with the conclusion that 'dog' applies to something if, and only if, there are things of the relevant sort; which is indisputable, but hardly helpful. The idiom of 'satisfaction' thus does little to advance our understanding of truth.

But the difficulties of the semantic account of truth in terms of predicate satisfaction become particularly apparent if we consider singular, i.e. non-quantified closed sentences. The idiom of 'satisfaction', as we have seen, had been invented as a convenient means of talking about predicates, or 'open' sentences. But singular sentences are sentences *without* variables. How, then, can an attribution of truth in such an instance be explained in terms of predicate satisfaction without a circularity which is even more blatant than the one we encountered above? Given that we are dealing with 'irreducibly' closed sentences, we cannot appeal to existential quantification as an explanatory device; even if existential quantification, on its own, could provide much enlightenment, which, as we have seen, is doubtful, to say the least. Thus 'Socrates is bald' *presupposes* the existence of a unique individual; it does not *assert* the existence of such an individual. But, then, what role might the concept of 'satisfaction' conceivably have in such an instance? To say that the sentence in question is an example of a 'predicate satisfied' is just another way of saying that it is grammatically complete, and this of course provides no clue as to what it means to say that it is *true*. On the other hand, to say that the sentence is true because if it is satisfied, it is satisfied by 'all sequences', is at best unhelpful, and at worst seriously misleading.

So the attempt to cast light on the 'equivalence schema' by appealing to the concept of 'predicate satisfaction' fails to come up with the goods. In point of fact, on closer inspection it turns out that if the concept of 'satisfaction' is used in anything other than a purely trivial grammatical sense, it *presupposes* an understanding of the concept of truth rather than providing a clarification of it. Thus e.g. whilst there are many terms which might be substituted for x in 'x is F' to yield a syntactically well-formed closed sentence, only some of them might make the sentence true, and it is just those that do so that may be said to 'satisfy' the predicate in a non-trivial sense. In short, we have to invoke truth in order to explain the concept of 'satisfaction', and the result is that we are back exactly where we began. The point is that the so-called 'semantic definition' remains not just circular (which is the fate few philosophical definitions can escape), but that it is circular in a frustratingly unenlightening way, and does little to broaden our insight into the nature of truth.

The equivalence schema and the problem of truth

To conclude, the argument that I have been advancing may be summed up as follows. *First*, the equivalence schema is not just unhelpful, but, as it stands, it is not even clear how exactly it should be understood. The only way to make it intelligible is by trivialising it to the point where it becomes useless, viz. by employing the predicate 'true' on both sides of the biconditional, and turning it into a straightforward identity statement. But, then, the schema cannot be used to underpin the redundancy thesis, let alone prove that truth is a logically simple notion.

Secondly, the equivalence schema does not enable us to understand what true sentences have *in common*. It says nothing about the nature of truth. It provides a kind of matrix of claims about particular sentences involving the predicate 'true', without making clear what exactly is the feature that such sentences are supposed to share. In a sense, it is like trying to explain what writing paper is by saying that it is the sort of thing that one is likely to find in the drawer, because it is usually kept there; leaving it to the person concerned to make an appropriate identification. At the same time, an attempt to turn the schema into something approaching a general theory by binding its variables to a general quantifier leads to insoluble ambiguities, for the topics talked about on the opposing sides of the biconditional are clearly different: whereas on the left hand side it is propositions that are being talked about, the topic of the right hand side are the relevant bits of reality.

Thirdly, the attempt to solve the problem by equipping the equivalence schema with a supportive definition in terms of the semantic concept of 'satisfaction' is unsuccessful. What the semantic account does is to state the conditions under which an open sentence can be turned into a closed true sentence. However, to state the conditions under which an open sentence can be turned into a closed true sentence still leaves us with the question, what is it for the sentence in question to be true? But quite apart from this, the statement of the satisfaction conditions itself, as it turns out, depends upon the prior grasp of the concept: the thesis that true sentences are true in virtue of being satisfied by all sequences of items from the relevant universe of discourse, as we saw, presupposes the notion of truth, without providing an elucidatory account of it. In addition, the concept of satisfaction tells us little of interest about singular sentences; yet it is just such sentences that serve as vehicles of a very large proportion of truth claims which are made in everyday life.

So the inevitable conclusion is that the semantic account so far from injecting substance into the equivalence schema, in the end leaves things pretty much as it finds them. Some logicians have of course taken the view that that is precisely where they *ought* to be, for the equivalence schema, in their view, was all that could be given in 'explanation', and is moreover all that we are likely to need. But I hope to have shown that they are mistaken.

3 The naturalistic approach to truth conditions

The account of truth based on the 'equivalence schema' discussed in the preceding chapter is concerned with form rather than content, and has been shown to be periphrastic and vacuous. Its underlying assumption is that any consideration of the issues relating to the content of what is stated or claimed to be true, beyond and above that which might give rise to paradoxes of self-reference or impinge upon the proprieties of syntax, is strictly irrelevant to the meaning of truth. But this is an untenable view, and moreover goes against what is our natural intuition. If our interest is not just in elucidating the logic of saying that something is true, but in establishing under what conditions thought exhibits reality, or how truth comes into existence, then content can hardly fail to be a main consideration. Facts come to light in virtue of *what* we say, not — not only, at all events — in virtue of *how* we say it. And this means that an investigation will have to be mounted into the constitutive features of the content. The questions that need to be addressed, are: What factors exactly are instrumental in shaping the truth-relevant content of a proposition? Where and how might a distinction be drawn — if a distinction indeed be necessary — between the specifically truth-relevant and the general propositional content? And in general, how does the meaning content of a truth claim relate to the latter's 'extensional' properties?

These are some of the issues that emerge from the collapse of the 'strategy of austerity', and they demand an in-depth non-formalist treatment. In the present chapter, and the subsequent two chapters, I propose to discuss three basic 'anti-austerity' strategies that might be pursued — and variously have been pursued, albeit often fitfully and unsystematically — in dealing with these issues. They represent the three types of approach or models of reasoning about truth which were briefly sketched out in chapter one, but which now require a more extensive airing. Each of them, as we shall see, brings important aspects to bear on the task in hand, although none of them, in the end, proves equal to its challenge.

I begin with the 'naturalistic' approach.

Structure and reference and the idea of an extra-linguistic reality

The naturalistic effort to pin down the constitutive features of truth-relevant content is inextricably bound up with an attempt to identify the constitutive features of what are assumed to be the 'bearers' of truth value. In contrast to the austerity thesis, the starting premise now is that, so far from being a simple logical notion, truth is a complex natural property of certain linguistic items, and an attempt is made, accordingly, to specify the conditions under which such items qualify as candidates for a significant attribution of truth.

The new approach brings about a radical change in philosophical landscape. Whereas the 'strategy of austerity' eschews any direct realist metaphysical commitment, and in general tends to assume an air of ontological neutrality, the key premise now is that there is an extra-linguistic world out there which pre-exists thought and is ultimately responsible for 'making' what we say true or false. The 'hook up' of thought with the world takes place via certain features of the content of truth claims. Such features can be specified in terms of the *logical structure* of what is asserted or said to be true, and the *referential properties* of the terms used. Any other features of the content are purely peripheral and incidental, and in so far as truth value represents our principal concern, they can be safely left to one side. 'Terms', incidentally, is here intended to include general as well as singular terms — with 'reference' being used deliberately in a broad sense, to cover extensions of concepts as well as individual designata of naming expressions.

However, as will become clear presently, the metaphysical realist commitment which underlies the naturalistic project leads to circular arguments which destroy its credibility. For whilst an explanation is sought of how thought 'hooks onto' external fact by engaging in an analysis of the truth-relevant content, an attempt is made at the same time to explain the truth-relevant content by invoking external facts. In short, it is by reference to external matters of fact that a clarification is sought as to how thought 'hooks onto' external matters of fact — with 'external' being interpreted here in an essentially metaphysical realist sense, i.e. as *unconditionally* external (rather than 'structurally', and hence conditionally, external, as I propose to use the concept; see later). Not surprisingly, neither structure nor reference can be given a satisfactory account on naturalistic premises, with the inevitable result that the concept of truth-relevant content remains ill-defined and obscure.

Does truth need a bearer?

Let us, first, look at what might appear to be possible candidates for 'truth bearers'.

Take sentences. A sentence is an ordered sequence of symbols; or — if it is a one-word sentence — is such as can, as a rule, be unscrambled into a string of symbols arranged according to certain canons of syntax.[1] Evidently not all ordered sequences of symbols lend themselves to acting, or are intended to act, as vehicles of truth claims. Those that are typically suited for this role are often characterised as 'declarative' or 'indicative', but this has only partly to do with syntax, and 'declarative' and 'indicative' are more illocutionary than syntactical designations. As hardly needs pointing out, depending upon the context and intonation, the same sentence may serve both as a vehicle of a question and as a vehicle of an assertion. And sometimes the intention behind the utterance may be simply to amuse, or to shock, or to provide a poetic insight through an unusual juxtaposition of images or the acoustic quality of the phonemes in verbal sequences specifically chosen for the sake of enhancing the sentence's resonance or rhythm.

[1] One-word declarative or indicative sentences are plentiful in highly inflected languages (e.g. Latin), whereas non-inflected languages like English have few such examples, although imperative one-word sentences abound, viz. 'Fire!', 'Help', 'Stop', etc.

In all such cases, both the syntactical structure and the verbal composition of the sentence may remain unaltered even though the meaning content of the message varies, and there is no question of making any truth claim in the ordinary sense of the term.

But, of course, even the use of an indicative sentence in what ostensibly looks like a factual claim need not necessarily give rise to considerations of truth or falsity; for example, when such a claim forms part of story-telling, or when it is made by an actor in the context of a theatre performance; or in general if it lacks what Frege called its 'usual force'.

In other cases, again, the question of truth or falsity, if it should arise at all, might do so only obliquely, by an inferential and often tortuous route; for example, when allegory or metaphor are involved, or the intention is merely to emphasise a rhetorical point. An indicative sentence is a vehicle that can carry a vast variety of freight, and what meaning content exactly a sentence does carry on a given occasion, and what kind of truth claim it conveys, will inevitably depend in large measure upon the circumstances and the conditions or utterance. This is particularly true of sentences that include speaker-related indexical expressions. Thus the semantical cargo of 'It is chilly today' will vary according as to when the statement is made, and 'I am here' will carry a different message depending upon who the utterer is and where he happens to be. And of course the converse holds too to a degree, viz. the same state of affairs can be reported by means of different sentences. If in conversation I say of an oafy windbag 'That man is an fool', I am merely emphasising not altering my abusive remark by adding a moment later, whilst accompanying my words, perhaps, with an appropriate indicative gesture, 'He is a fool' or 'Fool; that's what he is'. My purpose in employing a personal pronoun, changing the word order, modulating my speech, etc. is to ensure that the substance of my message gets through. (Notice, incidentally, that in the examples given 'he' is used logically on a par with 'that man', i.e. as a surrogate name, not simply as an anaphoric pronoun.)

But although the extensional aspect of the message in question need not necessarily be affected by such paraphrases, the meaning content may, and often does, alter, and this cannot be entirely irrelevant to truth. Sometimes a very slight modification, or unconscious lapse, or syntax, alone, may produce a radical change of meaning, with the correspondingly radical change in truth conditions; although in live communication, the meaning of the message can to some extent be protected from minor lapses of syntax or deviancy of idiom by a suitably modulated speech. The question how and to what extent a change of syntax may affect the meaning content in a given case raises some thorny issues to which I shall come shortly.

What needs to be particularly borne in mind is the role of the performative and generally episodic features of statement making in determining what is being conveyed on what occasion. Of course, in all statement making there are certain semantic constraints that have to be observed regardless; to do in particular with the general rules of coherence and contextual appropriateness, which set limits to what can be significantly said. But it is only in the concrete circumstances of utterance that a clear assessment can be made as to whether such rules are followed or deviated from; what the truth-relevant content is in the given case, and indeed whether a truth claim has been made at all.

Meaning content and truth relevant content

So what is it that might reasonably be described as a 'bearer' of truth value? Evidently it is not an indicative sentence. On the contrary, such a sentence, taken purely as a syntactical construction, must be regarded as truth-value neutral. But equally, it appears, it is not the entire meaning content of an indicative sentence; and if propositions are identified *tout court* with sentential meanings in this (all-embracing) sense, then the same is valid of propositions. If the meaning content taken in its entirety acted as a 'bearer' of truth value, then no two sentences which differed, however slightly or marginally, in respect of their meaning content could be said to convey the same state of affairs. Yet, as was noted earlier (see chapter 1), this conflicts with what seems to be plain common sense. We have no difficulty accepting that non-synonymous sentences can in principle convey the same states of affairs — and hence qualify as 'extensionally isomorphic'. Thus if 'The capital of England' and 'The largest city on the Thames' designate the same object, then if 'The capital of England is London' is true, it necessarily follows that 'The largest city on the Thames is London' is true also. The difference between the two sentences relates only to the 'mode of presentation', as displayed by their respective subject terms, but that does not affect their truth-relevant content'.[2]

What is more, the difference in the 'mode of presentation', it seems, can be as radical as we wish to make it, without this detracting from the extensional properties of the sentences concerned. Thus 'The mountain first climbed in 1953 by Hillary and Tensing is in Asia' and 'Mount Everest is in the world's largest continent' convey essentially the same state of affairs, although there is no overlap in their respective meaning contents, or 'modes of presentation'. All that is required in order that the two sentences should be 'extensionally isomorphic' is that they should have the same logical structure and that the range of application of their terms should be the same. Provided these two conditions are met, if either of them states a truth, then necessarily both do.

If, then, truth is going to have a 'bearer' (a notion, incidentally, which we shall have reason to reject, but now posit merely for the sake of the argument), then such a 'bearer', surely, can only be a *slimmed down* version of the content; viz. that portion of the content in relation to which different sentences can be said to be 'extensionally isomorphic'. The meaning content, taken in its totality, manifestly won't do; and if 'proposition' is identified with the meaning content in this sense, then propositions do not qualify as suitable candidates. It follows that if we wish to retain the term 'proposition' for that of which truth value is predicated, then we shall have to find a different way of specifying the typically 'propositional content' of sentential utterances, enabling us to draw a clear line between the propositional content in the strictly *truth-relevant* sense, and all the other, incidental and peripheral, aspects of sentential meaning.

Alternatively we might try a different tack, and look elsewhere for suitable candidates for 'truth bearers'. One possibility, which I shall discuss later on, is to adopt the pragmatist conception of truth as a property of *belief*. The advantage of the pragmatist approach is that it does not require that it should be possible for propositions which are non-synonymous to convey exactly the same, as distinct from merely *similar*, states of affairs. Consequently we don't have to take 'extensional isomorphism' too literally, and can adopt a more relaxed view concerning the truth-relevant content; for anything whatever that enters

[2] Concerning the meaning of the term 'mode of presentation' see chapter 1, footnote 5.

a given belief and is contextually conducive to its success becomes relevant to its 'truth'. There is therefore no need for a radically 'reductionist' treatment of the content. However, the problem is that in adopting a pragmatist approach one is almost inexorably driven to give up the thesis that the truth value of our utterances is determined by external matters of fact *independently* of any belief, and that is the price that the naturalistic philosopher — given his metaphysical realist commitment — is not willing to pay.[3]

Naturalistic reductionism

In the circumstances, therefore, his only option is to go for a 'slimmed down' version of the truth-relevant content, and, accordingly, pursue a *reductionist* path in his account of truth conditions. Put plainly, he has to show that all those aspects of the meaning content which cannot be defined in terms of 'structure and reference' can in principle be dispensed with without any loss of truth. As it turns out, all his efforts come to naught, for he invariably gets bogged down in tortuous arguments which expose the defectiveness of his premises.

Consider what is involved in naturalistic reductionism. With 'proposition' having been defined in terms of *truth-relevant content* of sentential utterance, the principal task becomes one of identifying the main constitutive features of such a content, with a view to rendering explicit that which makes a proposition capable of capturing a fact. The first step in pursuit of this objective is to try to show that the purely egocentric and self-reflexive features of utterance can be safely axed out of the sentential context; for example, by employing paraphrases which, whilst manifestly retaining all the information which is relevant to truth, involve no use of personal or demonstrative pronouns, indexical adverbs of time and space, tensed verbs, etc., and hence *any instruments of self-reference* which are normally associated with conscious language users. It is one of the fundamental tenets of

[3] The shedding of the notion that propositions which differ in meaning can nevertheless report the same state of affairs, as we shall see, leads invariably to a form of scientific anti-realism and the advocacy, by the radical pragmatists, of the view that no rival scientific theories are strictly 'commensurable' with one another. See chapters 5 and 6.

naturalism that the objective truth-relevant content, in principle, can be expressed *without* employing such expressions.

Nevertheless, an elimination of the egocentric features from the truth-relevant content is just the first, albeit an important, step in the naturalistic reductionist strategy. The ultimate aim is to eliminate not just the indexical features of meaning, but to get rid of meaning *altogether* as a separate and irreducible category. What matters in the end, it is claimed, are only the logical structure of the proposition and the referential properties of its constituent terms. Any feature of the content that cannot be accounted for in terms of structure and reference has to do merely with the 'mode of presentation', and is therefore incidental to the capacity of the proposition to have a determinate truth value; even though, admittedly, such features may be of some psychological interest, for example as a pointer to the attitude or likely behaviour of the language user. Thus what is relevant to the truth of 'There is no life on the Morning Star' is its specific logical form plus the fact that 'life' and 'The Morning Star' have the range of application they have. And that which makes this proposition convey the same state of affairs as 'There is no life on the Evening Star' is simply the circumstance that the reference of 'The Morning Star' and the reference of 'The Evening Star' are the same.

This is hardly a startlingly novel view. It is embedded in the methods and procedures of natural science, and its fruitfulness and heuristic value within the scientific context can hardly be disputed. Invariably those who pursue the reductionist policies in philosophical theory look to natural science for inspiration. But although fruitful in a scientific context, it is none the less a philosophically defective view, and the failure in particular to provide a satisfactory account of structure and reference — and hence of truth-relevant content — on naturalistic premises, shows why philosophically it cannot work.

One of the problems that immediately crops up concerns the relation between the conditions of meaningfulness and the conditions of truth. The naturalistic position is that the conditions of truth not only take precedence, but that the conditions of meaningfulness of everything that really matters in what we assert about the world can and should be defined *in terms* of the conditions of truth. Truth, not meaning, is the primary concept. But given the restrictive interpretation of truth-relevant content, such a position cannot be plausibly maintained — even if in a deliberate effort to make things easier for ourselves, we confined our attention exclusively to singular indicative sentences, leaving the complex issues raised by quantified, modal, optative, imperative, evaluative, etc. sentences to one side.[4] The thesis that the meaning content, in so far as it bears on truth or falsehood, can be specified in terms of the logical structure of the sentence (or sentences) concerned and the referential properties of their constituent terms, superficially attractive though it might seem, no sooner is it closely inspected than it can be seen to run into trouble, the simple reason being that we cannot even begin to know what the structure and the reference are in the given case without first comprehending the meaning content, not just partially or selectively but *in its totality.*

Meaning and the 'deep structure' of sentences

It is here that the naturalistic reductionist strategy begins to stall and flounder. Consider, first, some of the difficulties surrounding the concept of structure. One of the guiding principles underlying this strategy, as we saw, is that the structure of a sentence, in so far as it affects its truth conditions, is independent of its 'mode of presentation'. (I should emphasise that I am using here the term 'mode of presentation' in a broad sense, to include not only alterations of the meaning content resulting from substitutions of non-synonymous but coextensive terms within a sentence, but also the kind of semantic variations, however slight, as might occur when a sentence is translated into a different language, or such as may be brought about by syntactical re-arrangements of parts of sentences undertaken e.g. for reasons of emphasis, etc.) Two sentences that differ with respect to their 'mode of presentation' and their surface syntax, it is claimed, can nevertheless have the same logical or 'deep' structure, and it is this 'deep' structure, alongside the referential properties of their terms, that is instrumental in determining that aspect of the meaning which is relevant to their truth or falsehood.

[4] Not that singular indicative sentences themselves are without problems either, for depending upon the context and emphasis they too can carry a variety of other than purely factual cargo. Thus in current usage 'A is black' and 'A is a Negro' have different emotive connotations, even though they have the same truth conditions (or so it seems).

But granted that sentences which differ in respect of their surface syntax may sometimes turn out to have the same constitution at a deeper level, and, conversely, that sentences which appear syntactically similar on the surface may turn out to have a different logical grammar, the central point surely remains that this can be decided only by studying their *meaning content*. In order to find out what the 'deep' structure is in the given instance, it is necessary, first, to establish what message is being conveyed in the specific context in which the relevant sentence, or sentences, are used. It is only by grasping the meaning of the message in its contextual entirety that we can begin to sort out those aspects of the content which are from those which aren't relevant to its 'truth-value'. A decision, in short, as to what the 'deep' structure is in the given case can be taken only at the level of meaning. But — this is the difficulty that we are facing — if we have to identify those features of meaning which are relevant to truth or falsehood in order to know what the 'deep' structure consists of in the given instance, how can we then, without involving ourselves in a circular argument, invoke the 'deep' structure in order to explain those very features of meaning?

A note about terminology

I shall return to this presently. Before I do, it is necessary to interject a brief clarifying note about terminology. It will have been noticed that in drawing the distinction between 'deep' and 'surface' structure I have linked the former term with the traditional concepts of *logical structure* and *logical grammar*, rather than employing the latterly more fashionable term 'deep syntax'. Those among modern grammarians who have brought this term into prominence, whilst exploring the various semantical features of sentences with a view to laying bare their 'deep' syntactical properties, nevertheless tend to steer clear of the problem of *truth conditions*. Their starting premise is the familiar traditional rationalist thesis that behind the vagaries and varieties of surface syntax there are certain fundamental and invariant patterns and constitutive rules that govern the construction of intelligible sentences. Such patterns and rules, they claim, are 'innate', and account for our ability to manufacture significant sentences according to need, and in general to use language innovatively and successfully in transmitting the information we wish to transmit; in short, they account for our 'linguistic competence'.[5]

I shall not concern myself with these theories. As I have already made clear earlier on, there is no need for me to do so, for my main preoccupation is not with the mechanics governing the formation of significant sentences but with exploring the *conditions of truth*; and the traditional distinction between surface syntax and logical grammar (which I shall retain for the purposes of my discussion) has usually been associated with an interest in truth conditions.

The latter distinction, in the context of the naturalistic approach, as we saw, forms the basis of a radical reductionist programme. The interest is focused on those features of language which are regarded as being constitutive of the factual content of utterance, and are consequently held to be directly relevant to its truth value. The naturalistic philosopher characteristically takes an astringent view of factual meaning, and looks to 'deep' structures as a means of separating the essential from the superficial, unclear or ambiguous features of utterances. Whereas the grammarian is interested not in truth but in how language 'works', and is professionally committed to exploring all aspects of sentence formation, and in particular all variations of syntax that might have an effect, however slight, upon the meaning content of whatever sort, the naturalistic philosopher (and he is the principal object of my interest) confines himself to such features of syntax as affect what he sees as the specifically *truth-relevant* meaning content. Any aspects of meaning that do not — or, at any rate, *from his point of view* do not — enter into the truth-relevant content, are left out of consideration. What sets the naturalistic philosopher apart, in short, is his pursuit of truth conditions combined with an unremitting reductionism.

[5] I mean here in particular the grammarians who are concerned with the problems of the so-called 'transformational grammar'. See Noam Chomsky, *Syntactical Structures* (1957); also his 'Deep structure, surface structure and semantic representation' in Steinberg and Jakobovits (eds.): *Semantics: An Interdisciplinary Reader in Philosophy, Linguistics and Psychology*, 1971.

Alterations of surface syntax and the truth relevant content

Let us now look at some reductionist claims in respect of the alleged 'surface' features of sentences. The basic thesis, as we recall, was that in any given case the truth-relevant content — in part, at any rate — depends upon the 'deep' structure and is compatible with a wide range of surface alterations which, whilst signalling a change in the mode of presentation, nevertheless leave the deep structure intact, and are therefore irrelevant to truth conditions. But, of course, it all depends upon what form such alterations take, and in what context they are made. The difference between 'Torture is immoral' and 'It is immoral to inflict torture' leaves the essential grammar of the message unchanged, whilst 'Time is up' and 'The price of bread is up' have a very different logical structure, although their surface syntax looks very much the same.

There are countless examples from everyday life when we make use of different expressions or altered word order either in order to avoid tedious repetition, or to change weighting, or generally to instil a sense of urgency into what we say. Often such fluctuations of meaning as this might cause are too small or peripheral to have a significant effect on the essence of what is conveyed, and sometimes, as the first of our two examples above illustrates, a simple syntactical rearrangement of verbal material can be entirely superficial and negligible; although this is by no means always the case, especially in the context of live speech. Thus not only the 'mode of presentation' but the truth-relevant content itself may be altered by a mere change of intonation, without *any* alteration of either the verbal content or word order; and conversely, alterations of the content engendered by a change of syntax can to some extent be reversed by a suitably modulated speech.

In written language too in some cases minor syntactical alterations may have major consequences both for the meaning and the truth conditions. Sometimes small changes of syntax will leave the basic message intact, but at other times, depending upon the context, the very same syntactical modification may bring about a radical change of content, including the truth-relevant content. Often the change of the truth-relevant content, although quite substantial, is not immediately apparent. Thus 'The forest was destroyed by fire' and 'It was the fire that destroyed the forest' ostensibly report the same state of affairs; yet the difference between them is by no means simply one of emphasis. The second of the two statements, as well as involving a modification of syntax, carries with it an implicit reference to a *specific* fire-event, whereas the first statement is compatible with the occurrence of a succession of unconnected fire-events over an unspecified period. But, then, evidently the truth conditions cannot be the same in the two cases.

How difficult it can sometimes be to differentiate between 'surface' alterations and 'deep' structure (and, therefore, make out a convincing case for a reductionist treatment of truth-relevant content) is best illustrated by *passivisation*. The most dramatic changes of content occur when some quantified sentences are transposed from active into passive. Thus if everyone hates someone, it clearly does not follow that someone is hated by everyone. But even what at first glance looks like a perfectly innocent transposition of active into passive may signify important changes in emphasis and bring about a shift in truth-relevant content — and occasionally, moreover, it is *intended* that it should. Thus depending upon the context of utterance there may be more than just a superficial syntactical difference between 'Anytus hates Socrates' (*a property of Anytus*) and 'Socrates is hated by Anytus' (*a property of Socrates*). The 'reductionist' reply to this is likely to be that the two statements surely must have the same truth conditions, for they are both verified by the same fact. The active form of the statement and its passive counterpart do not refer to different sets of circumstances 'out there', respectively. If the 'voice' is changed, it is not the actual world that changes; it is merely our *representation* of it that does. But notice that this is a *metaphysical supposition*, which cannot be taken simply on trust. What we have before us are two reports which are structurally very different. The assumption that they both transmit, and are verified by, the same fact is clearly in need of some justification. The case of quantified sentences shows that passivisation does not *necessarily* leave things as they are. Why, then, one might wonder, should it do so in this case? Why should the 'deep' structure of the two reports — and with it, their *truth relevant content* — remain unaffected by the change of active into passive, and vice versa?

What the example of passivisation helps to bring out is just how difficult sometimes it can be to separate the apparently 'surface' features of an utterance from its 'deep' structure. Yet until this is sorted out, the naturalistic reductionist project in respect of the truth-relevant content cannot make much headway, and is destined to flounder in metaphysical generalities. We saw above that the assumption that 'Anytus hates Socrates' and 'Socrates is hated by Anytus' share the same 'deep' structure (whatever that might be) based squarely on the metaphysical premise that they are both 'made' true or false by the same matter of fact; which, it will be noted, is precisely the opposite of the kind of explanation that we have been led to expect, for on the naturalistic theory of truth conditions, as we recall, the assumption that two propositions convey the same state of affairs could only be justified with a reference to the identity of their structure and the co-referentiality of their terms. This is hardly accidental. In the absence of any clear notion as to how the active and the passive form might both be 'reduced' to the same basic logical pattern, the only way to maintain the illusion of their basic 'structural' isomorphism is to appeal to their 'extensional' isomorphism, and claim that since they 'obviously' both convey the same state of affairs and are verified or falsified by the same matter of fact 'out there', their deep structure surely must be the same. But quite apart from leaving us none the wiser about the 'deep' structure, the supposition that the same state of affairs is conveyed in both cases is far from 'obvious', and if it can be justified at all, then it is only on the basis of contextual and pragmatic considerations.

Conveying the same state of affairs and expressing the same truth

However, let us grant for the sake of the argument that the two propositions above are indeed extensionally isomorphic, i.e. that the extra-linguistic state of affairs targeted and conveyed in the two cases is the same; then the question which still remains to be answered is, in what sense exactly can they be said to express the *same truth*? Superficially this may seem an odd, even ludicrous, question to ask, but a moment's reflection is sufficient to see that it is neither. For why should the two statements be necessarily interchangeable with regard to *truth*? The passive voice alters the emphasis, and, depending upon the context, may introduce into the picture new facets of meaning which are cognitively important. Facts, after all, cannot be accessed except through specific 'modes of presentation', and passivisation changes the 'mode of presentation', sometimes very substantially. Why, then, should both the active and the passive form express *literally* the same truth? The naturalistic approach is committed to the view that they normally do (the sole exception to the rule, perhaps, being some quantified propositions). But once again this is an *ad hoc* hypothesis which needs to be argued for, and there are precious few convincing arguments on offer.

The tendency to take the view that passivisation — in a majority of cases, at any rate — is a matter of surface syntax and does not affect the 'deep' structure, and, therefore, has no implications for truth, stems from a reluctance to accept that a shift of the meaning content does occur in such cases, or if it does that it need be taken seriously. But a shift of meaning does occur, and it should be taken seriously. The meaning content is our only guide to the 'deep' structure — not some truncated or slimmed down form of the content, but the content in its entirety. For, despite appearances, there is no clear-cut distinction between the total meaning content of a proposition, on the one hand, and its 'truth-relevant' content, on the other. Any aspect of the content, however minor or peripheral, is implicated in truth in some way. This does not militate against the fact that non-synonymous sentences can in principle be extensionally isomorphic, even though — as we saw above — this may be difficult to justify in some cases. Sometimes the differences in meaning content can be quite sweeping, e.g. when a translation of an idiomatic expression into a foreign tongue demands the use of a completely different kind of metaphor as well as different syntax. Thus 'I am struggling to make ends meet' and 'Je tire le diable par la queue' place very different demands on our imagination. Nevetheless the striking differences in their imagery notwithstanding, they convey, one assumes, the very same sorry state of affairs. A successful translation is possible only on this basis. Yet it should be born in mind at the same time that this is a contextual and pragmatic decision, and it would be foolish to pretend that what the French sentence means to the Frenchman is exactly the same as that which the English sentence means to his English counterpart; and in so far as differences do exist, they cannot fail to colour the experience of truth in the two cases.

And therein lies the key problem for the naturalistic approach. For if whatever happens to represent the 'deep' structure in the given case is accessible only via the total meaning content, if it cannot be identified independently of such a content, then the claim that it is the 'deep' structure (in conjunction with whatever happens to be the reference of the relevant terms) that *determines* the content, or rather that part of the content which 'bears' upon truth, appears rather vacuous; for what it seems to amount to is no more than that in any given case it is the nature of the content that determines the truth-relevant content; as if we had not known that already.

In point of fact, the entire naturalistic theory of truth conditions here begins to come apart at the seams. An (indicative) sentence was said to be a valid vehicle of a truth claim if it was capable of having a truth value, and the conditions under which a sentence qualified as truth-value bearing were said to be explicable in terms of its structure — its 'deep' logical structure, that is — and the referential properties of its constituent terms. But given that the access to the 'deep' structure is possible only via the meaning content, the problem that immediately presents itself is, what criteria should be followed when the meaning content changes, even if the state of affairs targeted ostensibly stays the same? What aspects of meaning or syntax are and what are not relevant, and can be left out of consideration in deciding what state of affairs is being conveyed? A decision on this, as I have pointed out already, will have to be a contextual one, and will depend upon what in any specific set of circumstances we may consider to be important. But, then, what justification might there be for supposing that there is an 'externally' determined truth-relevant content, independent of the mode of presentation?

These are the difficulties that the naturalistic theory of truth conditions runs up against, and it is not immediately clear how they might be resolved, if at all. The only possibility, it seems, is to try as far as possible to underpin the idea of an externally determined truth-relevant content by making use of the notion of reference, and by providing, accordingly, a suitably *referential* analysis of the content. In short, one might begin with the following two assumptions: a) that the truth-relevant content, in any given case, ultimately depends upon, and can be articulated in terms of the attributes of whatever is *really* (as distinct from merely superficially or ostensibly) talked about, and b) that that which is being really talked about — i.e. the 'logical' as distinct from a mere 'grammatical' subject — in the final analysis is located, and can only be located, *outside thought*.

Referential analysis of content and the twin earth hypothesis

Let us now look at this in closer detail. The idea is that that which in a sentence is ostensibly talked about need not necessarily coincide with what is 'really', or 'fundamentally', talked about, and that in embarking on an analysis of the truth-relevant content we should always look for the *latter*. In other words, we should try to establish what the logical subject of discourse is in the given case, and, if need be, rearrange the sentence to make this explicit. Thus if by following this principle two different sentences can be arranged in a similar way, they will by definition have the same 'deep' structure. They will moreover have the same truth-relevant content, and hence the same truth-conditions, if it turns out that in all the relevant respects they convey the same information about the same object, substance or class of things, irrespective of their surface syntax. In order to exhibit their structure and core content, a certain amount of logical symbolism may be necessary; just enough to eliminate any ambiguity and make their truth-relevant features absolutely precise.

The next assumption, as we saw, is that the quest for logical subjects, if pursued with sufficient thoroughness, would invariably show that such subjects are located *outside* thought (in an unconditional, metaphysical sense of 'outside'). In support of this thesis, a thought experiment is sometimes invoked, involving the idea of a planet very similar to Earth — a *Twin Earth* of sorts — on which utterances of *identical sentences* would carry a different truth-relevant content, by virtue of being about *different* things. What a particular expression meant would depend upon the identity of the external object, or objects, aimed at in the given instance. Even what ordinarily pass for proper names would change their reference depending upon the context. Thus 'Newton' on Twin Earth would designate Newton's Twin Earth *doppelgänger*, with the result that 'Newton was struck on the head by a falling apple' would have a different truth-relevant content, depending upon *where* it is uttered. But the real problems would arise with descriptive phrases. Thus if 'Newton' were to be replaced by a descriptive expression, say 'The inventor of the Calculus' or 'The discoverer of the law of gravitation', then the situation would be even more precarious, for no description is *intrinsically* individuative of anything (think of Leibniz's rival claims concerning the Calculus). A purely descriptive reference may be contextually adequate, but it is never logically sufficient, except perhaps in the case of some abstract individuals (like numbers, for example). However specific or detailed such a reference might be, there is never a guarantee that it would hit a unique target, or indeed that it would hit any target at all.

But perhaps the clearest illustration of what is meant by the truth-relevant content being dependent upon external factors can be provided by considering *general terms*, in particular those referring to *natural kinds*. Take 'apple', for example. It is conceivable that whilst what are called apples on both Earth and Twin Earth look and taste exactly the same, and moreover are eaten for similar reasons, the apples on Twin Earth nevertheless possess certain properties, possibly as yet undetected, or unlikely ever to be detected, which the Earth apples do not have; in which case, clearly, there will be an additional reason why the proposition 'Newton was struck on the head by a falling apple' will carry a different truth-relevant content, depending upon where it is uttered, *irrespective of whether anyone is aware of the fact*.

The conclusion thus seems inescapable that the truth-relevant content of what is asserted or claimed to be true in any given case is ultimately determined not by any descriptive 'mode of presentation' (which indicates how things appear to, or are conceived by, a cognitive subject, or subjects, from their respective points of view) but by what happens *outside our mind*. Or, to use the familiar slogan, the meaning — the truth-relevant meaning, that is — of what we say about the world 'ain't in the head'.[6]

That this is a gross simplification, and is indeed untenable as a philosophical position will become apparent in a moment. The question that immediately presents itself, and cannot be given a satisfactory answer from a naturalistic point of view, is this: if logical subjects cannot be unequivocally pinned down descriptively, *how else can they be pinned down, if at all*? They are targeted in the context of a 'mode of presentation' (which embodies a specific point of view), and, for all we know, outside such a context they might not even exist.

[6] This slogan and the Twin Earth example have been made popular by the Harvard philosopher Hilary Putnam, but here I am not specifically concerned with Putnam's views, nor do I wish to suggest that — in his more lucid moments, at any rate — he was espousing the kind of radical naturalism that I am here criticising.

The notion of externality to thought and the problem of reference fixing

The main source of problems can be traced to the confusion — typical of the naturalistic approach — of the *externality* to thought with the *independence* of thought. 'External' is conceived in a metaphysical realist sense as 'unconditionally' or 'absolutely' external, rather than what might be called 'contextually' or 'relatively' external. As a result, that which is supposed to be the subject ultimately 'talked about', i.e. the world 'out there', is logically divorced from any descriptive characterisation, in such a way that it necessarily remains outside our grasp. Yet — and herein lies the contradiction at the heart of the naturalistic approach — that very world is at the same time supposed to determine the truth-relevant meaning content of our utterances!

There is clearly something deeply wrong about the notion that the identity of what in a given case is really being 'talked about', and with it the truth-relevant content, are ultimately determined by 'thought-independent' factors. Consider again the example of natural kinds. Apples on Twin Earth (it is argued) might have properties that Earth apples do not possess, and hence ostensibly the same statement involving a reference to apples will allow of different inferences, depending upon *where* it is made. Similarly, water, whilst qualitatively indistinguishable from Earth water, might nevertheless have a different chemical composition, in which case statements like 'Water quenches thirst' will have a different truth-relevant content; and so on.

But this is a matter of *definition*. The genus *apple* is not necessarily insufficiently determined because tomorrow we might come across another, as yet unknown, species of apples. If water had a different chemical composition, it would still count as water, provided it had all the other properties that we decreed water should have. We might of course change our criteria (as has in effect happened) by laying down that a specific chemical composition is an essential property of water, but that sort of decision is usually made on the basis of purely *pragmatic* considerations. Once such a decision is made, it necessarily follows that the watery substance on Twin Earth which tasted exactly like our water but had a different chemical formula would not qualify as water. The use of the word 'water' in the two cases would represent simply an irritating *homonymy*, and would not involve the same concept at all.

In short, the reference fixing in respect of the so-called 'natural kinds' is invariably a matter of a pragmatic decision, and is done, and can only be done, *descriptively*, via definitions of the relevant concepts. As the definition changes, so does the concept; but then there can be no question of any 'natural kind' — in so far as such a kind can be clearly specified at all — slipping through our conceptual nets.

What is more, everything that applies to *natural kinds* (like apples), applies even more to *artefacts*, which are defined not in terms of any 'natural' properties but strictly in terms of the function they perform, or the purpose they are intended to fulfil. Thus what makes a chair a chair or a hat a hat is descriptively laid down in relevant definitions, and provided we keep strictly within the confines of such definitions, there is no danger of such general terms ambiguously referring to different targets.

It is only certain specific classes of *individuals*, like physical particulars and persons, it seems, that cannot be uniquely captured by our descriptive nets, and they indeed do present special problems, about which I shall have something to say later on. By contrast, abstract individuals can be very accurately targeted. Numbers in particular provide the most conspicuous examples of this. A correct descriptive reference to the number *pi* will hit a unique target irrespective of when or where it is made, or by whom. No descriptive singular term referring to a mathematical object can hit alternative targets, whatever the circumstances of reference might be. Furthermore, descriptive terms referring to the so-called 'cultural objects', such as works of art or literature, seem equally certain of hitting unique targets. 'Madame Bovary' on Twin Earth, the duplicate writing effort and the mirror-image manuscript notwithstanding, does not refer to a numerically different literary work; although, clearly, the same does not apply to descriptive references to its *author*. Thus 'The author of *Madame Bovary*' on Twin Earth will evidently designate a numerically different, albeit qualitatively in every respect similar, individual. But, then, this is hardly surprising. Like any other similar descriptive singular term purporting to refer to a physical particular or a person, 'The author of *Madame Bovary*' is not intrinsically uniquely designative of anything in any case, i.e. it does not pick out a single individual as a matter of logic, although *contextually* it might well do so.

The causal theory of reference

I shall conclude my discussion of the naturalistic approach by considering another linchpin of naturalism, viz. the *causal theory of reference*.

The idea put forward is that the referential 'hook-up' with the world is achieved via certain causal relations that bring us into direct contact with certain entities 'out there', such as physical particulars and other persons. If a singular term succeeds in hitting a unique target, it is argued, then it is only thanks to such causal relations. In the context of our everyday existence we are engaged in a continuous traffic with external objects, which perceptually impinge upon us in a myriad of ways. From time to time, within the context of such a causal contact, we are moved to perform an act of naming, which establishes a unique link between the name and the object named. This accomplished, the name in question, packaged in suitably explicative descriptions, can then be passed on and used successfully by others, who themselves need never have been in direct contact with the object concerned, but who are nevertheless able to grasp the name's unique referential role by assuming it is causally grounded in an initial act of 'baptism'.[7]

In short, such individuative power as our referential terms possess derives exclusively from certain *causal relations*. But, of course, such a theory takes a realist thesis for granted. What is more, as we saw earlier, its realism is basically of a naive metaphysical variety. Physical particulars or types of substances are figured to be 'out there', lurking around and waiting, as it were, to emerge into the light of cognition by becoming causally involved with us, and to receive appropriate labels in the process. It is a pleasing notion, but not one to be taken seriously. There is nothing pre-fabricated or pre-existing out there, waiting to be labelled by us in this way. Rather it is we ourselves who exercise selection and classification, and generally lay down the conceptual frame of reference within which we conduct our exploratory activity. We are responsible for laying out the conceptual marker buoys to indicate where objects might be looked for, and how they are to be sorted out and identified.

The targeting of objects, that is, takes place in the context of our own interests and needs, and this unavoidably involves the use of

[7] Cf. S. Kripke: *Naming and Necessity* (1980).

classificatory descriptions of one kind or another. There is no such thing as targeting by 'pure ostension'. Every ostensive definition presupposes a degree of descriptive selection, without which no amount of ostensive signalling can pick out any individual object. If 'ostensive signalling' can serve as an individuative device at all, then it is only together with an act of — explicit or tacit — *classification*; even though, initially, the classification might be vague and general, and — in the light of modifications that subsequently might be made to the initial frame of reference — might very well be rejected as inaccurate.

So the conclusion that must be drawn is that *there is no individuation without classification*. Whoever named Socrates 'Socrates' was baptising a specimen of a particular sort. Proper names serve to select mooring points for multiple descriptive characterisations, but without any descriptive characterisations there is nothing to select. Besides, ostension is not always an option in any case. Thus the reference of 'the number two', in so far as it can be conveyed at all, can only be conveyed descriptively, but the expression 'the number two' is no less uniquely targeted for that. An object need not necessarily be ostensibly accessible in order that it should be targetable as a unique individual.

Moreover what applies to proper names applies even more to general terms, where the referential 'hook-up' is by definition achievable only through the vehicle of *description*. As we saw earlier, what counts as 'apples', or 'water', will depend upon the kind of characteristics that we definitionally associate with such things; with a decision as to which features are essential and which are accidental, and hence what criteria of classification are appropriate and should be applied in the given case, being based exclusively on contextual and pragmatic considerations.

None of this means, I should emphasise, that there are no genuinely extra-conceptual things out there, and hence that the realist thesis is false. It only means that the *metaphysical* realist thesis underlying the causal theory of reference, and implying that the extra-conceptual world is logically independent of and *antecedes* concepts, is false and should be discarded. The supposition that our (non-analytic) truth claims are targeted at a world of extra-conceptual things, as will emerge from our discussion, is a necessary structural ingredient, albeit not the only ingredient, of a theory of truth. The extra-conceptual world is not a figment of our imagination. But we 'discover' such a world — and can only 'discover' it — within a specific conceptual frame of reference which is of our own devising.

4 Truth and certainty

The naturalistic project, as we have seen, is vitiated by the dogmatic metaphysics implicit in its premises and gives a distorted account of the 'truth-relevant' content. The fault-line runs through its foundations, and cannot be repaired by tinkering with detail. The thesis that the content of a proposition, in so far as the latter's capacity to report a fact is concerned, is fixed by its truth conditions, which in turn are specifiable in terms of that proposition's logical structure and the referential properties of its constituent terms, founders on the inability to provide a satisfactory account of either structure or reference. We traced the source of the problem to the far too restrictive a view taken of the truth-relevant content, and the vain attempt to untangle this content from the other facets of meaning. The leading assumption was that the truth-relevant content can not only be differentiated from, but remains unaffected by any changes in the 'mode of presentation' (as enshrined in the relevant sentence), provided certain extensional properties remain preserved, and is in particular independent of any speaker-related indexical features of the content. This assumption, it turned out, could not be plausibly upheld. The mode of presentation is cognitively important, and in its entirety remains relevant to the truth conditions of what is claimed to be true. The truth-relevant content so far from being separable from the mode of presentation can only be gleaned through it. After all, in order to access the 'deep' structure behind the pluri-lingual diversity and episodic quirkiness of surface syntax, it is necessary first to understand what message is being conveyed when, and this demands that every aspect of the meaning content be taken into consideration. The access to structure, that is, leads through meaning, not the other way round.

The same goes for reference. It is only via descriptive contents that referential terms seek out their targets (although this does not mean that referring 'reduces' to describing). Even proper names, as we saw, presuppose a degree of descriptive classification before they can fulfil their naming function. With regard to the attempt to provide a causal explanation of the way referential terms 'hook onto' external objects, we saw that a causal theory cannot get very far without implicitly appealing to a framework of interpretation which dictates both the selection of the targets and the mode of reference in a given case; which, in turn, undermines the very premises upon which such a theory is based.

It thus seems that a radical re-examination is required of the topic of meaning content as a whole, and of the truth-relevant features of such a content in particular. The thesis that the truth-relevant content of a proposition is determined exclusively by its logical or 'deep' structure and certain things 'out there' which are independent of, and pre-exist all thought (whilst making their presence felt by causally impinging upon our perceptual mechanism) typifies the kind of metaphysical realism that guides and inspires the naturalistic effort, but cannot be underpinned with plausible arguments. This does not mean that realism in all its forms should be discarded. On the contrary, as our analysis will show, the idea of a world external to thought, or more accurately, external to acts of *thinking* — genuinely external, not just *conceived* as external — is an integral part of the general framework of truth conditions. But 'external' does not necessarily mean independent of, and pre-existing all thought. Naturalism habitually conflates these two ontological modalities. Yet they have to be carefully kept apart if absurdities are to be avoided, as will become increasingly apparent in the sequel.

The phenomenological approach and the central role of *mode of presentation*

The approach which I have dubbed 'phenomenological', and which I am about to discuss, stands diametrically opposed to naturalism, and is based on the following three assumptions: a) that a consideration of the truth-relevant content of a truth claim cannot be divorced from a consideration of the intentions and projects of the originator, or originators, of such a claim; b) that a truth claim must at least in principle be *decidably* true or false, or else it should be rejected as inappropriate; and c) that the decidability, or otherwise, of a truth claim depends on the possibility of evidence which is in principle accessible to direct experience.

If this is accepted, then it follows that there can be no clear-cut dividing line between the truth-relevant content and the 'mode of presentation'. That which is being talked about in any given instance is not logically independent of *how* it might be talked about. In a sense, the truth-relevant content and the 'mode of presentation', which now might also be called the 'intentional content', merge into one. In consequence, a firm platform for an analysis of truth-conditions will have to be sought in the first instance within thought itself; and, on the view under discussion, such a platform, and the ultimate mooring point of thought in reality, can be provided only by that which *cannot be coherently disbelieved.*

Decidability, justification and the idea of certainty

Let us now look at this approach more closely. The opening argument closely resembles the type of argument which, in a different context, is normally advanced against the Russellian 'predicates and variables' style of analysis of truth relevant content (see chapter 1). The key notion is that what is decidable depends upon what can appropriately be asserted, and what can appropriately be asserted, in turn, depends upon certain prior — tacit or explicit — decisions regarding the truth conditions in the context in which the relevant assertions are made. Thus if someone should assert that the coffee in the cup on the table is hot, and the cup turns out to be empty, then his assertion will have to be dismissed as inappropriate. Note that the speaker's intention is to say something about the coffee (which he assumes is there) not about the cup, still less about something or other that happens to have the properties of a cup and has coffee in it. It, therefore, won't do to paraphrase his assertion into an *existential proposition*[1], and pretend that what he is really saying amounts to a claim that there is something cup-like on the table which contains hot coffee, on the grounds that while the paraphrase is not exactly synonymous with the original it nevertheless expresses its truth-relevant substance, and is extensionally isomorphic with it. If all that is required is extensional isomorphism, then it would not matter whether we couched our paraphrase in terms of the properties of the cup, or the properties of the table. But the original assertion is about *neither* of these. It is about the coffee whose existence is presupposed; that's why the assertion is not false (which it would be if it were reducible to an existential paraphrase) but inappropriate.

As for what ostensibly are more problematic cases, such as propositions which seem decidably true or false even though they are about non-existent entities, such as characters in fiction, the phenomenological position is that basically here too similar conditions apply; in other words, the intention conveyed within the context of utterance should be our primary consideration. Thus it is perfectly legitimate, and is moreover true to claim that Hamlet killed Polonius, but only in as much as the claim is intended — and *accepted* — as a claim about a literary matter of fact depicted in the play; or, alternatively, because it is intended (if it is) as an elliptical claim about the author of the play who invented the incident.

The idea, in short, is that the truth-relevant content of utterance in all cases will have to be judged in the light of what the utterer intends to convey within a particular context of his utterance. An inquiry into the factors responsible for determining the truth-relevant content will thus have to involve an inquiry into the mental and speech acts of language users. It follows, among other things, that a considerably more flexible view will now have to be taken of truth-relevant content, and that, in particular — in contrast to the naturalistic approach — the indexical features of the content will now largely have to be allowed to stand. With regard to the question 'How does the propositional thought come to exhibit facts?', the phenomenological position is that an answer to this can be given only provided it can be shown that what is true is ultimately anchored in what can be known for *certain*. In order

[1] According to the familiar recipe suggested by Russell in his theory of 'definite descriptions'.

to make sense of truth claims, we have to appeal to the idea of evidence, and hence of possible knowledge; and this, in the final analysis, means presupposing the possibility of certainty; for without the possibility of certainty all knowledge dissolves into opinion, and it is in principle impossible to provide a satisfactory justification of any truth-claim; with the result that the ground of significance of truth claims is itself called into question.

Justification and true belief

My intention, in the following, is to pursue this argument to the limits to which it can be plausibly taken, with the aim of distilling from it those features that may usefully be retained from those that should be discarded. But, first, a brief clarifying note is called for regarding certainty. What this term signifies is not some irrational subjective 'feeling' of indubitability, or the strength of personal conviction. Rather, as the earlier reference to 'what cannot be coherently disbelieved' indicates, it involves a consistency test, which represents a final step in a rational vindication of belief. A belief qualifies as 'certain' when the consistency test reveals the absurdity, or incoherence, of entertaining its opposite. It is in this sense that certainty is sometimes taken by philosophers to represent the ultimate *point d'appui* of all rational thought.

This, of course, immediately raises a question about the criteria of consistency, and, as we shall see, such criteria are subject to certain contextual constraints, arising in particular from the use of language; which, in turn, sets strict limits to what any phenomenological project can accomplish. I shall have more to say about certainty shortly, and as regards the contextual constraints on consistency, and related matters, this will have to wait till the next chapter. At this stage, I propose merely to add a brief general comment about the relationship between justification and true belief.

The naturalistic position, unsurprisingly, is that the possibility of justification of a belief has no relevance to its truth or falsity. A belief may be true or false irrespective of whether it can or cannot be 'justified' in terms of possible knowledge, let alone in terms of what can be known for certain. Nevertheless a powerful argument against this view was already advanced by Plato. Without knowledge, Plato warned, true beliefs would reduce to so many lucky guesses, and there would be no guarantee that such guesses would be equally accurate on the next occasion. For what is true belief without knowledge? It is slippery and inconstant, and needs to be 'tethered' by 'working out the reason', if it is to endure.[2] A truth claim remains vacuous without the possibility of proof, and a proof depends upon what in principle can be known with evidence. The 'tethering' involves a process of *justification*; and — for Plato at any rate — this process ends with the knowledge of what cannot be rationally thought otherwise, and is the kind of knowledge that can flow only from *anamnesis*, i.e. from a recollection of the soul's original acquaintance with what had always been, and always will be, the case.

I should make it clear at this point, however, that what I call the 'phenomenological approach' goes beyond the mere demand that the true belief be 'tethered' to what can be known for certain, in as much as it involves the additional claim that a true belief could not even be significantly described as 'true' unless it were possible, at least in principle, for it to be 'tethered' to certainty in some way. The thesis, in short, is that truth and certainty are *logical bedfellows*.

Availability of the concept of truth and the idea of truthfulness

What rational basis might there be for such a view? One way of exhibiting the link between the two concepts might be to consider what I propose to call the *availability* of the concept of truth. In a universe populated by mindless robots who are mechanically constructing what from *our own* point of view appear like meaningful (true or false) sentences, the concept of truth is not available, and hence there is no notion of the possibility of something being true. Indeed it is doubtful if it makes sense to speak of there being such a thing as truth within such a universe at all, except from the point of view of someone like ourselves. If, however, the availability of the concept of truth is part of what 'truth' means, then certain important consequences follow. To

[2] 'True opinions are a fine thing and do all sorts of good so long as they stay in their place, but they will not stay long. They run away from a man's mind; so they are not worth much until you tether them by working out the reason.' *Meno*, 97e/8a.

begin with, to have the concept of truth, whatever else it might involve, must involve having the notion of 'telling the truth', and the latter notion, in turn, is inseparable from the idea of certainty in respect of the verifying evidence.

Consider a humdrum example. I see a friend standing on the edge of the pavement, craning his neck to scan the oncoming traffic and glancing occasionally at his watch. He is not altogether pleased to see me, and, disconcerted by my quizzical smile and anxious to be left alone, he tells me brusquely: 'I am waiting for a bus'. There are no bus-stops in the neighbourhood, and moreover I happen to know that buses do not use that route; but this does not affect either the content or the truth value of what my friend is saying. The question of truth or falsity, if it should arise at all, become here one of *truthfulness*. Provided my friend is familiar with the words he is uttering, then given he utters such words truthfully and is not merely making a facetious remark, committing a verbal error or engaging in some devious theatrical charade, what he says is true, even if it should happen that no buses are running — or even exist — anywhere. Conceivably he might believe that if he waited long enough, a bus would come down sailing from the sky.

Of course, this will not apply to any old statement he might make — at any rate, not in any immediately intelligible sense. Thus if he should tell me that he breakfasted on coffee and toast, or that he was wearing a Panama hat, or that the English Channel was twenty two miles wide at its narrowest point, the question of truth or falsity would have little to do with his own views on the matter. He might intend such statements as a joke, or deliberately try to mislead me, believing that what he says is in fact false. That his statements are true, if indeed they are, does not vouch for his truthfulness. But in the former case, *it does*. Provided he understands what he is saying, if what he says is true, then he is being truthful; and conversely, if he is being truthful, then what he says is indeed true (although he may have thoroughly disreputable motives for saying it). Truth and truthfulness here go *hand in hand*.

But why, it might be asked, should they go together *necessarily*? Surely the statement in question could be true without actually being *expressed*. The speaker, after all, might stay silent. He probably would have stayed silent if I had not intruded. Or, again, what is substantially the same state of affairs might have been expressed by a bystander in a third person idiom, viz. 'The man in a Panama hat is waiting for a bus';

in which case, clearly, the truth or falsity of the statement would have nothing to do with anyone being or not being truthful. But then, surely, the idea of truthfulness should be discarded as irrelevant to a consideration of truth value.

This criticism misses the point, for it overlooks the relevance of the availability of the concept of truth to the truth-relevant content in such cases. If, in the full knowledge of what he is saying, the person standing on the pavement — call him A, for convenience — declares that he is waiting for a bus, he must know whether he is telling the truth. Given that he has the concept of truth, his capacity to know whether he is telling the truth is part of the *meaning* of what he states. But a third person paraphrase of the same statement uttered by a bystander does not presuppose such a capacity on the part of the speaker.

This difference is crucial. The bystander's own sincerity is immaterial to the truth or falsity of what he, the bystander, is saying. Indeed he might be deliberately trying to tell a lie, and failing, without even realising it. By contrast, A's sincerity has a *direct bearing* upon the truth of A's own statement. If A is sincere, then what he says is true; if he lies, it isn't. This leaves plenty of scope for pretence. The possession of the concept of truth allows the possibility of acting *as if* one knew or told the truth on the given occasion. It therefore makes perfect sense to say 'A (or 'The man in a Panama hat', or whatever other description might be appropriate) merely pretends to be waiting for a bus'. By contrast, those who don't have the concept of truth cannot be liars either. My dog Caesar may be waiting for his food, but he cannot *feign* to be so doing.

Telling the truth and the verifying evidence

In short, the possession of the concept of truth, in as much as it involves the notion of *telling the truth*, also necessarily involves the idea of *certainty in respect of the verifying evidence*. This deviates from the naturalistic approach. From the naturalistic standpoint, the concept of truth has nothing to do with the availability or otherwise of verifying evidence, let alone with certainty as to what does or does not count as such evidence in any given instance. What is true is true, irrespective of whether it is known, or could be known to be so, let alone known for certain. But this position cannot be consistently maintained, if only because it ignores the direct relevance that the possession of the concept of truth has to the truth-relevant content in a wide range of cases.

Consider again the above example. A does not actually have to utter his statement in order that what he says be true; a third person can convey the same state of affairs, without A having to say anything. Nevertheless in such situations the underlying assumption is that if the state of affairs in question does obtain, A must in principle be capable of articulating the relevant thought. Furthermore, as we saw earlier, what A says cannot be true if, knowing the meaning of the words he utters, he is not being truthful, or if he himself is not in a position to *decide* whether what he utters is true. He must, that is, be capable of knowing for certain whether what he is saying is a *lie*. Given he understands the meaning of what he is saying, he cannot coherently claim 'I am waiting for a bus, but I cannot decide if, in fact, that is what I am doing'.

The point is that if A knows himself to be the subject of the experience, he must at the same time be able in principle to decide with certainty *what kind* of experience he is the subject of. Conceivably he might for one reason or another misdescribe what he experiences on a particular occasion, but if he knows the meaning of the words, he must be in a position to identify it in principle. His capacity to bear false witness testifies to that.

It follows that a grasp of the concept of truth presupposes and is inseparable from the grasp of what it means to 'speak the truth'. It is in ignoring this fact, among other things, that the formal-logical treatment of truth (discussed in chapter 2) goes awry. It assumes that the concept of truth is independent of, and can be treated separately from any other notions, and this view is plainly untenable. Similarly naturalism, whilst conceding the need for a broader approach to truth conditions, disputes that truth has anything to do with certainty, and in this it is equally mistaken. For, as we have just seen, the possession of the concept of truth entails the possession of the concept of truthfulness, and the idea of certainty in respect of the verifying evidence. To have the concept of truth is to know the difference between telling the truth and lying, i.e. deliberately uttering a falsehood; and it is impossible to have a clear conception of this difference without knowing what it is to be certain about the relevant *evidence*.

Indexical features of truth relevant content

But if so, then surely the speaker-related, indexical features of the propositional content cannot be entirely left out of consideration. Naturalism, as we saw, deliberately sets out to show that such features have no bearing on truth or falsity of what is claimed to be true, and can be safely axed, or at any rate paraphrased out of the propositional context. That part of the meaning content which affects the truth-value, as the familiar slogan has it, 'ain't in the head'. The scene is thus set for a policy of a systematic, and ultimately self-defeating reductionism; for the more assiduously such a policy is pursued the more absurd and unsustainable it is shown to be. In trying to filter out all the indexical features of meaning, naturalism, in the end, manages to throw away the baby with the bath water, for meaning in effect disappears as an independent category, to be replaced by an extensionalist notion of a proposition, with the 'truth-relevant content' allegedly being specifiable entirely in terms of structure and reference.

It was largely this austere notion of content that lay behind the theory, propounded by early Wittgenstein, according to which the process of semantic analysis of propositions must needs terminate with the so-called 'basic propositions', which, in turn, portray certain 'basic' states of affairs consisting of possible configurations of logically simple objects. The problem for such a simplistic theory, however, is that it can provide no explanation for such differences in content as do exist between non-synonymous, albeit strictly extensionally isomorphic, propositions. Yet the differences in meaning in such cases are real, and often considerable as well as important to those who assert such propositions, for they communicate the specificities of their respective points of view. So why should they not be relevant to truth? The only reply given to this is that such differences do not really matter in the long run; that all that matters as far as truth is concerned is the extensional isomorphism, and that any differences in meaning between extensionally isomorphic propositions will eventually fade away in the process of analysis to leave behind strings of identical elementary propositions. But they do not 'fade away'. When the man in a Panama hat tells me 'I am waiting for a bus' he identifies himself with a personal pronoun in a way in which he can never be identified with a descriptive phrase from another person's point of view. Nothing can identify him as uniquely as he identifies himself in that simple act of self-reference. But then, how can this fail to make a difference to the truth of what he says?

The 'austere' notion of truth-relevant content superficially commends itself on the grounds of its pragmatic advantage. It is contextually expedient to act on the assumption that substantially the same message can be expressed in a third person idiom, viz. by making use of descriptive referential expressions such as 'The man in a Panama hat', 'The man standing on the kerb', etc. Provided such expressions have the same reference, all the resulting propositions will be extensionally isomorphic, and *to all intents and purposes* will have the same truth-value. What is more (as we saw) additional practical gains are said to flow from a conversion of such referential expressions into pronominal phrases with variables.[3] Thus by converting 'The man in a Panama hat is waiting for a bus' into 'Whoever is wearing a Panama hat is waiting for a bus, and there is only one person wearing a Panama hat', we eliminate at a stroke all the ambiguities that beset the original proposition while preserving the essence of the message.

But while contextually this may bring some advantages, it is clearly logically inadequate. For, as has been shown, the uniqueness of reference cannot be safeguarded by relying on *predicates and variables* alone. What the speaker means by the word 'I' is not logically equivalent with any specific predicate, or set of predicates. If it were logically equivalent, then all distinction would disappear between existential uniqueness, on the one hand, and mere qualitative indistinguishability, on the other, and not even Leibniz, despite his *principle of indiscernibles*, which laid down that things are individuated by the predicates they have, was quite willing to contemplate such a possibility. Whilst arguing that there would be no 'sufficient reason' for there to exist qualitatively identical but numerically different individuals, he nevertheless had to concede that this was not *logically* impossible. But this means that a reductionist programme based on the kind of paraphrase suggested above cannot work. A third person paraphrase of 'I am waiting for a bus', along the suggested lines, *presupposes* the intelligibility of the first person report; it does not 'replace' it, or make it redundant. So far from being logically independent of such a report, it is *logically parasitic upon it*.

[3] See footnote 1 in this chapter.

Indexical features of content and the idea of consciousness

This granted, there are clearly important implications for a theory of truth. The full extent of these implications will become apparent as we continue our account of the 'phenomenological approach'. For the present, suffice it to highlight the following points.

The concept of truth-relevant content evidently must be taken in a broader sense than is allowed by, or is even compatible with, a naturalistic approach; in particular, it must be broad enough to incorporate indexical features of truth claims. This is not to deny that, within appropriate contexts, propositions containing such features might legitimately be replaced by extensionally isomorphic propositions *without* indexicals. Contextually information often can, and sometimes has to be whittled down to its skeletal essentials, so it might travel more easily. But this does not mean that indexical expressions are dispensable *altogether*; i.e. that they are altogether irrelevant to the truth-relevant content. If they made no logical difference, there would be a strict logical symmetry between statements in the first person singular and their third person paraphrases, both those involving the use of descriptive referential expressions and those of the more austere sort, involving the use of only predicates and variables. But, as we have seen, there is no logical symmetry.

Note that indexicality enters also into all the verbs descriptive of mental action — i.e. the 'intentional' verbs, such as the verb *to wait* in our example above — in this sense: that what is relevant to the truth or falsity of statements containing such verbs cannot be expressed adequately without making use of indexical expressions. Thus although 'I am waiting for a bus' and its third person paraphrase 'The man in a Panama hat is waiting for a bus' contextually convey the same state of affairs, the latter statement presupposes the kind of confirmatory evidence that can be articulated *only along the lines of the former*. The evidence, in short, contains certain features which can only be conveyed with the help of indexicals. We cannot reasonably say 'The man in a Panama hat is waiting for a bus, but he does not know he is', or 'is incapable of attributing the experience to himself', or 'is unable to understand the difference between having the experience now and having had it in the past', etc. The original statement cannot be significantly attributed a truth value without all these conditions obtaining.

Now it will no doubt be objected that this presupposes a specific view of persons, and it has to be conceded that, in a sense, it does. In general we think of persons as being endowed with the faculty of consciousness, and as being capable of ascribing experiences to themselves in the first person singular. This granted, it is obvious why 'The man in a Panama hat is waiting for a bus' cannot be treated as logically on a par with 'My dog Caesar is waiting for his food'. The former statement is incomparably richer in content, and licenses the kind of inferences about the subject of experience that cannot be legitimately derived from the latter.

The thesis that all truth should be grounded in certainty

Nevertheless it should be emphasised that these are merely preliminary moves in an argument which is considerably more ambitious in scope. All that has been shown so far is: a) that to have the concept of truth is to have the notion of telling the truth, and that the latter notion is inseparable from the idea of certainty in respect of the verifying evidence; b) that such evidence cannot be communicated without the help of indexicals; and c) that, therefore, wherever such evidence is involved indexicals form an important part of the truth-relevant content of the corresponding truth claims.

What I have termed the 'phenomenological approach', however, goes farther than this, in as much as it purports to show that all truth, in the final analysis, either rests on what can be known for certain, or else there is nothing whatever that can be significantly described as 'true'; with the role of indexical elements in the truth-relevant content, consequently, acquiring an even greater importance. This clearly is a much more problematic as well more ambitious claim.

In the following, I propose to look at this claim in closer detail. I should reiterate that my principal interest is theoretical, not historical or exegetic. As before, I am engaged in sketching out an ideal philosophical model, not expounding any specific theory, although, as everyone will recognise, there are plenty of theories which conform to this model in varying degrees, without necessarily coinciding with it in every particular. What specifically distinguishes the theoretical position that I am here outlining is the idea that the concept of truth cannot be divorced from the concept of evidence, and hence of possible knowledge, and that either knowledge rests on certainty or it becomes indistinguishable from opinion; and hence that truth ultimately must rest on certainty too.

The kind of certainty sought after might perhaps best be illustrated by considering certain infallible beliefs. In general we don't think of beliefs (especially other people's beliefs) as infallible: to believe that *p* is entirely compatible with *p* being false. Yet this does not, indeed cannot — *logically* cannot — apply to all beliefs. Admittedly it is conceivable, however unlikely, that all the beliefs I happen to hold at a given time might be false. But although all my actual beliefs might be false, it is inconsistent to suppose that any belief I might hold could be. Indeed either some such beliefs are true, or else there can be *no coherent concept of belief.*

It is here where we seem to enter the zone of certainty. For some beliefs are not just true, but cannot be other than true. Thus the belief that at least some (potential) beliefs are true is itself an infallible belief, for the supposition that none are cannot be consistently entertained. Here's why: If my belief that all beliefs without exception are false is true, then it is false; hence some beliefs must be true; hence my belief is *necessarily* false.[4]

A simple consistency test thus yields a necessary proposition: viz. that some beliefs are true cannot be false. Phenomenologically this is an exceedingly important result. For notice that the infallibility of the relevant belief is not explained from the necessity of the proposition believed, but rather the other way round: the necessity of the proposition in question is derived from the infallibility of the *relevant belief*; with the proof of infallibility being phrased in terms of the constraints on what can be significantly believed. If a belief is such that believing its opposite generates an absurdity, then that belief must count as 'infallible'.

Naturally not all propositions that can be infallibly believed are necessary truths. (I shall consider some examples of such propositions presently.) But some evidently are, and an essential part of the phenomenological argument is that their logical status depends upon the result of a phenomenological consistency test. The 'infallibility' of a

[4] Cf. my book *The Concept of Reality*, chapter 9.

proposition, that is, is derived from the incoherence that results from attempting — within the context of certain tacitly agreed assumptions — to believe its negation. This includes all the so-called analytic truths — both those whose analyticity depends upon the semantic overlapping, partial or total, of their terms (e.g. 'All bodies are extended', 'If x is red, it is coloured', etc.), and to trite tautologies (e.g. 'No married man is unmarried', 'It is raining or it is not raining', etc.), whose analyticity is grounded in the truth-functional definitions of the relevant logical particles (i.e. 'not', 'either-or', etc.). With regard to semantic overlapping of terms, the question which terms do and which don't semantically overlap can of course be a matter of dispute. Some philosophers, as is well known, have argued that there can be no clear or definitive *criteria* of semantic overlapping; and consequently that no possibility exists of deciding in a definitive fashion which propositions are, and which are not, analytic. However, I am concerned here not so much with the question of the criteria of analyticity as with the idea of infallible *belief*.

With this in mind, all that needs to be underlined here is this: that as a minimal precondition of coherent thought it must be possible to form a clear notion of what, in a given instance, one believes, and what one cannot self-consistently *disbelieve*. Phenomenologically all so-called 'analytic' propositions, in the final analysis, have to be tested, and can only be tested, as objects of belief on this basis. The idea, in short, is that a proposition qualifies as analytic only provided such a proposition is capable of generating an infallible belief by virtue of the fact that an attempt to believe the opposite could not be self-consistently entertained.

As it happens, there are a good many propositions — in addition to those normally described as 'analytic' in one of the two senses mentioned above — which seem to yield the same result. 'Nothing is blue and yellow all over at the same time', 'If the door is wooden, then it isn't metal', 'I could not have been Napoleon', provide some particularly striking examples. What is essential in all such cases, from a phenomenological point of view, is that a justification of the modal status of the proposition concerned — i.e. its necessity — ultimately can be provided only via a *phenomenological consistency test*.

Infallible beliefs and experience reports

But plausible though this may be, it is hardly sufficient to vindicate the phenomenological project in its entirety, and ensure its success. For what is needed, if this project is to succeed, is not just a phenomenological account of the conditions of coherent thought, but a clarification of the conditions under which thought *hooks onto* facts. What has been offered so far is merely a tentative explanation of the modal status of analytic propositions in terms of the infallibility of relevant beliefs, and an account of infallible belief in terms of a phenomenological consistency test; with certainty defined, accordingly, in terms of *what cannot be coherently denied*. But what we really need is a clarification of truth claims which purport to convey what the *actual world is like*. It is not simply the conditions of truth of 'analytic' propositions but of the propositions with hard factual content that need to be explained.

In short, if the phenomenological approach is going to work it is necessary to show that there exists an area of unquestionably certain *factual* knowledge which is capable of supporting the edifice of truth as a whole. But where might such knowledge be found?

Once again, the most promising, perhaps the only, option seems to be to look to one's own mental states, and in particular to the simplest form of such states, i.e. *sensory states*. Thus if I am in a sensory state S, then surely I can be certain that I am in that state. If I am hot, I cannot not be certain that I am hot. Of course 'I am hot', if true, is only contingently true; i.e. its negation does not generate any inconsistency. What is more, whoever utters such a statement might misidentify the experience, owing to a defective knowledge of the language. But if he uses the words correctly, and utters them truthfully, then surely what he says cannot be other than true. Above all, given the speaker understands what he is saying, he can be confident he is saying something true. The possibility of certainty (as with our earlier, somewhat more complex, example, viz. 'I am waiting for a bus'), is built into the truth-relevant content of what is uttered.

Looking at it from the opposite angle, if I am hot, I cannot — always provided I know what I am saying — without contradiction claim that 'I am not hot' and believe that I speak the truth when I utter my statement. In such a case, I can coherently believe only what I can truthfully avow.

The phenomenological approach and the foundationalist epistemology

What the experience reports, such as those above, seem to embody, then, is a unique combination of certainty with factual content. They provide solid intelligence about the actual world, in the sense in which those other candidates for certainty, viz. the 'analytic' propositions, evidently do not, nor cannot. 'Socrates is Socrates' does not require the existence of Socrates. 'An apple is not an orange' is true in any possible world, including those that have neither fruit. And the same applies to 'Nothing is blue and yellow all over at the same time'. By contrast 'I am hot', 'This feels heavy', 'I am in pain' supply concrete information, and since they can be infallibly certain into the bargain, might they not serve as a basis for evaluating *all* our beliefs? If a belief needs a validation, how might such a validation be provided if not in terms of precisely those beliefs that are self-validating? If knowledge requires a safe foundation, where might such a foundation be found if not in what can be known for certain? Here, then, it seems, we have all the clues we need. If our aim is to investigate the conditions of what can be significantly claimed to be true, we have to look to possible knowledge, and knowledge ultimately derives such authority as it has from what we have a right to be sure about, i.e. from the kind of information that we cannot self-consistently disbelieve.

A phenomenological theory of truth thus finds itself on a converging path with the 'foundationalist epistemology'. Most 'foundationalist' epistemologies seek to anchor knowledge in infallible beliefs in respect of what can be 'directly experienced', i.e. known by direct acquaintance rather than by inference. Admittedly there is a wide divergence of views as to what is or what is not accessible to direct experience. Thus whereas some epistemologists, in particular those pursuing the Positivist, i.e. the phenomenalist, verificationism, argue that the scope of direct experience is restricted to sensory states, sense contents, sense data, and such like, and that all other knowledge is purely inferential, others are ready to admit physical objects, and — in the case of the Platonists — even *universals*, into the realm of what can be directly known; with the Platonists, moreover, arguing that it is the knowledge of universals that comes first in the logical order of precedence. However, the main objection against all such epistemologies from the phenomenological point of view is that for the most part they still labour under the naturalistic preconceptions, and treat objects of knowledge, accordingly, as ontological items existing independently of the specific conditions under which they are recognised as being such and such; and hence are not sufficiently 'critical' (in the Kantian sense of the term).

The problem of specifying the content of infallible beliefs. The sceptical counter-argument

But leaving this to one side, what is of particular interest to us here is the general premise shared by what I have termed the 'phenomenological approach' with most such 'foundationalist' efforts, viz. that what is accessible to direct experience is a source of certainty, and that this is the place where one should look for a foundation of all factual knowledge and a criterion for evaluating the meaningfulness of truth claims. This premise, it turns out, is open to a devastating sceptical counter-argument.

The argument runs as follows. If, as the phenomenological epistemology assumes, there are infallible beliefs, how can such beliefs be *specified*? No sooner does one attempt to articulate one's supposedly infallible belief, than what one says becomes instantly susceptible of error. Thus I might misreport my belief because I am not sufficiently familiar with the words I am using, or because of an accidental, but unnoticed, misidentification or lapse of memory. Whatever my belief might be on a given occasion, I can never be entirely certain in respect of what is conveyed by my utterance. Moreover with every correction of verbal error there is a possibility of yet more error occurring. But if there can be no certainty about the accuracy of any *articulation* of belief, what justification is there in supposing that there actually are infallible *beliefs*?

If a belief is infallible — this is the gist of the sceptical argument — then it cannot be articulated, and hence no belief is infallible. The temptation invariably is to refer to mathematical theorems as objects of infallible belief. But mathematical theorems are rules that can be misapplied on the next occasion. In any case, they do not say anything about empirical matters of fact. Rather they are corollaries of certain a priori postulates and definitions. With regard to propositions that purport to provide information about matters of fact, including first person reports of own sensory states, their unavoidable corrigibility surely destroys the very basis of any 'infallibilist' epistemology. Suppose I have an experience which I report by saying 'I feel queasy'. The 'infallibilist' epistemology assumes that although I may commit a verbal error in reporting my experience, I cannot be wrong about the experience itself. But what is it exactly that I am certain about if no sooner do I give a name to it than I could be mistaken?

Can the sceptical argument be overthrown?

Is there a way of meeting these sceptical objections? There are, on the face of it, two possible ways of responding to them from a phenomenological standpoint. First of all, one might raise the question of the presuppositions underlying the use of the concept of error. The sceptic claims that I could always be mistaken in reporting my experiences. But how can I have a clear notion of what error is without at the same time having a notion of *absence* of error? Unquestionably, what I say may for a number of reasons give an inaccurate account of the actual state of affairs. But if I know what it is to be mistaken on a given occasion, I must also know what it is to be *right*. To take the above example again, how can I meaningfully say that I could be mistaken in claiming that I feel queasy if it is in principle impossible for me to know for certain that which I could be mistaken *about*? Surely if I can never be absolutely confident of having the relevant experience, I cannot claim to know what it is to make an erroneous report about it either.

There is one further observation that might be made in support of the above point. Consider what it is to have concepts. The sceptical position, carried to extreme, implies not only that every concept can be misapplied, but that there is no way of knowing with certainty on any given occasion whether a given concept has been applied correctly. But surely in the case of concepts of sensory states in particular, I cannot coherently claim both that I have a clear grasp of the concept F and that every single application of F might yield a falsehood. I cannot claim, that is, that I understand the concept of queasiness if I am unable, in principle, to know with certainty if I feel queasy. On the contrary — as we saw earlier — it is precisely because I am certain of the experience that I am able to lie, or mislead others, as to its occurrence.

Of course, the difficulty with this sort of reply to the sceptic is that it implicitly relies upon the division between the *private* and the *public* aspect of knowledge. But perhaps this cannot be avoided. The underlying assumption is always that I can be certain about my experience being of the given sort, even though my experience-*report* on any given occasion might be erroneous. The division that we have to confront here is thus between the corrigibility of the public report and the 'ineffable' inner certainty which, in a sense, remains unaffected by the public fate of my utterance. As I have said, this division may be unavoidable, and the best strategy is to try to find a rationale for it within a broader account of truth, rather than trying to 'eliminate' it, or pretend it is not there.

The Cartesian response to the sceptic

A *second* type of response to the sceptic might be along the familiar Cartesian lines. Descartes' strategy was to begin by conceding that the sceptic had a considerably more powerful case than was commonly allowed, and that neither a phenomenalist nor a Platonist epistemology was capable of seriously denting, let alone overturning, the sceptical argument. If it was going to be possible to arrive at certain knowledge and lay firm foundations for a theory of truth, Descartes was in effect saying, it was necessary to withdraw, temporarily at least, from the areas that could not be held in the face of a determined sceptical onslaught. Instead of insisting on the supposedly infallible knowledge of one's own sensory states, one should wisely decamp to the next available line of defence. Whereas it is quite possible that one may form a wrong notion of the sensory state that one happens to be in, one can at least be certain that one *thinks* that one's sensory state is of such and such a sort; or that one *thinks* that one's own verbal account of one's experience correctly expresses what one believes it does.

Descartes' *Cogito* experiment was thus intended to turn the sharp edge of the sceptic's argument against the sceptic's own position. But although this much is clear, the mechanics of this experiment are often misunderstood, partly due to Descartes' own insistence on dressing up his *phenomenological* analysis as a *metaphysical* argument. To begin with, it must be appreciated that 'I think' does not represent a proposition in the ordinary sense of the word. Indeed it is not a proposition at all. Rather — like 'I believe' — it is a truncated, grammatically incomplete expression. Thus in normal circumstances we use locutions such as 'I think that such and such', 'I believe that p'. By failing to keep a clear distinction between the phenomenological and the metaphysical aspects of his argument Descartes to a large extent himself contributed to a confusion over this, which, not surprisingly, was eagerly seized upon by his critics.[5]

The point is very simple: if 'I think' were a proposition in its own right, then a straightforward assertion of it would accomplish no more than is accomplished by any other proposition in the first person singular; for whoever asserts such a proposition refers to himself by virtue of the words he uses, the sole function of the first person pronoun being to point back to its utterer. It follows that if we have here a complete proposition, then the existence of the utterer is presupposed rather than entailed, and 'I think' — despite Descartes' protestations — accomplishes no more, and is neither more nor less certain, than 'I walk'. Neither of them is a necessary truth.

So what kind of certainty does *cogito* provide? Not a 'propositional' certainty, surely. 'I think', as we have just seen, should be read as 'I think that . . .', i.e. it is grammatically incomplete.[6] Descartes' analysis (at least in its phenomenological aspects) is concerned not with propositions but with *acts of thinking*, and the certainty that is supposed to flow from such acts. In other words, 'I think' signifies that whereby a

[5] There is a difference in logical grammar as between 'cogito' and 'sum'. Descartes (in *Meditation* II) refers to 'Ego sum, ego existo' as a *pronuntiatum* which is 'necessarily true each time it is expressed by me or conceived in my mind'. 'Sum' (or 'Ego sum') is certainly a *pronuntiatum* which is true by virtue of being expressed. But notice that this does not apply to *cogito*, which might well be false when uttered. Nevertheless neither 'sum' nor any other statement in the first person singular can yield the required certainty without thought; or, to use Descartes' expression, without being 'conceived' in one's mind. That is the key point. As to what is thus 'conceived' by me, this clearly can only be the circumstance that I have a thought *that* such and such (and hence that such thoughts have a bearer). In other words, the certainty is enshrined in the evidence that one has of the occurrence of a *thought that*.

[6] Sometimes it is suggested that 'I think' should be replaced by 'I am thinking', which is said to provide a more accurate rendering of *cogito*; but if the intention behind this suggestion is to make *cogito* look and sound more naturally like a complete proposition, then this shows a grievous misunderstanding of its meaning.

proposition becomes an object of thought; an act of thinking *that* something is such and such, or *that* something is the case; and the reflective awareness that one has of such an act. If I am thinking, i.e. having certain thoughts, then I can be reflectively certain that I am having such thoughts in the sense in which I cannot be certain that I am walking if I am walking. Descartes' thought experiment is designed to reinforce this conclusion, and relies heavily on the notion of *self-consistency*. Thus if I decided to take a radically sceptical attitude and doubt everything, I could not stick to my position without defeating my own objective. If I doubt that p is the case, I cannot at the same time coherently doubt that I doubt that p is the case; hence I cannot doubt everything. Whenever I think that such and such is the case I can be certain that I *think* that such and such is the case. The result of an attempt at a universal doubt is thus a discovery of the certainty of the occurrence of certain (*current*) thought acts.

What the *cogito* symbolises is thus at once the most universal condition of intelligible thought and something supremely trivial, viz. that any given thought at the time of its occurrence can be unmistakably known to occur as that specific thought and no other. I cannot both have the thought that I doubt everything and not be certain that that is the thought I am having. Whenever I think x, I can be certain *that* I think x.

It thus turns out that this kind of response to the sceptic is not that much different from the previous one, after all. The certainty that eludes the sceptic's arrows is the certainty of what cannot be coherently disbelieved irrespective of the unavoidable 'corrigibility', and hence a lack of complete certainty, in respect of what is *actually uttered*.

Yet it is an important response none the less, and should be taken seriously, even though it does not go anywhere near establishing what Descartes hoped it would. From the very beginning, Descartes presented his experiment with a universal doubt as part of a *metaphysical* project. Rather than confining himself to a phenomenological analysis of acts of thinking, as he should have done, he was anxious to prove the ontological separateness of the subject of such acts relative to extended matter. The subject of such acts, he argued, was a substantival I-mind — *mens sive animus* — entirely distinct from I-body. But the phenomenological experiment with a universal doubt, as Kant showed, could never shoulder such a metaphysical proposition. Kant's own comment on the Cartesian argument is scathing as well as deadly in its accuracy: 'That I distinguish my own existence as that of a thinking being, from other things outside me — among them my own body' — he points out — 'is an analytic proposition, for *other* things are such as I think to be distinct from myself. But I do not thereby learn whether this consciousness of myself would even be possible apart from things outside me through which representations are given to me, and whether, therefore, I could exist merely as a thinking being . . .'[7] It follows that there are no valid grounds for the claim that I can be 'more certain' of my own existence as a 'thinking being' than I can be certain of the existence of external things, still less for the supposition that my own existence as a 'thinking being' is causally unrelated to the existence of anything external. All that the *cogito* yields is the certainty that I am having certain determinate thoughts, not that thoughts could occur *independently* of whether there is anything external to thinking.

General propositions and counterfactual conditionals

None of this, it should be emphasised, entails that certainty is irrelevant to considerations of truth. Our discussion of the sceptical argument against the 'infallible beliefs' of the foundationalist epistemology, if anything, has established exactly the opposite. There is an idea of certainty of 'what cannot be coherently disbelieved' which, in a sense, is embedded in any truth claim, and which survives the sceptical attacks unscathed. We approached this topic earlier on in the chapter by exploring the idea of availability of the concept of truth. To have the concept of truth is at the same time to have the concept of *telling* the truth, and the concept of telling the truth is inseparable from the idea of certainty in respect of the *verifying evidence*. One cannot have the concept of truth without at the same time knowing that one cannot coherently disbelieve the experience which one can successfully dissemble about, or truthfully avow. What is more, there is a sense in which the possession of any concept demands the notion of certainty, in this sense: that to have a concept is to be in a position to decide whether a specific belief or experience associated with the application of that concept is of the relevant sort. Thus to have the concept of a

[7] *Critique of Pure Reason*, B.409.

chair is to be in a position in principle to decide with certainty whether something is or is not a *chair-perceiving* experience (irrespective of whether a chair is actually there).

But although the idea of certainty and the concept of truth are linked, truth is not grounded in certainty in the sense that it is through certainty, and through certainty *alone*, that thought achieves firm anchorage in reality, which is what the phenomenological model implies. There is a simple way of showing this, though not (as is often done) by trotting out facile 'realist' arguments.

Consider some obvious counterexamples. That all organic compounds contain carbon is true or false but it is not decidably true or false, let alone decidably true or false on the basis of direct evidence, unless containing carbon is taken to be part of what 'organic life' means, in which case the proposition is analytic. So if epistemic decidability on the basis of direct evidence is to be our criterion, it might be argued, we shall have to deny that general propositions such as this one can be meaningfully attributed a truth value, which surely is absurd. Similarly 'counter-factual' conditionals such as 'If the flood had not occurred, the dam would not have collapsed' which represent a mainstay of scientific reasoning would, on such as basis, have to be disallowed as valid candidates for truth claims, which is equally intolerable.

The answer to this from the 'phenomenological' standpoint is that such propositions presuppose a realist commitment, and once they are suitably paraphrased to remove such a commitment any conflict that might appear to exist between truth and the demands of certainty will fade away. Thus 'All organic compounds contain carbon' will have to be rephrased along the following lines: 'On the basis of the available evidence it is likely that we would detect the presence of carbon in any organic molecule we came across'. Similarly 'If the flood had not occurred, the dam would not have collapsed' would have to be reproduced, perhaps, in terms of belief, thus: 'On the basis of the available evidence it is reasonable to believe that we would not have seen the dam collapsing had the flood not intervened'.

In other words, the idea is that the problem can be resolved by avoiding any a priori metaphysical supposition about the world 'out there' and phrasing our truth claims in accordance with what is unequivocally decidable on the basis of the available epistemic evidence. But can this be done always?

Certainty and tense

Consider *tensed* propositions. On the Cartesian premises, I can be certain that a thought occurs to me now, but I cannot be certain that a thought occurred to me a moment ago, or that there was a past at all. But if there was no past, then there is no present either, and 'now' ceases to be a determination of tense. Of course, from a naturalistic point of view, this is all to the good, for a basic tenet of naturalism is that tense is not an essential feature of the propositional content anyway, and can be paraphrased out of the propositional context without any loss of truth. Thus the statement 'It rained yesterday', on naturalistic premises, reduces to 'It rains (tenselessly) on 11 August' (or whatever happens to be the date). However, as our analysis indicates, this view cannot be supported with plausible arguments. Indexical features cannot be removed wholesale from the truth-relevant content; and this *includes* indexical time. Today, yesterday, tomorrow, phenomenologically, represent irreducible modalities of temporal reference. It is entirely possible that today (or yesterday, or tomorrow) is 11 August, but it need not be. In my mind I might associate a specific date with the relevant indexical adverb, but it is equally possible that I don't, or that I have lost all track of calendar dates. Nevertheless this does not detract from the intelligibility of what I say; or from its objectivity, for that matter.

It is here that we encounter a difficulty. Phenomenologically the self-reflexive tensed indication of time conveyed by my statement ('It rained yesterday') remains this statement's irreducible feature; i.e. it cannot be replaced by a tenseless present without substantially altering its meaning. The point is that although in the context in which the statement is made, the indexical time determination does 'objectively' refer to a specific date in the calendar, nevertheless the calendar dates constitute a temporal series only in so far as they can be related to an indexically specifiable *present time*. The tenseless paraphrase of the statement, viz. 'It rains (tenselessly) on 11 August', by itself, gives no indication as to whether the event in question was past, present or future. By contrast, 'It rained yesterday' places the event squarely in the past. The use of tense thus helps to convey an essential piece of information that cannot be erased from my statement without altering its truth-relevant content. For what is communicated is not simply the place that the event occupies in a particular series of dates, but its *pastness*.

At the same time, 'It rained yesterday' manifestly cannot be known with certainty. I have a vivid recollection (or what I take to be a recollection) of yesterday's event, but I might easily be mistaken. Perhaps the event never took place. All I can be certain about is that I *think* that it rained yesterday, or that I have a memory-like experience to that effect. What is more 'It rained yesterday' cannot be known with certainty by anyone. The tensed structure of the statement anchors it firmly in the present, when the relevant evidence by definition is *no longer available*. A similar condition applies to 'It will rain tomorrow'. The evidence that will be available to a future witness is not available to me today, and the evidence available to tomorrow's witness will not be 'tomorrow' when it occurs.

It follows that if tense is an irreducible ingredient of the truth-relevant content, then tensed statements cannot be known with certainty *as a matter of principle*. And so we encounter a contradiction at the heart of the phenomenological approach, in as much as a systematic pursuit of the indexical aspects of the truth-relevant content turns out to be incompatible with the pursuit of certainty. An unexpected result indeed.

The phenomenological approach thus fails in the light of its own criteria. The question that cannot be avoided, is: What confers objectivity upon propositions about *order in time*? Even the indexical statement 'It rained yesterday', although it cannot in principle be grounded in certainty, clearly has an objective validity as well as a truth value. This is not simply because the evidence relating to the event in question, or its absence, is bound up with a large number of more or less institutionalised beliefs, which serve as my points of reference, and which I could not reasonably subscribe to without at the same time assuming that what happened today, yesterday or whenever, can be established from the relevant documents with a fair amount of accuracy, but because the event for which evidence is sought is commonly recognised as being located in an objective temporal sequence. The point is that we share certain *social beliefs* about time, which enable us, among other things, to understand how tensed propositions can express objective truths, which can be articulated in terms of socially constructed 'clock and calendar' systems, and how the truth-value of such propositions can be established. But the phenomenological approach, within its self-imposed remit, cannot rationally accommodate such beliefs.

5 Objectivity and the social construction of time

I now pass on to what I have called the 'socio-historical' approach to truth conditions, or the third type of account of how thought comes to exhibit facts.

The irony of the phenomenological approach, as our discussion in the previous chapter has shown, is that it ends up by being hoisted with its own petard. It purports to rehabilitate the indexical 'egocentric' aspects of truth-relevant content, which are regularly dismissed as non-essential or else quietly swept under the carpet in naturalistic theories, only to have its own inadequacy exposed by the difficulties generated by just such aspects; in particular, by the problem of objective validity of the indexical time determinations.

The point is that once it is conceded — as the phenomenological approach demands that it should be — that indexical time determinations are not merely an 'optional extra', or a piece of self-indulgent subjective embroidery which can be excised out of the propositional context without a loss of truth, but on the contrary form an important constituent feature of the truth-relevant content, the central issue that presents itself is no longer one of certainty, but rather one of deciding what confers *objectivity* upon such a content. It is not in virtue of being certain, or even being explicable in terms of what can in principle be known with certainty, but in virtue of satisfying certain *conditions of objectivity* that such contents are able to latch onto the world.

This, let it be stressed at once, does not mean that the idea of certainty has no useful role to play, and can be dispensed with altogether. On the contrary, as our discussion in the previous chapter has indicated, this idea must have a place in a comprehensive account of truth conditions. In point of fact, even the socio-historical approach, which I am about to discuss, does not altogether discard the idea of certainty, although it tends to downgrade it to the technical notion of what *contextually cannot be coherently questioned* (see later). What it deprecates is merely the radical Cartesian-inspired thesis that a satisfactory account of the meaning, as well as a justification, of truth claims can be provided only from the point of view of what *unconditionally* can be known for certain.

Note, however, that the shift of balance in favour of objectivity does not signal a vindication of naturalist objectivism. The naturalistic objectivism, as we saw, is typically *reductionist*, in as much as it deliberately sets out to show that any 'indexical' elements of the content — all, that is, speaker-related aspects of the 'mode of presentation' — can be removed from the propositional context without a loss of truth. Its core thesis is that the factors instrumental in determining the truth-relevant content of a proposition are explicable in terms of the latter's logical or 'deep' structure and the referential properties of its constituent terms, with such properties being determined entirely by external circumstances and not by any intentions or projects of language users. The idea is that by specifying the truth conditions in this way, one is *ipso facto* specifying the conditions of objectivity. But this was shown to be an untenable position. For the question that immediately presents itself is, how do we identify the 'external circumstances' independently of how such circumstances contextually present themselves to us? It is of no avail appealing to 'external circumstances' in trying to settle the objective truth-relevant content of a truth claim if the objectivity of an account of 'external circumstances' itself needs to be settled in the first place.

Objectivity and necessary order

So what does confer objectivity upon truth claims? Where does objectivity have its source? The strategy of traditional metaphysics was to seek an answer to this question by linking the concept of objectivity with that of a *necessary* order, and — at least as far as the physical world is concerned — by fusing the latter concept with that of a *causal* order. Objective world was thus conceived as a *causally ordered* world. This strategy was famously blown apart by Hume. For what exactly, Hume wished to know, was meant by 'cause' and 'causal order'? If 'A causes B' is intended to signify that there is a necessary connection between A and B, such that, other things being equal, B could not occur unless A did, then there is nothing in our experience to warrant such an assumption. All that we can say with a reasonable degree of confidence is that in a given type of circumstance A, as a rule, is followed by B, not that it does so come what may. So either 'A causes B' *reduces* to a statement of a regular sequential link between A and B, in which case the concept of cause (in so far as it is associated with a necessary connection) becomes dispensable, or else it does *not* reduce to a statement of such a sequential link, in which case we are faced with the problem of its objectivity, and, in consequence, find ourselves precisely where we began.

Hume himself had no answer to this dilemma, and, in Kant's memorable phrase, 'ran his ship aground on the shores of scepticism where it might lie and rot'.[1] Having masterfully pin-pointed the problem, he despaired of a solution, and — as Kant saw it — left the theory of science in a lamentable state of uncertainty and disarray.

But was Kant more successful in tackling the problem which made Hume falter? The solution he proposed involved an ingenious attempt to stand Hume's argument on its head. Hume raised the question about the grounds of objectivity of the causal hypothesis. In reply, Kant set out to prove that the idea of objective experience itself demanded a recourse to causality, and moreover that the two notions were so closely intertwined that neither of them could be given up without in effect giving up both — which, he claimed, could not be coherently done. The principle of causality was thus elevated by him from an unverifiable Humean hypothesis to the status of an a priori law, and was turned into a main instrument for drawing a distinction between subjective and objective order. It is through the mediation of causality, he claimed, that subjective 'judgements of perception' about sequences of certain phenomena in our experience are transformed into 'objective empirical judgements'. I perceive what looks like the sun shining on the stone, and feel the stone growing warm. But this, Kant points out, is just an

[1] *Prolegomena*, Preface.

accidental sequence of my experiences; little more than a 'rhapsody of perceptions'. It is only when this 'rhapsodic' sequence is brought under the concept of *cause* that the result is an objective empirical judgement, viz. 'The sun *warms* the stone'. In short, the supposition of the existence of causal relations, and hence of *necessary connections*, between events is a principal condition of the possibility of objective experience. Causality and objective order go hand in hand.

In his reply to Hume, Kant thus, in essence, reaffirmed the traditional view, according to which objective order presupposes a causal order, and hence the existence of certain 'necessary connections'; with — it should be emphasised — to him the all-important proviso that this view should be taken not as a metaphysical thesis about things (or events) in themselves but as an a priori epistemological requirement about *phenomenal objects*.

Nevertheless the price of this 'solution' to Hume's problem remained high, for it entailed a virtual identification of objective order with 'natural necessity', and an acceptance of a deterministically organised physical world. Indeed the seventeenth century's idea of a 'clockwork universe' was never far away from Kant's thoughts, even though the roots of his inspiration lay deeply buried in the rationalist tradition, which can be traced back to Plato, and which had always sought to link objectivity with necessity; not only in the physical world but in the *moral* sphere too.

A broader view of objectivity

Yet manifestly there is no need to appeal to necessity. 'The sun warms the stone' does not qualify as an objective empirical judgement because it conveys, or purports to convey, a necessary connection between two specific events that occur in close succession to each other. Rather its objectivity flows from certain theoretical premises, which have been found to work well in conjunction with the rest of our beliefs, and have, in consequence, acquired a degree of *institutional entrenchment*. And the same, surely, applies to any similar declarative propositions, *including* those which contain indexical features, and which, incidentally, both Kant and naturalistic metaphysicians exclude from their considerations, or at any rate take to be explicable (as far as their truth-relevant content is concerned) in terms of propositions which do not contain such features. Thus 'It rained yesterday' surely too, in the context in which it is asserted, carries an implicit objectivity claim; what is more, as we saw earlier, 'yesterday' in this case is not just a convenient indexical shorthand for an 'impersonal' calendar date, but represents a *constitutive part* of the truth-relevant content of what is said.

The point is that the problems posed by the propositional contents containing indexical elements cannot be resolved simply by applying to them a reductionist axe. Such a strategy is crude and ineffective, and soon runs into rocks. Indeed if there is a lesson to be drawn from the phenomenological critique of naturalism, outlined in the preceding chapter, it is precisely that such a strategy must fail, and that there is no real alternative to accepting that propositions with indexical features are on a par with other propositions as far as truth claims are concerned, and correspondingly adopt a more generous view of truth-relevant content. At the same time, it is clear that the truth conditions for such propositions cannot be uniformly specified in terms of what can be known for certain — tensed propositions in particular present an obstacle to this. But, then, there can be no question of certainty playing a central role in explaining the hook-up of thought with reality in such cases, let alone serving — in the spirit of the Cartesian project — as a guide for a rational reconstruction of the whole edifice of truth.

If, then, a satisfactory explanation of how such propositions latch on to facts is to be possible at all, then it is only through an exploration of the conditions under which they become capable of graduating from an expression of subjective beliefs to the status of 'objective' truths; and with the naturalistic account of objectivity in ruins, the only rational option seems to be to look for the clues to objectivity in the institutionalised forms of *social life*.

Theory of objectivity, theory of truth and the idea of objective time

This, in fact, is the line pursued by what I have called the 'socio-historical' approach; although, as will become apparent later on, the tendency to over-emphasise the socio-historical aspect of truth conditions leads to inevitable distortions, in particular by encouraging a conflation of the *conditions of objectivity* with the *conditions of truth*. I shall, however, reserve my final judgement about the socio-historical approach until I am ready to draw together the various strands of my argument, and compare with each other the rival theoretical strategies that I have been reviewing.

By way of a quick summary, the basic principles of the approach here under discussion may be stated as follows:

(a) *The criteria of what can or cannot be coherently and appropriately claimed to be true, and hence what qualifies as a valid truth candidate, cannot be defined independently of the social context and the institutional frameworks of social life.*

(b) *The conditions of objectivity of truth claims are in all essentials indistinguishable from the conditions of objectivity of knowledge claims. Objective knowledge and objective truth are to all intents and purposes identical concepts.*

(c) *The standards of objectivity at any given time reflect certain institutionalised, or intersubjectively entrenched, beliefs.*

The last of these principles has two important sub-divisions, with views diverging as to whether the standards in question are intrinsically relative and variable, or whether there exists a historical process of convergence to a universal norm. This as a rule betokens two different conceptions of truth. Thus the view that the historical and contextual variability of standards of objectivity is a permanent condition normally goes together with a relativistic conception of truth (I use the word 'normally' advisedly, without wishing to imply that the two are logically, or necessarily linked); whereas the view that the conditions of objectivity are subject to an historical evolution leading to a universal norm is usually connected with an evolutionary view of truth as being approximated in ever increasing degrees via the progressive expansion of knowledge, either as a result of some inexorable historical laws, or as part of some unfathomable divine plan.

Inevitably the notions of time and temporal order now move to the forefront of philosophical attention; with the source of objectivity of propositions about such an order being deliberately sought in the social context. Indeed one of the fundamental theses of the socio-historical model with which I am here concerned is that objective time is a *social construct*, and that the notion of an objective temporal order in the natural world ultimately owes its intelligibility to the conception that we have of a *social history*. The view, in short, is that the sequential order of the events 'out there' that come within the purview of natural science does not in itself necessarily constitute a temporal order, and moreover that, in the final analysis, such an order cannot even be described significantly as 'temporal' except in relation to a given historical present, and hence with a reference to the indexical, tense-laden, structure of the socially constructed time.

Serial and temporal sequences

Let us begin by taking a closer look at time indicative features of truth claims. We convey time and temporal relations by means of verbal inflexion and a variety of indexical devices which either implicitly or explicitly relate the various points in a temporal sequence to an experienced present. All such forms of time determinations can be grouped under the heading of 'tense'. Now the question that immediately presents itself, is this: Does tense represent an essential component of the truth-relevant content, or is it just a superficial grammatical feature which can be suitably paraphrased out of the propositional context, without thereby bringing about any substantial distortion of the underlying message, or an alteration of its truth-value? In other words, can order in time be successfully conveyed *without ever making use of tense*?

The naturalistic answer to this, not surprisingly, is in the affirmative. The view put forward is that tense, whilst being a convenient grammatical device is not logically necessary in order to express temporal relations, and consequently can be dispensed with or paraphrased away without this ensuing in any erosion of truth. But, as is already clear from our earlier comments on the truth-relevant content of tensed propositions, this is not a viable option.

Consider again our example from the previous chapter. 'It rained yesterday' reports an event which took part in the past relative to the time of utterance. The temporal relation is indicated by the tensed verb 'rained'. Now the suggestion is that tense here contributes nothing to the truth-relevant content, for the substance of what is said can be expressed adequately, and indeed with greater precision, in terms of 'tenseless present'. Moreover, it is argued, tensed statements, containing as they do an implicit reference to the time of utterance, themselves provide a clue as to their tenseless paraphrase. Thus the relevant message in the above example can be conveyed, with all the crucial elements of its content remaining intact, by saying 'It rains (tenselessly) a day before the statement is uttered' — or, if (say) 12 of August happens to be the date of utterance, 'It rains (*tenseless present again*) a day before August 12'. It follows that tense is not needed to express temporal relations. Whilst there may be an abundance of reasons why contextually we may find it useful to employ a tensed language, it is not logically necessary that we should do so. If the intention is merely to give a bare factual account of the situation, then tense can be safely omitted. Everything that occurs in the world (except, possibly, certain beliefs) can be accurately reported in a tenseless idiom. There are no intrinsically 'tensed facts'.

That this argument does not hold water can be seen by inspecting more closely the suggested paraphrase. Contrary to appearances 'It rains a day before 12 August' does not necessarily report a temporal relation, although in the context of our normal indexical (tensed) conception of time it generally does. The reason for this is that whilst 'before' and 'after' are indicative of a serial order, a serial order may but need not be temporal. Thus that the number 3 comes *before* the number 4 and *after* the number 2 in the number series is a logical not a temporal fact.

So the question that presents itself, is: what is it that makes a serial order *temporal*? The naturalistic answer to this question, as a rule, involves an appeal to causality. If a given serial order qualifies as temporal, it is claimed, then it does so only in virtue of certain causal relations. A temporal sequence at root is a causal sequence. It is not simply that time 'presupposes' a causal order: time is a form of causal order. It is causation that gives time its direction and makes it linear.

But this begs an explanation rather than providing one. A causal relation, alone, is not necessarily indicative of an order in time. Two events might very well be causally related, such that neither of them can occur without the other occurring also, without however being temporally ordered. Admittedly we generally talk of causes 'preceding' their effects, but notice that this *presupposes* a temporal linearity of causation. Yet why should a causal relation necessarily involve a linear temporal order? Imagine two persons engaged in a tug of war, pulling at a rope from opposite ends and working themselves to a frustrating equilibrium, with neither being able to force the other to yield ground. Then the explanation of the inability of either party to shift the balance in their favour lies in the strength of the pull exerted by the other — i.e. opposing — party, and the cause in such a case surely is contemporaneous with, rather then 'precedes', its effect.[2]

The point is that, so far from tense being replaceable wholesale by expressions supposedly conveying a tenseless sequential order, we need tense in order to make sense of any sequential order as temporal. In other words, we have to make clear when 'before' and 'after' are meant to be taken purely *serially* and when *temporally*, and in order to do this we shall have to resort to tense at some stage. If indexical time determinations were irrelevant and could be dispensed with, then there would be no possibility of indicating a distinction in the ordering relation as between 'It rains a day before August 12' and 'The number 3 comes before the number 4 in the number series'. Yet a distinction patently does exist, and it does make a difference to the truth conditions of the statements concerned.

Note, incidentally, that an indication of dates, alone, is not sufficient to convey time, for there is nothing *intrinsically* temporal in any system of dating. The specifically temporal meaning of a calendar system can

[2] For a causal theory of time see D.H. Mellor: *Real Time*, and for a criticism of Mellor's views as expressed there see my *Change and Selves*, pp. 60-63. In his more recent book *The Facts of Causality* (1995) Mellor tries to improve his earlier argument while at the same time raising the stakes by virtually treating causality and time as two sides of the same coin. It is not only that time does not flow 'independent of causation' (p. 4), he claims, but time is the very 'dimension of causation'. Causation has a single linear dimension and that dimension is time (pp. 234-5). It follows that causes always precede their effects, and that there can be no 'simultaneous' causation. Even what Kant called the 'form of *inner sense*' represents a causal sequence, such that the time order we perceive is in fact the 'causal order of the perceptions we see it by'. But, as in his earlier book, Mellor ends up by presupposing what he is attacking, i.e. he is relying on the grasp of a temporal order as temporal in order to explain the temporal linearity of causation. His thesis is that causation links facts, and that no fact provides its own explanation. From this he derives the conclusion that causation must be a linear sequence, and that causes must *temporally* precede their effects (pp. 234-5). But if I drink water, I must swallow it, and while 'swallowing water' helps explain what happens when I drink it, it does not follow that the relevant events necessarily precede each other in time.

be made clear only with the help of indexical time determinations, and presupposes the grasp of an order in time. Here too tense plays a key role, and cannot be removed without altering the truth-relevant content of what is said. Thus if 'rained' in 'It rained on August 11' is replaced by a tenseless present, then all that the statement reports is a relation of correspondence between two items belonging to two different series, respectively; one series being a series of events and the other being the series of calendar dates. In respect of its logical structure it is virtually indistinguishable from a statement such as e.g. 'The position occupied by letter C in the alphabet corresponds to the position occupied by the number 3 in the number series'; in other words, it does not communicate anything temporal at all.

Tense and substance

Verbal inflexion and indexical temporal adverbs are our principal linguistic tools for conveying temporal continuity and temporal change. It is with their help that we articulate our basic temporal intuitions, in particular as embodied in the notion of individual substance as an enduring subject of altering attributes. If the mechanism of tense were unavailable, this concept of substance would to all intents and purposes become inoperable, and the same would apply to a whole array of associated ideas and categories upon which we normally rely in making sense of our experience. Time, as Kant demonstrated, is a necessary precondition of the applicability of *all* epistemic categories (including causality), but what is often overlooked, and needs to be particularly underlined in the present context, is that this condition requires, and can be fully articulated, only in a *tensed* idiom.

Needless to say, this does not mean that temporal relations cannot under any circumstances be expressed in terms other than tensed propositions. It would be foolish to make such a claim. Contextually we often transmit temporal messages in an 'uninflected', tenseless mode, and do so quite successfully. General causal propositions in particular provide good illustrations of 'tenseless' reporting of typically temporal sequences. This is not what is in dispute.

What is less obvious, but is none the less true, is that tenseless reports cannot be understood as conveying temporal relations unless within a broader epistemic context they can be related to facts about temporal order that we most naturally express by employing tense; or, broadly speaking, unless they can be explained in terms of the ideas of *past*, *present* and *future*. If, however, this is true — as I claim it is — then this has significant implications for a theory of how thought comes to express what actually is the case. Indexical time, it turns out, cannot be 'eliminated' from the truth-relevant content. That we often find it convenient in conveying temporal relations to use a form of 'tenseless' present does not show that tense is logically redundant, and is therefore ultimately irrelevant to any considerations of truth. On the contrary, the grasp of temporal relations as temporal goes hand in hand, and is moreover inconceivable without a grasp of tense.[3]

Objective past

But if tense is not logically redundant, then the main problem that presents itself is one of accounting for such objectivity as attaches to tensed accounts of temporal relations. What makes such reports *objectively valid*? 'It rained yesterday', despite its indexical features, communicates an event that forms part of an objective temporal framework. What it says is that an event took place at a specific point in time in what is a real, not an imagined past. In other words, an objectivity claim is a constituent part of its structure. Yet on what grounds can a significant distinction be drawn between a 'real' and an 'imaginary' past? Indeed what assurance do we have that there exists such a thing as a real past at all? The obstinacy with which common sense clings to this notion — as the long line of philosophical sceptics has never tired of repeating — is not a substitute for a rational argument. Unlikely though it may be, it is not inconceivable that there is no past time; and if the past is fiction, all time is fiction.

These are extreme views, but they are not obviously incoherent. So the question is, why should they be false? Attempts have sometimes been made to show that they cannot be squared with our concept of *memory*. The argument to this effect runs approximately as follows. We

[3] For more discussion of time, tense and related topics, see my book *Change and Selves*, chps. 3 and 6.

generally accept that a significant distinction can be made between correct and incorrect memory. But if no past exists, all memory claims are incorrect. What is more, given the premise that there is no past, then by definition all memory claims are false. But if it is impossible for memory claims to be correct, then there can be no coherent concept of memory. Hence past cannot be fiction.

This is a flawed argument, for what it shows is merely that a distinction between correct and incorrect memory is logically connected with the *idea* of a real past, not that there is such a past. The point is that the *rationale* of the distinction between 'correct' and 'incorrect' memory is itself in need of clarification, and this is precisely where the difficulty lies. For one can hardly appeal to this distinction in order to prove the reality of the past, if, in turn, one has to invoke the reality of the past in order to clarify this distinction.

Incontestably we do have a notion of a *real* as distinct from an *imaginary* past, just as we have a conception of a defective or inaccurate memory. But there is a certain disconcerting vagueness about both these notions. What is needed is a clear statement of the conditions under which they can be significantly applied. The question that has to be addressed, in short, is, what justifies the distinction between 'I am representing to myself the event E as having occurred in the past' and 'The event E occurred in the past'?

Remember that what we are concerned with here is not simply the position of the event within a specific sequence of events, but its *pastness*; i.e. its temporal not its purely serial placing. That an event forms part of an ordered series, as we saw earlier, does not necessarily mean that it forms part of a *temporal* series, and it is of course the latter series, and in particular the *objectivity* of such a series, that is of interest here. In other words, the question is: What makes an objective temporal series possible? Or, phrased differently, what confers objectivity upon propositions about order in time?

Social construction of the past

It is the thesis of the 'socio-historical approach' that these questions cannot be answered without presupposing the existence of a community of certain consciousness-endowed beings, who interact with one another within a certain institutionalised framework of social life. The idea of a 'real', or rather 'objective', past — 'real' is here explained in terms of 'objective', rather than the other way round — is seen as being logically inseparable from the idea of a community of such beings. Whilst each individual member of the community has his or her own experience of temporal flux, the notion of an objective time presupposes, and cannot be made sense of without the idea of *shared* time; the time, that is, of a society of contemporaries and near-contemporaries, who are directly or indirectly involved with one another in a variety of ways, and who perceive themselves as successors to the generations which preceded them.

Consider this more closely. A central feature of the approach under discussion is the assimilation of 'real' to 'objective' in respect of temporal relations. Real time is treated as indistinguishable from objective time, and objective time is interpreted as a socially constructed time. This runs counter to what we ordinarily take to be the case. Thus we tend to take for granted that time flows from past to future regardless, and that the order in which the events take place 'out there' is independent of any perceived order. But, of course, our ordinary common or garden notions are not always the most reliable guide, and what seems 'natural' to believe in this case tends to produce the kind of naturalistic metaphysics, which was considered earlier, and found wanting (see chapter 3). For, as we saw, there is not much intelligible sense that can be extracted from the idea of an observer-independent temporal order 'in itself'. And if so, then the question becomes simply one of drawing a distinction, under the general heading of 'perceived order', between subjective and objective temporal sequences. This is what lies behind the assimilation of 'real' to 'objective' in respect of temporal relations, and is the source of the thesis — which I shall uphold, despite my criticism, to be aired in a moment, of the socio-historical approach in other respects — that objective time, ultimately, has to be seen as a *social construct*. This, it should be emphasised, does not mean that no temporal order exists 'in reality', and that all time is fiction; it only means that the concept of reality has to be modified so as to incorporate the social conditions of temporal ordering.

In other words, the main question that we have to ask ourselves, is: under what conditions do propositions about temporal order qualify as valid truth candidates? And an answer to this question will have to depend in part — indeed, from the socio-historical approach, it will depend *wholly* — upon the answer to another question, viz. What confers *objectivity* upon such propositions?

I should reiterate that what is at issue here is a temporal, not just any old serial order; i.e. the kind of order that can only be conveyed in terms of the ideas of present, past and future. A temporal placing of an event, as we saw, is not simply a matter of indicating its serial location. Rather, it involves situating it, often indirectly and circuitously, but none the less unmistakably, in relation to the *present* time, within a chronometric system which reflects the contextually prevailing conception of *history*.

The idea of history and the contextuality of temporal placing

If this is granted, then it follows that the objectivity conditions will necessarily be context-relative, with the general framework for such a temporal placing being provided by the relevant *institutionalised system of dating*. In the Western world, this as a rule means the Christian calendar. But there is of course a multitude of different dating systems, and while some of them are more elaborate and comprehensive than others, none of them is necessarily more 'objective' or provides a more reliable vehicle of temporal reference than any of the other available options. When a chronicler records that Marco Polo visited China during the Ta Yuan dynasty, or that Martin Luther started the Protestant Reformation in the 5th year of the reign of Leo X, such statements are no less capable of objective validity than any of their 'neutral' or ostensibly 'science-based' paraphrases, involving the use of 'impersonal' systems of temporal placing. The objectivity of any dating system depends on its respective *institutionalisation* within the given social context. What is more, any 'concordances' as between such systems will in turn themselves depend upon certain criteria that derive what objectivity they possess from their respective institutional entrenchment. As for the chronometric systems used in natural science, they can be intelligibly said to record temporal rather than serial relations only within the context of our general grasp of time, as conveyed in the tensed chronology of everyday discourse.

The concept of an objective temporal order is thus inseparable from the concept of *history*; and the concept of *history* is a quintessentially social concept. We view time as history stretching from past to future, from whatever position we ourselves happen to occupy in this process; which means that propositions about historical order will necessarily be *tensed* propositions, and hence will incorporate an implicit reference to the present time, although (as was shown earlier) without thereby necessarily forfeiting their objectivity. If there is a 'real time', then it is only in the sense of an objective historical time, and the objective historical time is a *socially constructed time*.

It is indeed difficult to see how such a conclusion could be avoided, or what plausible arguments might be adduced against the view that the objectivity of a temporal order presupposes, and is therefore conditional upon, the existence of certain social institutional structures and the multifarious forms of social intercourse that take place within such structures. A physicist might speak of 'atomic clocks' and similar serial mechanisms for expressing temporal relations, but his use of temporal order concepts, if closely examined, can be seen to be essentially parasitic upon the notion of historical time. For there is no clear sense that can be attached to the notion of a 'unidirectional' objective clock-and-calendar time which is entirely independent of any social framework; not simply because as a matter of fact clock-and-calendar systems are invariably social constructs, designed with a specific purpose to help relate past happenings to contemporary events, but because — once the metaphysical notion of a temporal order 'in itself' has been discarded — the *very notion* of an objective temporal order could not be made intelligible without recourse to such structures.

An order qualifies as temporal, then, only in so far as it can be expressed in terms of a chronometric system which relies on the ideas of past, present and future; and such objectivity as attaches, within such a system, to propositions about order in time cannot be explained without a reference to the social world. This naturally does not exclude the possibility of events 'out there' being ordered in a serial, non-temporal sense. On the contrary, a closer inspection shows that a naturalistic notion of an atemporal serial order 'out there' is presupposed by any truth claim concerning order in time; and hence that temporal and atemporal serial order concepts are *structurally interlinked*.

The thesis that what applies to propositions about order in time applies to all propositions

I shall return to this later on. For the present, it should be emphasised that with regard to the sources of objectivity (of the truth-relevant content), on the philosophical model here under discussion, what applies to propositions about order in time essentially applies to *all* propositions, i.e. we shall have to look for such sources in the institutionalised structures of the social world — although the propositions about order in time retain a special status, in as much as they provide a means of indicating the specific reference points within the general framework of socially constructed historical time in respect of which the objectivity conditions of any other propositions with factual content are to be judged.

It follows that a decision as to whether a proposition qualifies a valid truth candidate or what exactly constitutes its truth-relevant content, will now have to be made on grounds that deviate in important respects from either of the two types of approach discussed previously. Thus, in contrast to the 'phenomenological' approach, there can no longer be any question of insisting that the truth-relevant content, as a condition of its meaningfulness, be in principle analysable in terms of certain states of affairs which are accessible to 'direct knowledge'. The notion of the Cartesian certainty now goes out of the window. Similarly the naturalistic policy of wholesale reductionism, specifically in respect of the indexical features of propositions, and especially the policy of separating the conditions of truth from the conditions of knowledge, must on the present view be rejected as flawed and unworkable. The position now rather is that truth and knowledge are intimately interlinked, but that the linkage takes place not via certainty but via *objectivity*, which is regarded as a fundamental requirement for both.

The immediate effect of this, however, is that it encourages a conflation of the conditions of objectivity with the conditions of truth. Since the truth-relevant content is assessed entirely in the light of the conditions of objectivity, all distinction disappears between the *truth-relevant* and the *objective* content; although, in a deliberate opposition to the naturalistic policy of radical reductionism these concepts are now interpreted in a fairly broad sense. In short, the general thesis now is that it is only by satisfying the conditions of objectivity that a proposition qualifies as a candidate for inclusion into the stock of objective knowledge, and conversely that it is only by qualifying for inclusion into the stock of objective knowledge that a proposition can be significantly described as *true*.

The concept of truth *simpliciter* thus gives way to the qualified concept of *objective* truth; with objective truth and objective knowledge being treated virtually on a par. The argument now is not only that the conditions of objectivity are the same in both cases, but that it is only by exploring such conditions that we can gain a clear insight into either concept.

The socio-historical approach and the world of common sense

Evidently there are powerful common sense considerations that favour such a view. For where might the clues to the 'objective' content of our utterances be found if not in the rules, procedures and rituals that govern our social existence? Ideas and theories in terms of which we make the world intelligible to ourselves all presuppose a social environment. They are the fruits of the many-faceted intersubjective traffic of information and intellectual cross-breeding that go on unceasingly within the social context of which we are part. Not only do the notions which nourish and shape our thoughts about the world sprout and evolve in such a context, but all our utterances acquire what objective meaning they possess from the same source. What is more, it is only via certain institutionalised rules and testing procedures within such a context that any hypotheses or theories that we may advance can acquire the status of objective knowledge. But, then, how can an inquiry into the conditions of knowledge and truth be sensibly separated from an inquiry into the emergence and the development of *social institutions*?

The view thus naturally suggests itself that the existence of an interactive social world should be accepted as a primitive fact which in one way or another affects the meaning of all our utterances. This granted, there is precious little sense that could be attached to the 'foundationalist' efforts of the Cartesian-inspired epistemology and the kind of certainty to which this epistemology aspired. From the 'common sense' point of view, the sceptic is not an opponent who needs to be taken seriously, for his case is vitiated by the tacit premises on which it depends. Thus by making use of language, he is implicitly placing himself within the institutionalised framework of the social world, and thereby conceding what he is overtly attacking. Descartes' error was to credit the sceptic with more destructive power than he could conceivably have at his command; with, as it turned out, disastrous consequences, for, in a desperate bid to reach safe ground, Descartes only managed to paint himself into a corner, with little hope of regaining the territory which in a foolish and unnecessary tactical manoeuvre he had yielded to the enemy in the first place.

Contextual unquestionableness and the institutional framework of human discourse

It is largely such common sense considerations that underlie modern anti-Cartesian 'social epistemology' and its inseparable stable-mate, the 'sociology of knowledge'; although, as we shall see presently, there are important differences of opinion as to how precisely an inquiry into the socio-historical conditions of knowledge and truth ought be pursued.[4] First, a brief note must be interjected concerning the interpretation of certainty as 'contextual unquestionableness'.

[4] The anti-Cartesian 'social epistemology', which in recent times has drawn much inspiration from the work of the later Wittgenstein, can be traced back to Hegel. For although Hegel applauded what he saw as the principal Cartesian insight concerning the 'unity of thought and being', he regarded the Cartesian conception of the mind as too narrow and abstract, and lacking in appreciation of the mind's 'external manifestations' in the physical world and human history. But the most demonstratively anti-Cartesian in his approach was of course that well-known maverick Hegelian Karl Marx, who saw objective knowledge, in effect, as a function of *production*; with 'production' being interpreted by him as a typically *social phenomenon*. ('Production by an isolated individual outside society — a rare exception which may well occur when a civilised person in whom the social forces are already dynamically present is cast by accident into the wilderness — is as much of an absurdity as is the development of language without individuals living *together* and talking to each other.' *Grundrisse*, Introduction.) From his point of view, accordingly, the sceptic should be dismissed as a crank or mere mischief-maker, and the idea of the so-called 'presupposition-less' epistemology as a defence strategy against scepticism is just a product of muddled thought. In the *German Ideology*, he and his co-author Engels characterise their own method of approach in the following terms: 'This method of approach is not free from presuppositions; on the contrary, it starts with real presuppositions and does not abandon these presuppositions for a single moment. Its presuppositions are human beings . . . in their actual, empirically perceptible process of development under definite conditions.' (Marx/Engels, *Die Deutsche Ideologie*, Collected Works, Vol. 3, p. 27, Berlin, 1962.)

I said earlier that the rejection of the Cartesian conception of certainty, demanded by the socio-historical approach, does not necessarily mean an abandonment of the idea of certainty altogether, although it does entail a significant re-interpretation of the concept. In this sense: that whereas Descartes began by divesting himself of all presuppositions about 'external' reality and looked to the certainty of the *cogito* to furnish him with an Archimedean point from which to conjure up the world back into existence, certainty is now taken in a more limited, mundane sense of what *contextually* cannot be coherently questioned. The idea is that within any area of discourse there are certain underlying premises which cannot be impugned without casting into doubt the very frame of reference within which the discourse is being conducted. In short, if certainty is available at all, then it is only in a restricted but none the less effective form of 'unquestionableness', within the given context, of the premises upon which the meaningfulness of reasoning within that context depends.

Unquestionableness, however, is a consequence of the *institutionalisation* of certain rules and practices that underlie a successful communicative intercourse. Any successful exchange of information, indeed any form of intersubjective co-operative effort, demands an institutionalised framework of rules, within which different participants, or groups of participants, perform different but mutually recognisable roles. Such institutionalised set-ups may have different degrees of complexity and they can be of varying duration, but irrespective of how primitive or short-lived they might be, or how often the participants change their roles, there are always certain rules to be followed, and the intersubjective intelligibility of what is going on in any given instance, indeed any decision as to what can be meaningfully said or asserted within such an institutional framework, will depend upon such rules.

These, then, are the guiding principles that animate an inquiry into the links between the institutionalised forms of social life and the objectivity conditions of significant knowledge and truth claims. Institutionalisation as a form of social entrenchment of certain rules and practices is seen as providing a frame of reference not only for assessing the significance of social actions but also for evaluating the objective content of utterances, including any truth claims, that are made within the relevant social historical context. Moreover the argument is that the whole machinery of concepts in terms of which we make the world intelligible to ourselves is crucially influenced by the rules, written or unwritten, that form the institutional basis of our social life. For — to quote a well known sociologist of knowledge — 'men do not confront the world from an abstract level of a contemplative mind as such, nor do they do so exclusively as solitary beings. On the contrary, they act with and against one another. These persons, bound together into groups, strive in accordance with the character and positions of the groups to which they belong to change the surrounding world of nature and society or attempt to maintain it in a given condition. It is the direction of this will to change or to maintain, of this collective activity, which produces the guiding thread for the emergence of their problems, their concepts, and their forms of thought'.[5]

Variability of the objectivity criteria. The relativistic perspective on knowledge and truth

But whilst this may seem plausible as a general hypothesis, there are difficulties in interpreting the historical evidence. With regard, in particular, to the problem of objectivity, the question is, how exactly should an inquiry into the social roots of objectivity of significant knowledge and truth claims be pursued? There are two main possible types of approach, which I shall call the *relativistic* and the *evolutionary* approach, respectively, both of which suffer from debilitating drawbacks; the latter approach, perhaps, more so than the former. (Following my usual practice, I shall continue talking principally in terms of ideal models or types of argument, rather than engaging in discussion of specific theories, which may or may not conform to a given model in every particular.)

The starting position in both cases is the same, viz. that the clues to the objectivity of the truth-relevant content of what is said or asserted should be sought within the institutionalised framework of social life. Such objectivity as attaches to our utterances derives ultimately from certain institutionalised rules and practices that are operative within the given social context, and reflects the strength of their social

[5] Karl Mannheim, *Ideology and Utopia*, London, 1960, p. 3.

entrenchment. ('Institutionalisation', I should emphasise, is used here in a sufficiently wide sense to embrace *any* form of intersubjectively established practice.) It follows that objectivity is not a fixed commodity, but on the contrary it varies and alters in response to changes that take place in the relevant institutional framework. Some social institutions clearly are more durable than others, but they are all subject to modification and change; and with the change of institutions the criteria for assessing the objective truth-relevant content of our utterances will change too.

But now the question arises, should the diversity and variability of institutional frameworks, and with them the variability of objectivity criteria, be accepted as a permanent condition, or is there an underlying evolutionary pattern, leading to certain universal standards? What I have called the 'relativistic' approach takes the former view; the argument being that a decision as to what constitutes the objective meaning of a given assertion or utterance, and indeed a decision as to what qualifies as objective knowledge, will depend upon whatever institutional structures happen to be contextually relevant. An inquiry into the objectivity conditions, therefore, will require a painstaking exploration of the network of the institutionalised and semi-institutionalised rules, customs and rituals that characterise social life in its appropriate historical setting. Such exploration will have to eschew any 'universalist' claims, and it will have to refrain from making any value judgements. 'Universalist' claims are out of place, because there is no privileged frame of reference, and hence no fixed vantage point from which the objective content of an assertion or belief can be specified in a unique fashion. All that can usefully be done is to investigate the relevant social-historical conditions, and base one's interpretative models upon the results of such an investigation. Above all, one should refrain from any value judgements, for there is no universal standard to which individual beliefs or truth claims must conform. The sole objective should be to try to explicate the objective content of truth claims by relating the ideas and premises that underlie such claims to the appropriate social context, rather than foisting upon them an alien frame of reference.

Some sociologists of knowledge have tried to moderate such relativism by drawing a distinction between the propositions about social phenomena and the propositions of natural science, on the grounds that the latter, unlike the former, are possessed of a certain universality of meaning that requires a different, *trans*-contextual and *trans*-historical, type of treatment. But the difference, such as it is, is relative rather than fundamental. Indicative propositions of either sort convey certain states of affairs in the light of certain tacit and/or explicitly stated theoretical premises, and their objective content changes with a change of such premises. It follows that there is nothing permanent or universal about the objective content that any such proposition may carry. Its objective content will depend upon whatever theoretical premises happen to be operative at the time, and so inevitably will its truth-value. Such premises normally form part of a system of beliefs which in the relevant historical context characterises the prevailing 'view of the world', but there is nothing intrinsically permanent about any 'view of the world'.

Nevertheless, whilst the context-dependence of the objective content can hardly be disputed, the tendency to identify the objective with the *truth-relevant* content creates obvious difficulties. Thus given that the objective content in any given case is to be judged in terms of the criteria operative within the relevant socio-historical context (whatever such a context might be), then, given the assumption that the objective and the truth-relevant content are the same, the problem arises, how, if at all, can on such a basis a valid comparison be drawn between different assertions — or between mutually competing theories, for that matter — which purport to be about the 'same' states of affairs? If those features of the content which are relevant to truth depend upon, and can only be decided with respect to, a particular socio-historical context, then with a change of the context different criteria will apply, and no meaningful comparison will be possible.

The evolutionary perspective

The evolutionary approach, notably, is not plagued by such problems — or if it is, then it is to an incomparably lesser degree. For the key assumption now is that there is an unequivocally identifiable general pattern of social evolution, and hence a universal frame of reference, which makes it possible to give an accurate interpretation of the objectivity conditions of the truth-relevant content in any given case.

Thus whereas the relativistic approach often demands a long and painstaking examination of the historical context, which in the end may yield no more than tentative hypotheses, the evolutionary approach by contrast stakes out in advance its general bearings. The relativistic position is that the objective content of truth claims cannot be adequately or appropriately judged except in terms of the ideas and categories that are current in the relevant social context, and hence from an insider's point of view; and that for this reason any external interpreter who has no first hand knowledge of such a context, and is therefore reduced to constructing interpretative models in terms of the ideas that are current in his own social and cultural environment, inevitably ends up by providing a false account of the facts. By contrast, the evolutionary view is that an external interpreter, equipped with the knowledge of the 'historical laws', is infinitely better placed to assess the objective content of what is stated or asserted, now or at any other time, than those who are responsible for making such statements or assertions but lack a clear grasp of the historical circumstances, or the general direction in which history is moving.

But the problem for an 'evolutionary' theory — depending as such a theory inevitably does on the idea of a privileged frame of reference — is that it has to assume that the criteria for assessing objectivity conditions as defined by the theory are not *themselves* subject to evolutionary change; for if they are, then the theory cannot provide the universal interpretative model that it purports to provide. Yet why should such criteria remain impervious to change? If the claim that such a theory provides a privileged and moreover universally valid frame of reference cannot be justified within the framework of the theory itself, as it evidently cannot, then there is nothing else left to underpin such a claim except personal preference and relativism seems to be the only alternative.

If, on the other hand, it is true, as is claimed it is, that there is a point when it becomes possible to identify a universal pattern of historical development, then the conditions of objectivity can be defined in terms of that pattern, and we can avoid the undesirable consequences of the relativistic option. There is thus a pleasing prospect of reconciling the demands of objectivity, universality and certainty. Not surprisingly, evolutionary theories have often been used as ideological weapons by would-be social engineers and political visionaries, with all too well-known results. Such theories are invariably based on ill thought-out premises, and the efforts of their proponents to justify their claims by an appeal to what is sometimes fondly called the 'scientific method', as might be expected, yield few solid arguments and a large amount of bogus science.

Objectivity and historical time

But leaving such distortions to one side, the general argument concerning the social roots of the objectivity conditions remains largely intact. Evidently what is true is true universally but *not unconditionally*, and amongst the conditions that the truth-relevant content must satisfy are the conditions which lay down what can and what cannot be coherently and appropriately claimed to be the case, as distinct from how in the given circumstances things might appear to be. Such conditions, however, cannot be explained without a reference to the institutionalised forms of social life. The socio-historical approach, in *both* its versions, is premised on this key assumption.

This marks an important new departure as compared with the theoretical models discussed previously. On the naturalistic model objectivity is seen as being vested in certain mind-independent things and their causal properties. But this, as we saw, merely encouraged a reductionist treatment of the truth-relevant content, with the result that all the 'ego-centric', indexical features of the content were consigned to the ignominy of the subjective 'mode of presentation', and declared to be irrelevant to truth. By contrast, the socio-historical approach takes a much broader view of the truth-relevant content, and looks for the roots of objectivity in the social sphere.

That there is a need for a more comprehensive concept of truth-relevant content, as we saw, is shown in particular by the propositions involving indexical *temporal determinations*, such as temporal adverbs and inflected verbs. For if, as must be conceded, such propositions are not logically eliminable, if they are needed to express that which makes a temporal order *temporal*, then the inevitable question is, what does confer objectivity upon such propositions? How do they come to express facts? The naturalistic attempt to deal with this problem by providing an account of what passes for an objective temporal order in causal terms was shown not to work; for if all that the causal link between A and B indicates is a necessary connection between A and B, then such a connection does not have to involve time — events may be necessarily inter-linked without being temporally ordered; and if, on the other hand, the causal connection is interpreted in terms of a temporal succession, then a grasp of time is *presupposed* rather than explained.

In short, we are faced with the problem of accounting for the objectivity of propositions about order in time, and it is difficult to see how this problem could be resolved without a reference to the context in which the subjective experience of temporal flux becomes incorporated into an institutionalised conception of *history*. For what is objective time? It is not the Newtonian *absolute time*, which 'flows equably' from past to future regardless.[6] It was Kant — long before Einstein — who put paid to any such metaphysical notion. 'Time', Kant warned, 'is not something which exists of itself, or which inheres in things as an objective determination, and it does not, therefore, remain when abstraction is made of all subjective conditions of its intuition.'[7] In other words, no intelligible sense can be extracted from the idea of *noumenal* time, or time 'in itself'. But, equally, a causal account of temporal order, as we saw, cannot get very far for the simple reason that the idea of a causal sequence already presupposes a grasp of temporal succession. And if so, then an account in terms of an institutionalised, socially based, conception of history as anchored in a phenomenologically shared present, seems the only sensible alternative.

Indeed what I have called the socio-historical approach goes beyond this, in that it uses the notion of historical time not only to highlight the framework within which truth claims are actually made but to indicate where the objectivity conditions of any such claims should be sought. This too is hard to fault; for where else might such conditions be found? The coherence and appropriateness, and along with this, the objective content, of what we say about the world have to be judged in the light of the rules and institutionalised standards that are operative within the relevant social context. What confers objectivity upon our truth claims, ultimately, are the ideas and rules that are implicit in the

[6] Cf. *Principia*, the Scholium following the Definitions.
[7] *Critique of Pure Reason*, B 49.

kinds of the institutionalised activities that, directly or indirectly, we engage in together with other humans within a broader framework of our common existence.

But while all this can hardly be disputed, the socio-historical approach nevertheless goes awry, in particular by treating not just the conditions of objectivity but the conditions of truth in their entirety exclusively from the point of view of historical time. This clearly must be rejected. The point is that the historical order would be little more than an organised fiction if it was not based on an atemporal natural order. In other words, to say that a particular event E occurred at a particular point in history is to claim two things: a) *that E has a place in historical time*, and b) *that E has a place in a natural order*. But the premises of the socio-historical approach leave no room for a meaningful distinction between the two.

6 Truth as a species of good

The critical account of the 'socio-historical' approach in the preceding chapter completes my discursive exposition of the three basic styles of approach to an analysis of truth-relevant content. Each of these styles of approach — or methods of explanation — highlights one specific aspect of the task in hand, but in preferentially weighting that aspect at the expense of the others it gives a slanted account of the issues involved, and is severely limited in what it can achieve.

The aim in all three cases is of course the same, viz. to clarify the conditions under which significant truth claims can be made by identifying the factors that are instrumental in determining the truth-relevant content of truth-claims. But the answers given are different, and whilst not entirely false, individually they are nevertheless out of kilter and incomplete. From the *naturalistic* point of view, the truth-relevant content is determined by structure and reference, with the latter in particular depending upon certain external matters of fact, not upon any intentions or projects of individual language users. The *phenomenological* approach seeks to clarify the truth-relevant content by relating it to certain states of affairs that are in principle accessible to direct knowledge, and hence can be known for certain. Finally, the *socio-historical* approach looks for clues to the truth-relevant content in the conditions of objectivity. Each of them offers a tantalising glimpse into the inner mechanics of the problem without ever being able to encompass it in all its complexity.

For on closer inspection it turns out that all the three key notions involved, viz. the notion of 'external' states of affairs, the notion of certainty and that of objectivity have a role to play in an explanation of how thought hooks onto the world. Our analytical discussion of the respective theoretical models in the preceding three chapters unmistakably points in this direction. However, before I embark on a more detailed exploration of the structural links between these notions and the general implications that this has for a theory of truth, it is necessary to address certain major issues which have been left in abeyance so far, and which have to be sorted out before we proceed.

One such issue concerns the possible candidacy of *belief* as a bearer of truth-value, and, in connection with this, the pragmatist conception of truth as a belief that guides successful action. The pragmatist conception seems to tie up naturally with the socio-historical approach, in particular with what I called its 'relativistic' version. Indeed in some ways the relativistic version of the socio-historical approach and the pragmatist theory of truth may be regarded as parts of the same body of doctrine. Another outstanding, and equally important, issue that needs to be addressed concerns the relationship between the scientific and the philosophical method of explanation, in so far as this bears on the problem of truth. In the present chapter and the chapter that follows, I propose to discuss these two issues in turn.

The 'occurrence' of truth

Consider pragmatism first. The instantly appealing feature of pragmatism is its typically 'dynamic' approach to truth. Truth does not pre-exist out there, independent of our involvement and waiting to be 'discovered'; rather it *comes into being*; it is *brought about* by our action. 'The truth of an idea' — writes W. James — 'is not a stagnant property inherent in it. Truth *happens* to an idea. It *becomes* true, is *made* true by events. Its verity *is* in fact an event, a process: the process namely of its verifying itself, its veri-*fication*. Its validity is the process of its valid-*ation*.'[1] [All the italics in the quotation are James' own.] Truth materialises, that is, when a belief is put to work, and only then. This, essentially, is a sound insight, although, as we shall see, what the actual occurrence of truth involves is not quite what James had in mind.

[1] *Pragmatism*, in 'William James: Pragmatism in Focus', ed. Doris Olin, 1992, p. 100.

Another attractive trait of pragmatism is what might be described as its anti-reductionist tenor. For although especial emphasis is placed on empirical verification, the latter concept is not taken in the restrictive phenomenalist sense in which it is taken, for example, by the Positivists, viz. as involving, ultimately, a reduction of all meaningful propositions to propositions about sense contents, sense data, and such like. The pragmatist approach is far less doctrinaire, and the epistemological dogmatism of the phenomenalist variety in general tends to be spurned in favour of more inclusive criteria of significance.

Nevertheless this should not be taken to mean that the pragmatist generosity knows no bounds, and that any proposition whatever could validly be accepted as significant, provided it satisfies certain basic grammatical proprieties. Pragmatism is an empiricist doctrine which from its inception has been motivated by a strong anti-metaphysical bias. The principle vigorously defended by both Peirce and W. James is that nothing should be allowed to escape empirical tests. All ideas that we entertain must be capable of being explained, or 'cashed', in terms of their observable consequences if they are to make clear sense. Indeed either they can be 'cashed' in terms of 'experience' or else should be discarded as vacuous.

Moreover it is only within an empirical context that beliefs can qualify not just as meaningful but 'true'. For a belief is true, it is argued, only if it 'pays' to entertain it. This in general means that it should work well in conjunction with certain other beliefs which we already hold, and use as our frame of reference on the basis of their proven success. Nevertheless any such system of beliefs necessarily remains a fluid structure; i.e. it is subject to a continuous adjustment and modification in the light of new experience.

The central idea is thus that we should look at truth via the notion of a belief that 'works'. Every belief is to be treated essentially as a rule for action. If, within a specified context, such an action leads to success, then that is what is meant by saying that the belief is true. Truth is that which is better for us to believe. In short, it is a *species of good*.

The view that truth is a property of belief

Two objections against this view immediately spring to mind. The first is that a definition of truth in terms of belief obscures the distinction between belief and the object of belief. It conflates the truth of *what is believed* with the correctness, or justifiability of the *belief*. A belief, surely, is correct or incorrect depending upon whether that which is believed, i.e. the relevant proposition, is true, *irrespective* of whether it is believed. If A believes that p, it is the belief-independent truth or falsehood of p that makes A's belief correct or incorrect; and it is the availability in principle of the relevant evidence that provides its 'justification'. But the idea of correctness and the idea of justification *presuppose* the concept of truth rather than helping define it. In short, the objection is that without possessing the concept of truth we cannot even begin to explain the properties that make a belief true. And if so, then belief cannot be regarded as a 'bearer' of truth.

A second objection is that an interpretation of truth as a property of beliefs, if pushed to its logical conclusion, leads to a virtual destruction of any serviceable notion of reference. What is at stake here has to do with a problem which has preoccupied us from the beginning. Normally we take it for granted that non-synonymous propositions can be 'extensionally isomorphic' in the strict sense of conveying the same state of affairs — for example, when non-synonymous but coextensive terms are substituted for each other. Thus 'The inventor of Analytical Geometry is lost in thought' and 'The author of *Meditations* is lost in thought' are isomorphic in this sense. If the relevant terms have the same reference, then if either proposition is true, both are. But if truth is a property of belief, then the reference is a function of belief, and it will no longer be possible a) to draw an unequivocal distinction between *actual* and *intended* referents. All referents will come, in effect, under the heading of 'intended' referents, and the realist conception of a world external — *actually*, not just posited as, external — to acts of referring will no longer be rationally sustainable; and b) given that the reference is determined by the mode of intending, there will be as many referents as there are modes of intending; which means that there will no longer be any strict coextensiveness between terms, and hence no extensional isomorphism based on the identity of reference. The consideration of reference in any evaluation of truth-relevant content will in consequence reduce to considerations of practical consequences of belief.

Peirce's theory of meaning and truth

I shall come back to these objections shortly. First, let us cast a brief glance at Peirce's operationalist account of meaning. It should be emphasised at once that both Peirce and James use 'meaning', basically, in the sense of what I have called 'truth-relevant content'. Thus when Peirce speaks of the need for a reliable method for 'making our ideas clear', what he wants to say is that a reliable method is needed for elucidating the truth-relevant content of utterances. Such a method, if it is to have any real value, will in his view have to be based on a consideration of the practical consequences of belief, or, expressed differently, on the practical consequences of supposing something true. What matters, in the end, is what difference an idea or concept — as deployed, that is, in a truth claim — makes in terms of observable effects. As a matter of fact, Peirce at one point goes so far as to suggest that one could not properly be said to entertain an idea of anything whatever unless such an idea was related to sense experience in some way.[2]

As an illustration of what he has in mind he provides an operationalist definition of the concept 'hard'. We generally regard something as hard if, among other things, it won't be easily scratched by other substances: it is in this sense that we call diamond 'hard'. But 'hardness' is not a quality that 'inheres' in the diamond, and pre-exists its sensible effects. There is nothing contradictory in supposing that a hard body remains soft, *until* and *unless* it is touched. Such an assumption would involve a 'modification of our present usage of speech with regard to the words hard and soft, but not their meanings'.[3] In other words, the ascription of a property to a thing makes clear sense only in respect of the results obtained (or obtainable) via an operationalist test. The property 'hard', like any other property, is the

[2] 'Our idea of anything is our idea of its sensible effects; and if we fancy that we have any other we deceive ourselves . . .' *Writings of Charles Peirce* (Indiana University Press, 1986). Vol. III, p. 266.

[3] Ibid., p. 267.

propensity, under given conditions, of an object or substance to react or behave in a certain way. But, then, there is nothing improper in describing a diamond now as 'hard' and now as 'soft', according to circumstances.

The underlying message is thus that in trying to clarify the truth-relevant content of an utterance we should carefully avoid any metaphysical assumptions, and rather than attributing to things certain intrinsic qualities, focus on their behavioural characteristics, or the propensities to behave in a certain fashion within the general context of our interests and needs. Moreover since all we ever need to know are just such contextual behavioural characteristics (i.e. what Peirce generally calls 'sensible effects') the idea of an 'external' identical substance is shown to be void of content.

This approach, however, soon hits choppy waters, as demonstrated by another of Peirce's own examples — although Peirce himself seems curiously oblivious to the difficulties involved. Thus he goes on to claim that his theory is capable of handling not just relatively simple cases, like that of diamond, but also highly complex issues such as that of *freewill*. The question 'Do we have a freewill?', according to him, boils down to the question 'Could we have acted otherwise than we have done, if we had so willed?' And the answer to this, he claims, cannot be a straight 'yes' or 'no', for this is not a question of fact, but of the 'arrangement of facts'. Thus if, given that I do sometimes experience shame and regret, I feel on a particular occasion that I ought to blame myself for having done wrong, then a clear implication is that had I willed it, I should have acted differently. If, on the other hand, a different consideration is brought to bear, viz. that a temptation, or urge, to act in a certain way, if sufficiently powerful, would have produced the relevant effect anyhow, then by definition I could not have acted otherwise than I did. In short, it is all, it seems, a matter of how I *retrospectively* see my actions.

But this is a facile, not to say slapdash, handling of a thorny issue; for the implication is that the existence of freewill is contingent upon the occurrence or non-occurrence of feelings such as 'shame and regret', which in concrete circumstances prompt us to 'arrange facts' retrospectively in such a manner that freewill fits into the picture. As a consequence, the idea of a moral agent who remains responsible — and hence could be held to account — for his or her past actions is reduced to nonsense, for the same action, on two successive occasions, could with *equal justification* be judged as 'free' or 'not free', depending on how the agent felt at the time.

The pragmatist account of meaning and the fragmentation of reference

But leaving the specific problem of freewill to one side, the 'operationalist' treatment of meaning, as indicated earlier, has considerable implications for the notion of reference. Thus the supposition that literally the same object can be addressed from different points of view is now seriously called into question. Similarly the inference seems to be that there is no rational basis for the assumption that two propositions can convey literally the same state of affairs, unless, that is, they happen to be completely synonymous (which on the pragmatic criteria can never be guaranteed in any case). There is thus implicit in the above approach an *anti-realist* bias which, despite the occasional inconsistencies and hesitations in the writings of individual pragmatists, remains one of pragmatism's most distinctive features.

At first sight, the suggested general strategy commends itself as eminently sensible. Given the concept F, one should ask oneself what (contextually) verifiable consequences follow from the supposition that something is F. The process of 'making our ideas clear' (to use Peirce's phrase) thus becomes a matter of elucidating the truth-relevant content of relevant propositions. Moreover, the idea is that in pursuing this task one should focus specifically on the way in which such a content translates into certain contextually specifiable *activities*, rather than seeking to spell out such a content in terms of certain metaphysical entities and their 'intrinsic' properties.

Unfortunately the farther one travels along this path the more difficult it becomes to find a justification for retaining the principle that identical topics can be referred to under different descriptions, i.e. via different meaning contents, which forms part of the elementary epistemological luggage of common sense. This is not simply because in any given case a pragmatist analysis of the content, however painstakingly pursued, is unlikely to establish beyond all reasonable doubt the identity of the items talked about, but because it cannot do so *as a matter of principle*.

The point is that if the reference of an expression depends on its descriptive content, which in turn is specifiable in terms of its 'sensible effects', i.e. in terms of its contextual *pragmatic consequences*, then only those expressions which strictly coincide in respect of their pragmatic consequences — and are therefore equisignificant on the pragmatist criteria — can be said to have the same reference (or, in the case of general terms, to have the same extension). But of course few expressions, if any, are likely to qualify on such criteria, for there are inevitably going to be variations, however minimal, in the pragmatic consequences from one context to another, or from one occasion to the next; and in as much as such consequences do vary, there cannot be any 'fixity' of reference. Yet we do accept, and act upon, the assumption that different terms, and indeed different, non-synonymous sentences — their differences in meaning notwithstanding — can be extensionally isomorphic. Moreover either this is possible, or the notion of reference ceases to have any clear meaning.

This is the heart of the problem. For if the contextual pragmatic consequences are to be our only guide, then it is literally impossible for two *non*-synonymous terms to be co-extensive in the above sense, because such terms would inevitably differ in respect of their 'sensible effects', and pragmatically there is no other way of defining reference. Thus 'The Morning Star' and 'The Evening Star', in as much as they differ with regard to meaning, will necessarily differ in respect of their pragmatic consequences; and if so, then it is no longer clear on what grounds it could reasonably be claimed that they nevertheless designate literally the 'same' object — or anything at all, for that matter. The most that might be claimed is that the *belief* that they do has 'useful consequences'; but this is a vague notion which does nothing to resolve the problem, for not only is the belief in question compatible with its 'object' being fictional, but it is not at all certain how might such a belief be 'cashed' in terms of the criteria of meaningfulness actually put forward.

This of course is not to deny that in normal circumstances a decision as to whether two descriptive expressions have the same reference is generally guided by pragmatic considerations. What is at issue is something quite different, i.e. whether the very notion of an identical object acting as a target of different (non-synonymous) descriptive symbols, can be made sense of in terms of a pragmatist theory of meaning, and the answer to this must be no. The point is that on pragmatist premises the supposition of the identity of reference under different descriptions represents a metaphysical hypothesis, which can never be 'cashed' in terms of any 'sensible effects', and consequently should strictly be regarded as pragmatically vacuous.

Yet clearly it is not vacuous; for if the reference automatically shifted with every shift of the meaning content, however slight, we could not talk about *any* topic whatever in non-synonymous utterances, and as a result there could be no meaningful disagreements about the accuracy or appropriateness of what is said on any given occasion. No two non-synonymous utterances could be treated as 'commensurable' with one another in respect of the state, or states, of affairs 'talked about'; with the inevitable consequence that there would be little or no room left for any meaningful argument, for we would all end up talking at crossed purposes.

Interestingly enough, the idea of 'incommensurability' of different contents, which is directly linked with the difficulties involved in accommodating within a pragmatist account the notion of the identity of reference under different descriptions, has come to occupy a significant place in modern pragmatist theory of science, and I shall have to say more about that in a moment. For the present, suffice it to point out that the abandonment of the identity of reference leads naturally to anti-realism, and, along with it, to a repudiation of the notion that the truth-relevant content of truth claims is determined, even in part, by the circumstances external to and independent of belief.

The criteria and the meaning of truth

Notice, incidentally, that none of this necessarily involves a rejection of the general notion of truth as consisting in things being as they are said to be. We have already seen that this notion may but need not necessarily be interpreted in the sense of the 'correspondence theory', and is in fact compatible with any number of rival views. The pragmatist objection against it is essentially the same as the one brought against it in chapter 2, which is that whilst it is not wrong it is *vacuous*. To say that truth consists in things being as it is said they are is to provide a nominal rather than a real definition of truth; and the same goes for any other similar formulations, such as that a proposition is true if it expresses a fact, or that p is true if p is the case. It is to supply a lexical definition of 'truth', whereas the objective must be to provide a substantive account of the *concept*.

But whilst the pragmatist objection against such 'lexical' definitions is that they are vacuous, the objection against the classical correspondence theory, with its implicit idea of 'mapping' or 'picturing' extra-linguistic, mind-independent facts, is that it is rationally unsustainable. For what 'external' fact might be 'mapped' or 'pictured' by the non-existence of the Marsians? The sheet of paper on which I am now writing is not green, but there is no pre-existent fact of its non-greenness, which I 'portray' in my statement. In rejecting such metaphors, the pragmatist is rejecting the metaphysical myths surrounding the notion of correspondence, and with excellent reason. However, he goes beyond this by rejecting *any* notion of a belief being 'made' true by mind-independent facts. In recent philosophy, there have been attempts to modify the traditional correspondence theory with a view to strengthening it and making it more plausible, by in particular decoupling it from the damaging metaphysical notion of 'mapping' extra-linguistic facts, and making the correspondence conditional, rather, upon certain *conventions* that govern the way we talk about, and describe segments of reality.[4] But in so far as such a repair work on the correspondence theory still retains the idea of propositions being 'made true' by external facts, it continues to incur pragmatist criticism. For the pragmatist does not see truth in terms of a reportage on 'external' reality but in terms of beliefs, which if put to the test lead to certain results. If truth is 'made' by anything — writes James — it is made 'just like health, wealth and strength are made, in the course of experience'.[5]

Propositions, in short, cannot be detached from beliefs, and treated as being true or false regardless. Nor can there be any question of beliefs being true in virtue of 'agreeing' with mind-independent facts.

[4] The well known attempt to reform the correspondence theory along these lines is due to J.L. Austin. See: 'Truth', in J.L. Austin, *Philosophical Papers*, ed. J.O. Urmson and G.J. Warnock, 1970.

[5] *Pragmatism*, p. 107.

Rather the 'agreement with reality' is now interpreted in the sense of a process of a successful application of belief. It is a process that leads to certain solutions that *work*. To quote James again: 'Agreement . . . turns out to be essentially an affair of leading — leading that is useful because it is into quarters that contain objects that are important. True ideas lead us into useful verbal and conceptual quarters as well as directly up to useful termini. They lead to consistency, stability and flowing human intercourse.'[6]

Now the standard objection against such an approach is that it involves a confusion of the *meaning* with the *criteria* of truth. For why, it is asked, should the criteria whereby a belief qualifies, or is accepted, as true be relevant to the meaning of truth? The pragmatic (contextual) test of success and usefulness, whilst conceivably offering a convenient means of deciding, in a concrete case, whether the belief in question is true or false, does not, nor can it, help throw light on what truth means, and it is the meaning that we are after. A belief might be true even if there are *no* obvious criteria for testing it.

However, this objection, plausible as it might seem, on closer inspection turns out to be less damaging than might be thought. For if one is to provide a non-trivial account of truth, then such an account can hardly fail to provide a criterion for applying the concept: a criterion for its application is part and parcel of its 'content'. James' response to the above objection, accordingly, would be that a definition of truth has to incorporate such a criterion, or else it does not qualify as a 'real' definition of the concept of truth at all.

The concept of inquiry

This response is basically correct, even though the criterion that James himself supplies, as we shall see, is defective, and must be rejected. However, before I say more about this, it is useful, for reasons of comparison, to look first at Peirce's treatment of truth in closer detail. What will emerge is that although Peirce is in some ways a more subtle thinker than James, it is James who is a more consistent pragmatist of

[6] Ibid., p. 106.

the two. This will at once help to throw the basic difficulties that pragmatism faces into clearer relief.

The problem of truth, according to Peirce, is a problem of a 'fixation' of belief. The opposite of belief is doubt, and doubt is an unsettled state of mind and a source of irritation which issues in a struggle to attain a state of settled belief. Peirce terms this struggle 'inquiry'. The purpose of inquiry is to try to eliminate the 'irritation' of doubt not just temporarily but permanently. This inevitably remains a distant goal, for such settlements of belief as lie within our grasp are invariably fragile and fleeting. The process of inquiry will therefore have to continue indefinitely into the future.

This invites obvious criticism. Surely our aim is to attain not to a permanently settled belief but to a *true* belief. We hold a variety of different beliefs, and conceivably some of them may be so well entrenched that they are never seriously challenged, but this does not make them immune from falsehood. A settlement of belief, even a permanently settled belief, can be achieved by any number of means. People might be brainwashed or hypnotised. If all that we are after is a settlement of belief, why should the process of 'inquiry' necessarily continue indefinitely into the future?

Peirce's answer to such criticism, such as may be gleaned from his various comments, falls into two parts. *First*, he insists that there is no need specifically to emphasise that the aim of *inquiry* is to attain to a 'true' opinion or belief. 'We may fancy' — he writes — that this is not enough for us, and that we seek, not merely an opinion, but a true opinion. But put this fancy to a test, and it proves groundless; for as soon as a firm belief is reached we are entirely satisfied, whether the belief be true or false. And it is clear that nothing out of the sphere of our knowledge can be our object, for nothing which does not affect the mind can be the motive for mental effort. The most that can be maintained is, that we seek for a belief that we shall *think* to be true. But we think each of our beliefs to be true, and, indeed, it is mere tautology to say so.'[7]

This, to put it mildly, is a shaky piece of reasoning. To begin with, the claim that 'nothing out of the sphere of our knowledge can be our object' is hardly something that can be accepted without argument. In

[7] Ibid., p.248.

making this claim, Peirce seems to be alluding to Kant, but if so, he is misreporting Kant's view. Kant claimed that nothing that falls outside the conditions of experience can be an object of knowledge, which is not quite the same thing. Kant used the term 'object of knowledge' in the technical sense of 'phenomenal object', but, as he himself conceded, there is a perfectly intelligible sense in which we can distinguish between objects of knowledge and objects of *thought*, or objects of *belief*. Evidently not everything that can be thought, or believed, is necessarily cognitively accessible. Anything whatever can be an object of belief, including *contradictory propositions*, but it is logically impossible to know such propositions to be true. To 'know' that p is the case is incompatible with p being false; but evidently anyone can consistently believe a falsehood.

It follows that, contrary to what Peirce claims, it does make sense to say that what we are after is not just a settlement of opinion but a settlement of *true* opinion, or belief. In one respect, though, Peirce is certainly right. Given the rules of common usage, if I believe that p, then it follows that I *think* that p is true. I could not consistently claim both that I believe that p and that I hold p to be false. Nevertheless the question is not whether I or anyone else believe that p, and hence *think* it true, but whether we are right in believing it. The objective, that is, is not to attain to a state of belief 'untroubled by doubt', but to attain to truth.

Consider now the *second* part of Peirce's answer (or what may be taken to be his answer) to the above criticism. The process of 'inquiry', he claims, cannot be arrested artificially. The search for truth has to go on, and a permanent settlement of belief cannot be manufactured at will. He examines, and rejects in turn, three different methods of settling belief prematurely, which he calls the 'method of tenacity', the 'method of authority' and the 'a priori method', respectively, and finally decides in favour of the method of natural science, which, being open-ended, is in his view the only one suited to the inquiry's august purpose.

It is instructive to see how he arrives at this conclusion. The 'method of tenacity', he explains, is simply holding fast to one's beliefs come what may, and this clearly cannot be right, even though personally it might be gratifying to a degree. A belief is in the nature of habit, and clearly there is a measure of reassurance to be derived from clinging to one's own habits regardless, despite the inconvenience that occasionally one might have to endure in consequence. Such an attitude, though, cannot be sustained for long, for within a social context one is confronted with a multitude of opposing views, and eventually one is forced to accept that other people have as much right to their opinions as one claims in respect of one's own. The facts of social life thus act as a corrective to any inflated sense of self-righteousness, and much as we dislike conceding that we might be wrong, the 'method of tenacity' is not likely to produce the lasting solution we need.

But suppose now that a belief acquires a sufficiently strong following, or becomes part of the institutionalised ideology of a powerful state, and is imposed and maintained by force. This method of settling belief — the 'method of authority', as Peirce calls it — is by far more efficient as compared with the 'method of tenacity', and, backed by the resources and the coercive power of the state, may produce quite spectacular results. Yet this method too comes to grief in the end, because heterodoxy and internal dissent, which can never be entirely eradicated, keep gnawing at its roots, with the opponents of the official ideology drawing inspiration from the knowledge that at other times different doctrines have held sway, none of which was necessarily superior to any of the others, let alone being incapable of improvement.

Finally, there is the 'a priori method', favoured by metaphysicians, which involves appealing to what are supposed to be the unfailing rational insights. The assumption here is that there is a stock of a priori truths which are accessible to any rational being and which represent the ultimate court of appeal in any adjudication as between competing beliefs. This method too, claims Peirce, is unsatisfactory, since the alleged a priori insights are difficult to distinguish from what happens to be the prevailing fashion or an idiosyncratic personal preference. As a result, the process of inquiry is effectively downgraded to 'something similar to the development of taste'.[8] Not surprisingly, metaphysicians have never been able to resolve their differences and agree on what such a priori and universally binding insights really are.

---

[8] Ibid. p.253.

The only rational alternative, therefore, concludes Peirce, is to look to science for guidance. The method of natural science represents the only reliable vehicle for resolving disagreements, in such a way that anyone who is endowed with the normal rational faculties would, if presented with the relevant empirical evidence, arrive in the end at 'the one true conclusion'.[9]

The illusion of permanent settlement belief

This view rests on three main premises, all of which have since come under severe attack, not least by the pragmatists themselves: first, that it is through science, and science alone, that we cumulatively gain reliable knowledge about what the world is 'really' like; secondly, that the method of scientific investigation is superior because (as Peirce claims) in contrast to other methods 'no doubts about it arise from its practice'; and thirdly, that for this reason alone, if for no other, science is competent to pronounce on matters of fact in any sphere or field of research, and therefore act as an impartial arbiter between conflicting beliefs.

Few pragmatists today would wish to subscribe to any of these premises. This is not simply because an agreement as to what the actual facts are in a given case may be as difficult to achieve in science as anywhere else, but because it is generally realised that the theories and models of science are designed primarily to show how certain hypotheses and procedures lead to certain results, not to provide a picture of what the world 'out there' is really like. In insisting that science should act as the ultimate arbiter for settling beliefs Peirce was hoping to avoid relativism. By contrast those pragmatists who have a clearer grasp of the scientific practice, and are therefore far less confident about what science can achieve, are led, in varying degrees, to draw relativistic inferences. Inevitably this has revived some old problems, as well as bringing some new ones in its wake. Thus the problem of *reference* in particular has come back to pursue the pragmatist inspired theory of science with particular virulence.

---

[9] Ibid. p. 254.

There is no need for my purpose to engage in a detailed discussion of the debates that animate the philosophy of science at the present time. Nevertheless a few words of comment are called for about the thesis which has sparked off these debates, and which marks a radical break with the Peircean conception of truth as a 'permanently settled belief', and signifies a return to a more relativistic, and, in a sense, more genuinely pragmatist notion of truth. What I have in mind is the thesis, mentioned earlier in passing, of the so-called 'incommensurability' of scientific theories.

This thesis has received a number of different formulations in pragmatist literature, some rather strident and radical, others more cautious and subdued. In its most carefully thought-out, and most plausible, version it was introduced into the debate by Thomas S. Kuhn as part of his now widely known theory of 'scientific revolutions'.[10] Kuhn's basic contention is that there is no such thing as a fixed and universally valid 'scientific method', and hence no universal criterion of what does or does not qualify as 'genuine' science. What passes for 'normal' science in a given historical context conforms to the prevailing 'paradigm' within that context, i.e. it represents a set of entrenched beliefs, rules and values which lay down how scientific research ought to be pursued, and which usually can be traced to, and are frequently consciously associated with, some particularly striking or important scientific theory that, for one reason or another, has come to be accepted as a model of what good science should be like. The contextual paradigm not only supplies the vital reference points for evaluating scientific research, but generates a range of puzzles that such a research is called upon to address. From time to time, the theoretical machinery of the paradigm proves unequal to the puzzles thus generated, and the ensuing crisis may lead to a revolutionary 'paradigm shift'. The old reference system of beliefs, rules and values is replaced by a new one, which thenceforth becomes the new norm — until at some future date fresh problems give rise to yet another revolutionary change; and so on.

Two features of this model are directly relevant to our discussion, and need to be highlighted in the present context. *First*, although

[10] *The Structure of Scientific Revolutions*, second edition, 1970.

'paradigm shifts' do occur, there is no absolute necessity that they should. Thus it is conceivable that, for one reason or another, people might decide to hang on to the same paradigm, or theoretical frame of reference, regardless. In short, such weaknesses as might afflict the given paradigm need not necessarily lead to any 'revolutionary' change of orientation; or, if a change does take place, it might be a regressive change to an earlier theoretical model. It follows that there is nothing necessary about 'scientific progress'. *Secondly*, there is no cumulative evolution of scientific knowledge, such that changes of paradigm 'carry scientists and those who learn from them closer and closer to the truth'.[11] Such progress as takes place concerns the improvement in puzzle-solving, usually within the context of a consensual paradigmatic frame of reference. But there is no progress in the sense of a steady upward rise in the amount of knowledge and the degree of verisimilitude of representation of what the world is 'actually' like.

If this is granted, then of course it follows that there can be no neutral trans-paradigmatic criterion, which might enable us to make a comparison between different scientific theories with a view to deciding which of them provides a 'more accurate' account of facts. A genuine comparison between rival theories can be made only with regard to their relative success as puzzle-solving instruments within some broader framework of assumptions, to do with what such theories are expected to accomplish. But there is no independent way of deciding whether they are about literally the same 'external' states of affairs at all.

Evidently all this is in full harmony with the pragmatist approach to meaning and truth — at least in the version sketched out by James. We saw earlier that one of the consequences of this approach was that there could be no valid basis for the assumption that two terms which differ in meaning content could nevertheless have (literally) the same reference, for different criteria for reference fixing would automatically apply in each case. This is now taken on board as a fully fledged part of the doctrine, with the thesis of the 'incommensurability' of different scientific theories signifying a virtual acceptance of a *pluralism of reference*. In other words, it is effectively conceded that there is no single thing or set of facts that the ostensibly mutually competing

[11] Ibid. p.170.

scientific theories are about, and that such comparisons as may profitably be made between them concern exclusively the results that their use may lead to in specific contexts.

The relativist conception of truth

The old Peircean vision of a 'permanently settled belief' thus in effect disappears from view. Instead we now have a much more modest — and, it should be added, much more pragmatically consistent — account of what truth claims 'really signify'. Peirce was talking of what he called 'inquiry' (by which he meant scientific inquiry first and foremost) — if pursued 'sufficiently far' — leading to a resolution of doubt in such a way that certain beliefs or opinions would come to be accepted by all rational beings. Indeed, truth, to him, signified the kind of opinion which was 'fated to be ultimately agreed to by all who investigate'.[12] The essential proviso in this account was that the inquiry should be pushed 'sufficiently far', or as far as it could rationally and profitably be pursued. This is a somewhat vague concept, but perhaps this was deliberate. The inquiry, obviously, may at any stage produce an acceptable, even a permanently acceptable, belief, but this is not enough to give us the meaning of truth. Truth, rather, Peirce was anxious to emphasise, is what everyone, or rather every rational being, would assent to if the inquiry were to be carried as far as it could possibly go. The choice of the broad, all-inclusive phrase 'as far as it could possibly go' enabled Peirce to assert the converse of his definition as well, viz. that if a belief was accepted as a result of a sufficiently prolonged inquiry (such that there could no longer be any rational grounds for doubting it), then that belief would be true. In other words, the two formulations essentially come to the same thing: truth is the belief that could stand the test of a prolonged inquiry, and, *conversely*, the belief whose acceptance by all rational beings would be ensured by such an inquiry is true.

But all these are mere metaphors, with little if any testable content. The trouble with Peirce's definition was that it could not properly be squared with his own pragmatist premises. In an effort to escape from

[12] 'How to Make Our Ideas Clear?', *Writings*, Vol. 3, p. 273.

relativism, he stretched his notion of a 'permanently settled belief' to the point where it became pragmatically vacuous. This was well noted by James, among others, who for this very reason increasingly came to emphasise the aspect of 'utility'. Thus, for James, the Peircean conception of truth as that which was destined to be accepted by all at the end of a prolonged inquiry represents no more than a notion of 'that ideal vanishing-point towards which we imagine that all our temporary truths will one day converge . . . Meanwhile [James continues] we have to live today by what truth we get today, and be ready tomorrow to call it a falsehood.'[13] In short, truth as an end of inquiry lies *beyond the pragmatic horizon.*

Peirce's inconsistency exposes the dilemma that any pragmatist faces in attempting to reconcile the universalist demands of truth with the inherently contextual properties of belief. In trying to resolve this issue, Peirce eventually came up with a definition which in effect separated the idea of truth from the consequences of belief. Truth is the sort of belief that is 'fated' to be agreed upon in the end, whatever its consequences. But this is not a solution, but a fudge. For there is a wide scope for rational argument in respect of most of our beliefs. But even if a belief were such that it could not be rationally challenged, this still would not of itself ensure its eventual acceptance by 'all who investigate'. The definition, therefore, is worthless; quite apart from the fact that its implicit anti-relativism stands in direct opposition to what remains a fundamental distinguishing feature of the pragmatist approach, viz. that the only way to obtain a clear sense from 'p is true' is to investigate the conditions under which p, in conjunction with the rest of our beliefs, may be said to 'work'.

Does truth have a cash value?

It was of course precisely in an effort to restore the link between truth and the consequences of belief that James was so anxious that one should explore what he called the 'cash value' of truth claims. Either we steadfastly pursue this course or we are more likely than not to lose our way in the mire of metaphysical metaphor or beguiling but slippery

---

[13] *Pragmatism in Focus*, p.109.

trivialities. A truth claim promises certain results, and should, accordingly, be viewed with an eye to its practical consequences. Such a claim becomes fully intelligible only when it is translated into an operation, an action, to which attaches a certain *value*. The concept of truth, in short, has to be approached from the perspective of the investigative action and the empirical tests whose results *matter* to us. In making a truth claim we are, in effect, making a recommendation as to what is good to believe, or rather what is *better* to believe, because if acted upon it is more likely to produce success. In this respect, James and the majority of subsequent pragmatist writers are far more consistent than Peirce.

Now, of course, with regard to the basic principle that guides them, viz. that truth *matters*, that it has a *value*, this is hardly something that one would wish to quarrel with. For if truth did not matter, why should we prefer it to falsehood? Truth matters because it makes a difference to our survival. We are not contemplating the world as disinterested onlookers, but are actively involved in trying to alter it and shape it to satisfy our desires and our needs. An account of truth has to take this into consideration. Pragmatists are justifiably dismissive of the 'spectator's view' of the world, embedded in classical metaphysics. Far from being mere spectators we are doers and makers who employ certain conceptual tools for certain specific ends, and it is only in the context of this doing and making that such concepts make clear sense.

But while one may readily concede all this, the extent to which this should serve as a basis for a definition of truth is far less certain. For it is one thing to say that truth is important to us, that it matters, and quite another to define truth in terms of beliefs that matter, because they are conducive to successful action. That truth matters is self-evident. But that truth matters because it is the sort of belief that is conducive to successful action runs counter to what we instinctively know to be possible, viz. that on occasion success might be achieved with falsehood too. Now it will no doubt be said that whilst false beliefs might produce success in the short term, it is the true beliefs that are bound to triumph in the end. Maybe. But notice that this hypothesis, in the strictest sense, cannot be justified on pragmatist principles. For how do we know that true beliefs are more likely to lead to success in the long run? If the criteria of success are defined contextually, and can only be defined contextually, then there is no pragmatic sense in saying that 'true' beliefs will in the end prevail over the 'false' ones. Conceivably they might never do so. It follows that from the pragmatist point of view, the only sensible course is to forget about the long term, and equate truth literally with what *contextually* works. This presumably is what James meant by saying that 'we have to live today by what truth we get today, and be ready tomorrow to call it a falsehood'. A consequence of such a view, however, is that all distinction disappears between truth and what is regarded as true on the basis of its contextually perceived 'success'. Now although the act of regarding or believing something to be true, as was remarked earlier (chapter 1), is an important ingredient in the 'occurrence' of truth, they are by no means identical, whereas a consequence of James' view is that it is strictly impossible for something both to be regarded as true, *because* of its perceived success, and to be false in actual fact.

We thus run into difficulties regardless of whether we interpret truth in terms of belief that is conducive to successful action, or define it, with Peirce, as a belief which is 'fated to be ultimately agreed to by all who investigate'. For it turns out that neither of these conditions is necessary let alone sufficient for a belief to be true. That a belief is destined to be universally accepted does not necessarily make it true, for there is nothing incoherent in the idea of a universally accepted but *false* belief; and, with regard to the view that true belief is conducive to successful action, it is clear that, contextually, false as well as true beliefs can be instrumental to success.

Fragmentation of reality and truth

An attempt to explain truth in terms of properties of belief thus inevitably ends up by missing its target. This should not come as a great surprise, for, as we saw earlier, such an approach deliberately ignores one of the main components of truth by underplaying the 'externality' of states of affairs targeted in truth claims in favour of the notion of belief triumphant. The driving concept now is that of a belief that 'works', and this radically alters the stakes. The point is that if truth is a property of belief, then all reference is a function of belief, and a distinction between actual and intended referents can no longer be given any clear meaning. There will be as many referents as there are modes of intending, with the result that it will no longer be possible to explain how two different contents can be 'extensionally isomorphic'. I have spoken earlier of the pragmatist notion of the 'incommensurability' of ostensibly rival scientific theories. If no clear sense can be attached to the supposition that such theories are about the 'same' things, then it follows that it is meaningless to describe any such theory as 'true' and its competitors as 'false', and our preference for any of them will be guided exclusively by whatever happen to be our goals at the time. Moreover if all truth claims are incommensurable in this sense, then clearly there will be no possibility of transmitting the 'same' states of affairs in non-synonymous sentences, for such states of affairs cannot be meaningfully said to exist. As a result, we will all end up talking at crossed purposes, unless we happen to share literally the same beliefs.

Pragmatism thus not only favours a pluralistic conception of the world, but it suggests the kind of pluralism from which any sense of cohesion is absent. For there is no universal binding agent to hold all the individual elements of reality together, and any successful communication of information from one point to another will by definition remain a hit-and-miss affair. As a result, reality is reduced to a random aggregate of essentially unconnected fragments, and any claims about the world as an integrated whole will have to be rejected as strictly void of meaning.

7 Truth and philosophical explanation

The lesson of the last chapter is that an interpretation of truth in terms of preferable — because 'successful' — belief, and hence as a species of good, results in relativism and a virtual abandonment of the idea of fixity of reference in different cases of referring. The world falls apart into isolated fragments, with communicative contacts across different areas or types of discourse becoming a matter of coincidence, a pure fluke. Instead of a single concept of truth, we seem to end up with a plurality of contextually defined concepts of truth, with only a faint 'family resemblance' between them, for all distinction seems to fade away between what is true and what on some contextual criteria is seen to 'work'.

Yet this surely goes against what truth claims are meant to convey. Admittedly there are always contextual constraints on what can be meaningfully asserted or claimed to be true. These are not just formal logical constraints but specific categorial rules that lay down how certain concepts or types of concepts may be appropriately deployed in propositions. Moreover such contextual constraints can and often do change. The criteria of what does or does not qualify as a valid truth candidate reflect the contextually prevailing institutionalised standards, and such standards are not set in granite for all eternity. Nevertheless truth claims, within the compass of such constraints, do not purport to express merely what is good to believe, but what is true. The supposition, that is, is not just that certain specified criteria for judging or believing a proposition true are fulfilled, but that the conditions of *truth* are fulfilled.

Such conditions, however, are not fulfilled simply because there is a belief which contextually leads to success or works well in conjunction with the rest of our beliefs. This is neither a necessary nor a sufficient condition of truth. The conditions of truth such as are enshrined in the meaning of a truth claim, as we saw, demand the existence of a particular *extra*-linguistic state of affairs, whose propositional expression satisfies the norms of objectivity and can be an object of someone's infallibly known belief (see chapter 4) — *irrespective* of what such a belief might entail.

Necessary and sufficient conditions and the nature of philosophical explanation

Consider this now in the context of a broader question concerning the nature of philosophical explanation. What is it to provide an explanation of the claim that p? There is a snap answer to this, of course, viz. that to claim that p is to claim that things are as it is said they are. But such an answer is also the most inane. If our concern is with how thought 'hooks' onto the world, then it is necessary to take what is said into consideration. A simple account in terms of 'things being as stated' is not going to be sufficient.

In chapters 3-5 I discussed certain basic theoretical models which address themselves specifically to this task. However, the difficulty with all such models, as we saw, was that their respective accounts are invariably one-sided; with each of them selectively emphasising certain conditions while ignoring or underplaying the importance of others; whereas a close analysis suggests that the different conditions to which they respectively give precedence are in reality all inter-dependent, and are all necessary as well as being jointly sufficient for the occurrence of truth.

This has been the main burden of my argument so far, and will be set out in more systematic detail in the next chapter. In the meantime, some elucidatory observations are called for regarding the necessary and sufficient conditions, with a view to highlighting the distinction between the philosophical and the scientific (in a narrow sense of 'scientific') type of explanation. A scientific explanation is normally couched in terms of possible scenarios; the main aim being to set out, in a hypothetico-deductive form, the *sufficient* conditions of the occurrence of the given phenomenon, or phenomena, whilst at the same time scrupulously refraining from making any claims regarding the necessary conditions of their occurrence. Similarly any speculation is shied away from regarding possible necessary links between alternative explanatory models. The general assumption, on the contrary, is that such models need not be logically linked at all, and that the choice between different explanatory options in any given case should be guided exclusively by contextual and pragmatic considerations.

By contrast, the insistence on the *necessary* as well as the sufficient conditions goes back to the essentially rationalist belief that the constitutive features of reality are all interconnected, in such a way that the world can be made sense of entirely in *its own terms* (which, contrary to what one is sometimes led to suppose, does not necessarily enter as a premise into a scientific explanation; see later). However, rationalism should not be confused with determinism: the belief that the world can be made sense of in its own terms does not demand that it be conceived as a deterministically closed system, although the classical European metaphysics is full of examples of such a confusion. To say that p is true is to imply that the world at the relevant time is so arranged that p comes out as true. But it does not follow from this that anything that takes place in the world is necessarily dependent for its occurrence upon everything else that occurs in it, now or at any other time, such that if an event takes place, it *must* take place if it is to be intelligible at all.

Hypothetico-deductive method of explanation and the D-N model

In what follows, I shall look at this issue more closely, by in particular comparing a standard model of scientific explanation, where truth does *not* play a key role, with a philosophical model, in which it does; whilst at the same time highlighting some typically metaphysical distortions of the latter model.

Consider, first, the hypothetico-deductive method of explanation as exemplified by the familiar *deductive-nomological* (D-N) model. Explanation is here portrayed as an inferential sequence, with a general ‘law-like’ proposition — as distinct from what are taken to be merely 'accidental' generalisations — acting as a major premise, with the minor premise, or premises, setting out the specific conditions under which the conclusion, or the *explanandum proposition*, follows as a matter of logical necessity. Thus given that all lead is toxic, it necessarily follows that if x is lead, x is toxic. Why does the apple fall from a tree? Because all bodies attract each other in proportion to their mass and in inverse proportion to their distance from each other, and the dehydrated stem of the apple is no longer strong enough to compensate for the gravitational pull resulting from the presence of a larger mass. Why does A have the *flu*? Because he caught the virus, and other things being equal, all unimmunized persons who catch the virus develop the symptoms of the disease. Given the truth of the premises, the truth of the conclusion follows with deductive certainty.

Admittedly it is not always easy to decide which generalisations do and which do not qualify to act as 'law-like' major premises. If on my entering the room the lights came on without the switch being flicked, or any other events normally associated with the flow of electric current being triggered off by my action, this is likely to be dismissed as a mere coincidence. But if this happened a sufficient number of times, irrespective of the state of the electrical circuit, then there might be valid grounds for an appropriate inductive generalisation; and, consequently, for making the relevant inferential predictions. My entering the room, in such a case, would be a sufficient condition of the lights coming on.

The distinction between 'law-like' and 'accidental' generalisations is based on the assumption that some events are causally linked, whereas others occur in close sequences which are purely coincidental. But this assumption is an ontological hypothesis which need not feature in descriptions of what, in a given set of circumstances, actually takes place. The point is that a decision as to whether a given generalisation is 'accidental' or 'law-like' will inevitably be a contextual decision, and will depend on a whole constellation of currently held beliefs.

Another observation that needs to be made at this point is this. The major premise in the D-N model, more often than not, will be a probability statement; that is, the explanatory process — save in the unlikely circumstance when all the specimens of the relevant sort have been literally gone through — will begin with a probabilistic hypothesis, such that the prediction as to the occurrence or non-occurrence of a particular phenomenon will be phrased with rather less than complete certainty. Nevertheless the premises will entail the corresponding degree of *likelihood* of the explanandum proposition being true, and in this respect the structure of inference will not change. The explanation will count as adequate provided the link between the premises and the conclusion — irrespective of whether we are dealing with universal or probabilistic premises — is one of logical entailment.

Of course, the necessity with which the conclusion follows in a D-N inference does not presuppose the necessity of the premises. It is an essential feature of the deductive-nomological model that it provides only the *sufficient*, not the necessary conditions of the truth of the explanandum. Compelling though an explanation might be in the given instance, it is always possible that an entirely different but equally plausible set of premises might be found which would yield exactly the same result, or the same explanandum proposition. If p be the explanandum proposition, then, as far as the inferential relationship is concerned, no particular set of premises has the monopoly of the conditions that entail the truth of p. In other words, the possibility can never be excluded of (equally valid) *alternative* explanations that p.

At the same time, it is important to bear in mind that a given set of sufficient conditions in respect of a given explanandum proposition does not cease to be sufficient if the theory is rejected. The explanatory inference is a hypothetical syllogism, which if correct, remains *always* correct. If the explanation provided none the less proves to be wrong, it is wrong not because within the context of the explanatory inference the sufficient conditions cease to be adequate to prove the conclusion — this is a logical impossibility — but because, on some specific criteria, a different set of sufficient conditions are found to correspond more closely to our experience, or, in the light of some other assumptions, are found to be more appropriate or fruitful.

Of course, an entirely different situation arises if the explanandum proposition *itself* is altered or rejected on the grounds that it misreports the event or the state of affairs to be explained. If that happens, then a different set of sufficient conditions is likely to become necessary in any case.

Criticism of the D-N model

Consider now some criticisms of the above model. There are basically two types of objections that might be directed against it: one general and philosophical, the other rather more specific and practical.

The principal philosophical — or, in a narrow sense, 'metaphysical' — objection concerns the question of adequacy of explanation, and runs as follows. A statement of the sufficient conditions in the spirit of the D-N model, providing, as it does, an explanation in terms of 'possible scenarios', neither answers nor is capable of answering the question *why*, in the given case, things are as they are. It merely shows how under certain specific conditions things are likely to turn out. But to provide an explanation in terms of possible scenarios is not to explain why the world is thus and not otherwise; and, from a philosophical point of view it is the latter explanation that ultimately we should strive for.

Note, incidentally, that this objection does not question the appropriateness or general usefulness of the D-N model in a scientific context. It is obvious that for practical purposes we have to rely on such sufficient conditions as we can find, or such as seem contextually appropriate, and construct our inferences accordingly. Often there is a choice between what seem to be equally plausible alternative scenarios, allowing equally successful predictions regarding the occurrence, or non-occurrence, of a particular event. But — this is the gist of the 'philosophical' objection — *predictions* are not the same as *explanations*. To be able successfully to predict the occurrence of a particular event is not to explain what was necessary for its occurrence, and hence in one sense it is not to explain it at all. To revert to the idiom of propositions, an explanation, if it is to be philosophically satisfactory, cannot be simply a matter of contextually indicating certain sufficient conditions that entail p; rather it demands a clarification of certain conditions that *must* be fulfilled for p to qualify as true.

I shall return to this objection later on. What I have called the 'practical' objections are of two sorts, and may be briefly stated thus.[1]

[1] For more details about these objections see Michael Friedman: 'Explanation and Scientific Understanding' and Peter Achinstein: 'The Illocutionary Theory of Explanation', both in *Theories of Explanation*, ed. Joseph Pitt, 1988.

First, the D-N model does not take into consideration the conditions under which an explanation is understood and accepted as an explanation. The tendency rather is to dismiss such considerations as having no bearing on the nature of explanation as enshrined in an objective and impersonal deductive argument. The basic view is that a D-N explanation, if valid, remains valid regardless, irrespective of whether it is accepted, rejected, or misunderstood. Yet surely things cannot be left there. For even if it is conceded that acceptance or rejection make no difference to the validity of an explanatory inference, the question still remains, what makes such an inference *explanatory*? Not all logically valid inferences automatically qualify as such. Some are trivial and unilluminating, and of no interest to science. But, then, explanation cannot simply be equated with valid inference. We need some criteria for sorting out genuine from fictitious, or trite explanations. Some deductive arguments are accepted as explanatory because they enhance our understanding of the relevant constellation of phenomena, while others are rejected because they don't. Thus in the context of the theory of gravitation we explain the range of tides from the position of the moon and the sun; we do not seek to explain the position of the moon and the sun from the state of the tides.

A second type of 'practical' objection is that the D-N model ignores, or brushes aside as unimportant, the illocutionary and pragmatic aspects of explanation. It focuses exclusively on the inferential relationships between certain sentences. But sentences and their logical relationships cannot be divorced from the living context in which language is used and explanations proffered. The exaggerated emphasis placed upon the 'objectivity' of explanation leads the advocates of the D-N model to portray explanations as some kind of ideal logical models, which subsist *independently* of the acts of explaining. But explanations are not archetypes of proofs that subsist in an ideal Platonic realm prior to being deployed. They fulfil their function only through the activity of explaining. But then it is necessary to take into account the contextual and pragmatic aspects of the explanatory act, for depending upon the circumstances of utterance, the intentions of the speaker or the specific emphasis that he/she lays upon the various aspects of his/her message, ostensibly identical sentences may carry very different propositional contents, and consequently convey very different kinds of explanation.

Explanation and entailment

Both these objections are well-founded, and clearly have to be taken seriously. Nevertheless it is important to realise that they do not challenge the main principle embodied in the deductive-nomological model, viz. that any reasoned explanation can be expressed as an inferential sequence, such that the premises entail the conclusion. This principle remains intact. In addition, the above objections are entirely compatible with another key assumption of the model, viz. that the premises in any given instance supply only the sufficient not the necessary conditions of the truth of the conclusion (the explanandum), and consequently that there can always be *alternative* explanations. All that such objections show is that entailment, *on its own*, is not sufficient; that it is not the whole story. In short, the deductive-nomological model is criticised not so much because it emphasises the aspect of entailment, but because it tends to *identify* explanation with entailment, without at the same time providing any clue as to the conditions under which an explanatory entailment qualifies as explanatory.

But the question that needs to be asked is not simply under what conditions an explanatory entailment qualifies as explanatory, but why should an explanation necessarily take the form of entailment? For it is not at all obvious that every explanation could, or should, be pressed into the same mould, i.e. that it should assume the form of *proof*. The thesis that it should, and must, depends, amongst other things, upon another assumption, viz. that all explanations are ultimately reducible to explanations of certain *propositions*, and we shall see that this simply is not the case. Secondly, and just as importantly, even if it is accepted that an explanation must take the form of proof, the question still remains, what makes such an explanation not just formally valid or contextually appropriate, but adequate in a *philosophical* sense of the term?

Why, for example, is it enough, if indeed it is enough, to confine oneself to *sufficient* conditions in constructing explanatory inferences? Or, to turn the question the other way round, what is wrong, if anything, with the argument that an explanation which does not include the necessary conditions cannot properly be said to account for the *truth of the explanandum*? These issues have to be confronted sooner or later. In order to show what is at stake here, let us consider accounts of actions.

Explanations of actions and explanations of propositions about actions

To give reasons for an action in terms of the agent's own motives manifestly is not to provide any proof: the relationship between the reasons given and the actions entered into is not one of logical inference. This, after all, is hardly surprising. The sort of questions that may appropriately be asked about actions are not such as can be reduced without further ado to questions about the corresponding *propositions*. It is one thing to explain why an action is undertaken, and quite another to explain how it comes about that the *proposition descriptive of that action* is true. But then an explanation here cannot be a matter of simple derivation from certain general hypotheses.

In point of fact, the reason, or reasons, that motivate an action need not feature in an explanation of the relevant proposition at all. Conversely, an explanation of the truth conditions of the proposition in question need not enter into, or form part of, a motivational account of the relevant action for such an account to be contextually adequate.

Consider an example. If, say, A happens to have kippers for breakfast, it is clearly not going to be very difficult to find a set of premises such that the proposition 'A is having kippers for breakfast' comes out as true. But it would be foolish to pretend that such premises, while providing an explanation of how 'A is having kippers for breakfast' can be true, at the same time provide an account of that which makes A's eating kippers an *action* rather than (say) an instance of mindless or somnambulic behaviour, and it is the *former* that needs explaining. A's reason, however, may be anything at all. It may be that he is partial to kippers, or just wanting a change from his usual breakfast fare, or acting on the assumption that eating kippers will help improve his memory.

Now there are two ways in which one might try to bridge the gulf which separates explanations of *actions* from explanations of *propositions* reporting, or descriptive of, actions (and thereby restore the idea of explanation as proof). First, one might try a reductionist approach, with a view to assimilating actions to natural events. If actions and natural events could be treated on a par, then such differences as exist between explanations in terms of motives of agents and explanations in terms of the sufficient conditions of the propositions descriptive of the given action, or actions, being true, would surely fade away. All phenomena, actions included, would become amenable to explanations in terms of possible scenarios, as exemplified by the normal employment of the D-N model.

A second way of bridging the gulf might be to concede that the difference between accounts of actions and accounts of natural events is indeed fundamental, and cannot be brushed aside, while at the same time trying to maintain the general principle of explanation in terms of sufficient conditions; by, for example, introducing into the inferential sequence certain general premises that describe the agent's likely behaviour in terms of his/her aims or (habitual) inclinations and desires, thereby allowing for the *explanandum* proposition, i.e. the proposition reporting, or describing the relevant action, to be inferred in the usual way.

Neither of these two options produces the desired result, as I will show presently.

The insufficiency of 'sufficient conditions'

With regard to the attempt to assimilate actions to natural events, it is sufficient for our present purposes to highlight one specific ingredient of actions, viz. that of *trying*.

Take the above example again. There are clearly two aspects of A's having kippers for breakfast that need to be distinguished from each other: (i) the plain fact of kippers being eaten, and (ii) A's *trying*, or making a deliberate attempt, to eat kippers. It is the latter feature that resists a reductionist analysis and confers upon what is reported by (i) the character of an action. So the question that needs to be asked, is: What might count as an adequate explanation of (ii)?

Evidently the choice is vast. Any motive whatever that A may decide is an adequate reason for him, *is* an adequate reason. But while A's own motive, in the given circumstances, represents an adequate explanation of his attempting to act in a particular manner, it is clear that there is no relation of *logical entailment* as between any such motive and A's attempt to do anything at all, let alone between his motive and his actually performing an action of a specific sort. A's motive may be his desire to improve his memory, or grow 10ft tall, or even to make himself invisible; and of course his motive for engaging in the same kind of action, or attempting to act in the same way, may vary from one occasion to the next. Admittedly, such motives are often likely to be dismissed as silly, or in some sense inappropriate. But however odd or unlikely they might appear to the agent's *audience*, they are not disqualified as genuine motives on that account. Any motive whatever can be legitimately given in explanation of an action, or rather of an *attempt* to act in a certain way, provided it is inspired by an earnestly held belief.

The crucial point here is that there can be no logical inference from any such motives to the agent's attempted *actions*. Whatever it is that in given circumstances motivates A to act, or attempt to act, in a particular way, does not provide a necessary let alone a sufficient condition of the *proposition* to the effect that A acts, or attempts to act in such and such a way, being *true*. Or, to put it the other way round, no motive that A might give in explanation of his action can ensure against such a proposition being false. But, then, the discrepancy between explanations of actions and explanations of propositions reporting actions cannot be swept away, and the reductionist programme must fail.

Consider now the second option. The basic suggestion here is that rather than resorting to extreme measures, such as a wholesale reductionist assimilation of actions to natural events, which clearly leads nowhere, we should try instead to accommodate such differences as do exist between these two types of phenomena *within* the general framework of the D-N model; by in particular taking care to select the appropriate general premises (or general hypotheses) in the two kinds of cases, respectively. Thus in the case of actions, we shall have to look for premises which will enable us to make the desired derivation on the basis of what the agent would rationally choose to do, given his general aims and beliefs. For example, if A desires to improve his memory and moreover believes that eating kippers will definitely have the effect hoped for, then the rational thing for him to do (as indeed for anyone else in similar circumstances) is to eat kippers. A's desire to achieve a specific result, combined with his belief as to how this result might best be achieved, imposes certain rational constraints upon his action.

This sounds plausible, but it won't work, for the simple reason that different agents are prone to act differently even if they happen to have similar desires and hold similar beliefs. Just how an agent will act in given circumstances, or whether he will act at all, will depend not simply on the specific desires that he might have at the time, and the beliefs that he happens to entertain as to what might best satisfy those desires, but on a whole range of other factors; to do, in particular, with his temperament and traits of character. An explanation of his action, therefore, will necessarily have to take such factors into consideration. And even this conceivably might not be enough, for no general premise derived from the agent's observed character traits is necessarily an unfailing guide as to how he will act on the next occasion. Every situation differs in however slight a degree from every other, and just how the agent will act will depend in large measure on his state of mind at the time. Besides, our character traits are not immutably fixed in advance (even though they may be influenced to some extent by certain genetic predispositions) and may, and sometimes do, change. What is more, even to the extent to which they are relatively stable, it is not unknown for people occasionally to act 'out of character'. Yet to act 'out of character', or even irrationally, is not necessarily to act without a reason.

Needless to say, this is not to deny that we regularly make predictions about the likelihood of other people's motives or actions by generalising from their past behaviour or known character traits. There is after all no other method of inter-personal interpretation available. Yet the possibility of error is never far away. For the problem is not simply one of explaining 'A is *likely* to try to do x at t' but 'A tries to do x at t'. A may be likely to try, without actually ever trying. He might desist from trying, for another, stronger motive might intervene at the critical moment. Or again, he might fail to try despite all his internal urges and inclinations, because at the critical moment he might suffer from the weakness of the will.

So the conclusion is that the second option too fails to cure the problem.

The price of proof: The necessary conditions of truth

The only possibility, it would seem, of preserving the form of proof with regard to an explanation of 'A tries to do x at t', is to include the *necessary* as well as the sufficient conditions into the inferential sequence. Let us see how this might be done.

Our problem, articulated in terms of propositions, as we recall, was this: if 'A tries to do x at t' is true, under what conditions is it true? Now the easy answer to this, as we saw, is that 'A tries to do x at t' is true provided A tries to do x at t; but that is next to useless. In order to explain how 'A tries to do x at t' hooks onto reality it is necessary to explain why A actually does make the effort to do x at t, and this is far from simple. He may be conditioned to act in a certain way by his temperament or character traits, or by some overpowering urge that gripped him at the time, and yet he may fail to try. If the explanation consists in an inferential sequence such that the explanandum proposition is entailed by the premises, then clearly none of these conditions will be sufficient to guarantee the truth of the conclusion. What they can ensure, at best, is its *probability* not its truth. But, then, it is not until we strengthen our premises with certain necessary conditions that we can ensure that the inference does indeed go through.

In concrete terms, the explanatory sequence will have to include either a general premise to the effect that when A, for whatever reason, makes up his mind to do x, he manages to make the attempt; or, at the very least, the condition that if A *at time t* feels sufficiently motivated to do x, he finds it in him to make the move. Unless such a condition is fulfilled the explanandum proposition cannot be proved.[2] Of course, whilst an account of why 'A tries to do x at t' is true, if it is to be adequate, it must include a statement of the necessary as well as the sufficient conditions, it does not follow from this that the action in question was bound to take place, only that it was bound to take place provided (with all the other conditions obtaining) it was willed by the agent.

Now clearly not all explanations need include necessary conditions in order to qualify as explanations. Nor, as we saw, do all explanations

[2] The full inference might take the following form:

Whoever eats x, eats kippers
A makes a deliberate effort to eat x at t
If A resolves to eat x at t, he manages to make the attempt
A is aware that eating x is eating kippers
A eats x at t
A deliberately eats kippers at t

necessarily take the form of entailment. It is one thing to ask 'Why does A try to eat kippers?' and quite another "Why is 'A tries to eat kippers' true?" In normal circumstances, it suffices, in answer to the former question, to state A's actual motive at the time. The latter question, however, demands a different approach altogether. The proposition contained within it requires for its explanation a statement of certain necessary as well as sufficient conditions of its truth, and the motive that A may have for acting as he does need not feature in such an explanation at all. Thus the fact that A as a rule enjoys eating kippers may be relevant to his trying to eat them. But although he may be motivated by any number of reasons to try to eat them on a particular occasion, there is no relation of logical entailment as between any such motive and his actually making the attempt.

The curious result that this leads to is that whereas in the given circumstances the reason, or reasons, given by A may be contextually perfectly adequate to explain why he is trying to do x at t, no such reasons are adequate to explain why 'A is trying to do x at t' is *true*.[3] But in addition, whilst there may be any number of alternative, mutually unconnected, motivational explanations of A's action, there can be no entirely unconnected sets of premises which are all equally able to explain the truth of the relevant proposition in accordance with the canons of the deductive-nomological model.

What this shows is thus, first, that explanations of actions and explanations of *propositions* reporting actions cannot be treated on the same logical footing, and, secondly, that as far as propositions reporting actions are concerned, our interest in truth cannot be satisfied with a simple account of sufficient conditions. The characteristic feature of the D-N model is that in principle there can always be alternative, mutually independent, explanations of the same explanandum proposition. But, as we have seen, this does not work with propositions such as 'A tries to do x at t'.

[3] See my paper 'A Paradox of Explanation' in *Synthesis Philosophica*, Vol. 9(1), 1994.

The pursuit of truth and philosophical explanation

In point of fact, it is possible to go further, and argue that with regard to truth conditions what applies to propositions reporting, or descriptive of, actions, applies essentially to *all propositions*. Thus if p is true, whatever p might be, it might be argued, an explanation of its truth cannot be adequate in a philosophical sense unless it includes the *necessary* as well as the sufficient conditions of p. This has always been one of the central tenets of metaphysics, and is one that I wish to uphold, although, as I have already made clear, the deterministic inferences that have sometimes been derived from it in metaphysical theories are unwarranted, and must be rejected.

A scientific explanation, as we saw, need never go beyond a statement of sufficient conditions; but, then, unlike a philosophical explanation, a scientific explanation is not really concerned with truth at all. Rather its primary purpose is to explain how certain conditions lead to certain results, or generally to construct certain 'models of prediction'. Accordingly, accounts of phenomena are provided in terms of possible scenarios; with past events 'retrospectively' predicted from certain hypothetical premises. The main underlying principle is that no such account can rationally be treated as definitive, or 'intrinsically' more correct than any possible alternative.

But this clearly is not sufficient to explain what is meant by a truth claim that p. Thus while in principle there is no difficulty in accepting that there could be any number of different predictive accounts of Socrates' death, the assumption underlying the claim that Socrates dies is that certain conditions must exist without which 'Socrates dies' *could not* be true — even though this does not entail the 'necessity' of the actual event. For practical purposes, of course, any old account might do. Possibly the drinking of the hemlock precipitated Socrates' death, or it may be that his friend Krito's uncontrollable weeping broke his heart. There is a wide range of possible scenarios, all of which at one time or another conceivably might be accepted as providing suitable explanations of what took place; but if an explanation is to be *philosophically* adequate, then, it seems, it will have to include the necessary as well as the sufficient conditions of the truth of the explanandum.

The point is that the interests of philosophy are not safeguarded by simply sketching out possible scenarios, showing how, under certain circumstances, things are likely to turn out. The principal philosophical task is to determine what conditions *must* obtain for thought to express what actually is the case, not simply to construct theories that contextually 'work'. For if all that is available, or can ever be provided, are alternative sets of sufficient conditions, then no explanation will be able to provide a full insight into what makes p possible. For p to be possible the world must be structured in a particular way, although it does not follow from this that the world must contain every feature it does contain, viz. that all its properties are its *defining* properties. In short, it does not follow that an explanation in terms of the necessary and sufficient conditions makes sense only on the assumption that everything that occurs *has* to occur thus and not otherwise. That this is not so has been shown by our discussion of actions. Whilst an account of what is involved by the claim that A tries to do x at t must include the necessary as well as the sufficient conditions if it is to be adequate, this does not make the reported action a 'necessary' event if the relevant claim happens to be true.

This may seem obvious, yet it is not all that obvious, and the tendency to link the explanation in terms of the necessary and sufficient conditions with the idea of 'ontological necessity' is not an uncommon occurrence in philosophical tradition.

Scientific and philosophical explanation Newton and Leibniz

In the remainder of this chapter I propose to look more closely at the motivations as well as the implications of such a linkage by in particular considering the views of Newton and Leibniz. This will at once help cast additional light on the different concerns of science and philosophy, respectively, as well as exposing the metaphysical misconceptions concerning the nature of philosophical explanation. Consider, to begin with, Newton's account of the sources of motion and gravity.

Central to Newton's position is the concept of *inertia* as a fundamental defining property of material bodies; and, connected with this, the distinction between *inertia* and what he calls the 'impressed force'. These ideas go back to Galileo, and in a more explicit form, to

Descartes, who in his *Principles of Philosophy* famously claimed that bodies by nature tend to persist in the same state, and 'what is once in motion always continues to move' unless and until compelled to change its state by external causes; a principle which became enshrined in Newton's First Law of Motion. There was thus in Newton's approach, from the very beginning, the underlying assumption of a fundamental cleavage between a 'passive' and an 'active' principle in nature; with *inertia* (which somewhat confusingly, he also terms 'force') representing the former, and the 'impressed' force, or the Cartesian 'external cause', representing the latter.

The second key assumption upon which Newton's approach is based is that motion in mechanical processes, so far from being self-sustaining, is continuously on a downward path. Motion, he says, is 'much more apt to be lost than got, and is always upon the Decay'.[4] It follows that unless the loss of motion was restored in some way, all mechanical processes would cease eventually, and the world would grind to a halt. This, according to Newton, is prevented by gravity and what he calls 'fermentation'. Indeed '. . . if it were not for these Principles', he writes, 'the Bodies of the Earth, the Planets, Comets, Sun, and all things in them, would grow cold and freeze, and become inactive Masses; and all Putrefaction, Generation, Vegetation and Life would cease, and the Planets and Comets would not remain in their Orbs'.[5] However — and herein lies the main source of the controversy — unlike *inertia*, Newton argues, neither gravity nor fermentation are inherent to bodies, so they must come from an *external source*.

Given his scientific concerns, Newton understandably feels somewhat chary of going into detail about the specific nature of this external source, but if what he says in *Opticks* about gravity and fermentation is taken in the broader context of his theological convictions, then there can be little doubt that for him the ultimate source and the sustaining cause of motion, indeed of all change, lies in the *divine agent*.[6]

[4] *Opticks*, London 1952, p. 398.

[5] Ibid., p. 399f.

[6] In a letter to the theologian Bentley in 1692, commenting on the suggestion that in addition to the force of attraction, a so-called 'transverse impulse' was needed in order to explain the possibility of a circular revolution of the planets around the sun, he says explicitly: '. . . ye motions wch the Planets now have could not spring from any naturall cause alone but were imprest by an intelligent Agent.' Newton to Bentley, 10 December 1692. See *Correspondence* Vol. III, Cambridge 1961, p.234. See also letter to Bentley of 25 February 1692(3), p.254.

The picture that thus emerges from Newton's account of motion is of a clockwork universe which would cease ticking were it not for the continuous intervention of its creator, who supplies the required impulse to keep it in operation. It was this kind of scenario that Leibniz found unacceptable on both philosophical and theological grounds; although, as we shall see presently, the theory that he devised in an attempt to solve the problem was itself seriously flawed.

Leibniz's argument ran as follows. The supposition that God finds it necessary to 'wind up his watch' from time to time in order to keep it ticking cannot be reconciled with the idea of an all-powerful as well as rationally acting agent, for it would imply that God either accidentally or deliberately created a defective world. But if God had accidentally created a defective world, this would signify an imperfection on his part, which is incompatible with his nature. If, on the other hand, he deliberately created a defective world, he would have acted without a sufficient reason, and this again would be contrary to his nature. It follows that the only rational assumption is that the world, once created, functions in accordance with a pre-established order, without needing any subsequent repair work by his creator.

The key plank in Leibniz's argument is what he calls the principle of *sufficient reason*, i.e. the principle 'that nothing happens without a reason why it should be so rather than otherwise'.[7] Unfortunately in his criticism of Newton in particular, as I will show presently, this principle becomes the source of some conspicuously faulty reasoning.

In one sense, it has to be conceded that Leibniz's objections against Newton's position have an instant appeal, for they deprecate the use of *ad hoc* hypotheses in order to resolve an awkward problem. Confronted with the difficulty presented by the attrition of motion in mechanical processes, Newton postulated what can only be described as a miraculous external intervention, aimed specifically at maintaining the world in good repair. In reply, Leibniz, whilst only too ready to concur with the view that the world could not subsist without God, who 'preserves it in being', finds it intolerable that God, having brought the world into being, has to go on tinkering with his own creation. It is, he

[7] See 'Letters to Clarke', in G.W. Leibniz: *Philosophical Papers and Letters*, A Selection Translated and Edited, with an Introduction by Leroy E. Loemker, Second edition, D. Reidel, Dordrecht-Holland, p.677.

argues, contrary to reason to suppose that the world is the sort of mechanism which grinds to a halt or breaks down from time to time like a bad watch. What Newton overlooked was that the attrition of motion does not affect the total *quantity of force*, which surely remains unchanged.[8] But then there is no need for a constant external intervention to keep the wheels of the world turning, as Newton, mistakenly, assumed.

What does count as adequate explanation?

But leaving aside the attrition of motion and the precise nature of the relationship between the total quantity of motion and the total quantity of force, the main philosophical disagreement between Newton and Leibniz is over what constitutes an *adequate explanation*. This disagreement, I think, was due in large measure to the fact that Leibniz, much more so than Newton, was anxious to maintain a close link between *explanation* and *truth*.

The point is that Newton, even when making use of theological hypotheses, was guided principally by pragmatic considerations. His approach throughout was that of a practical scientist. By contrast, Leibniz's reasoning was inspired by certain typically metaphysical preoccupations about the completeness of explanation. Whereas Newton's explanations, in effect, were couched in terms of sufficient conditions, Leibniz, for his part, relied on what he called the 'principle of sufficient reason' as a main explanatory tool. The principal difference was that an account in terms of 'sufficient reasons' was supposed to provide the *necessary* not just the sufficient conditions of things being such and such (or events occurring as they do); with — in Leibniz's case — the notion of a rationally organised world being stretched to the point where it became difficult to draw any clear distinction between what was occurring accidentally and what necessarily.

In laying emphasis on 'sufficient reasons' (as distinct from 'sufficient conditions') Leibniz was echoing the long established rationalist metaphysical tradition, which since the time of Plato had always been guided by two key principles, viz. a) that reality can be

[8] Cf. Ib. p.713.

made intelligible only on the assumption that everything that happens in the world happens for a reason which determines why it should happen thus and not otherwise; and b) that all things are interconnected in such a way that nothing that takes place could fail to take place, or be different to what it is, without everything else being different, and hence without ceasing to be explicable within the world that we actually occupy. Leibniz added to this his own specific theological gloss to the effect that there would have been no sufficient reason for God to arrange things differently to what they actually are, for God, he argued, acts in accordance with his nature, and hence 'rationally', only in so far as he creates the best world possible out of an infinity of options available to him. Conceivably God could have made a different choice, if he had so desired. But if he had, his action would have been strictly irrational, and hence unintelligible; and hence nothing whatever would be intelligible.

Two kinds of explanation

It is not difficult to see where this argument goes wrong. Leibniz conveniently slurs over the distinction between *acting for a reason* and *acting with a sufficient reason*. Evidently an explanation of an action, as distinct from an explanation of a mere 'behaviour', demands an account of the agent's own reasons. But such an explanation, as we saw earlier, is intelligible not because of any 'necessary link' between the reason given and the action performed, for there is no such link, but because it conforms to our notion of a *free agent*. Acting for a reason is entirely compatible with there being alternative and equally valid or adequate reasons for a given action, whilst acting with a 'sufficient reason' (on Leibniz's view) excludes such a possibility. Yet clearly any reason that a free agent perceives as sufficient for him to act as he does in pursuit of his goals *is* a sufficient explanatory reason for his action.

Interestingly enough, Newton's model of explanation *does* leave room for such a possibility. Newton sees God as a free agent, who is not constrained by any so-called 'principle of sufficient reason'. God acts freely, and whatever motive he might have for acting as he does is a sufficient explanatory reason for his action. It is therefore not inconceivable that it suited God to create the world as a rather less than perfect clockwork. That the world is thus and not otherwise is simply because, for whatever reason, God *wished it so to be.*

What is remarkable is that Newton as a scientist did not find such a hypothesis in the least embarrassing. He was apparently quite prepared to countenance the fact that there was no unitary system of explanation. God's actions, like actions of any other free agent, he seemed to be saying, were subject to different principles to those that govern the physical universe. In other words, there was a basic dualism of freedom and necessity, and, accordingly, two different types of explanation. This dualist conception, as is well known, was subsequently given a philosophical underpinning by Kant. By contrast, Leibniz was trying to bring all events under the umbrella of his principle of 'sufficient reason', which he saw as a key to all rational explanation. The world, he was saying in effect, could not be made rationally transparent unless it was possible *in principle* to explain why things occurred thus and not otherwise, and Newton's idea of an interventionist God who constantly kept tinkering with his own imperfect handiwork made this impossible.

Rational transparency of the world and the idea of necessity

There are basically two questions that arise here, both of equal importance. First: Does the rational transparency of the world demand that the world be conceived as a unitary system?, and secondly: Is it a condition of the rational transparency of the world that everything that occurs in it should occur thus and not otherwise? On Leibniz's premises these two questions are not only intimately connected, but they both have to be answered in the *affirmative*.[9] And that is false.

Admittedly Leibniz was justified in questioning the philosophical adequacy of Newton's approach. The procedure that Newton followed, as I pointed out earlier, was essentially in accord with the method of explanation in terms of sufficient conditions as exemplified by the N-D model. Any hypothesis, including the hypothesis about free agents unconstrained by external factors, was in principle admissible,

[9] Note that Leibniz's thesis that the world consists of mutually independent individual substances, or monads, does not conflict with the idea of a world as a rationally ordered unitary system (from God's point of view).

provided contextually it led to fruitful results. To Leibniz, however, this was philosophically unsatisfactory. Philosophy, as he saw it, was interested in truth not results; i.e. it looked for an explanation which would show not simply how things worked out under different scenarios, but *why* things happened as they do. But whilst we may broadly agree with him on this, it does not follow that the question *why?* can be given an intelligible answer only if a reason can be found why anything that occurs has to occur thus and not otherwise.

Not surprisingly, Leibniz, as a consequence of his view of explanation, found himself in difficulty over the question of free will. His interpretation of the conditions of the rational transparency of the world clearly did not leave much room for free action, and this was understandably fastened on by Newton's spokesman Samuel Clarke. He pointed out to Leibniz that his approach led to a 'universal necessity and fate, by supposing that motives have the same relation to the will of an intelligent agent as weights have to a balance, so that, of two things absolutely indifferent, an intelligent agent can no more choose either than a balance can move itself when the weights on both sides are equal'.[10] The point is that given the way in which the 'principle of sufficient reason' works, if two different ways of acting lead to the same result, then there is no sufficient reason for preferring one to the other, and hence no rational way of choosing between the two.

Leibniz had no convincing reply to this criticism. All he was able to say in his own defence was that his thesis that everything that occurs — if it is to be rationally explicable — has to occur in accordance with the principle of sufficient reason, did not imply that it was *logically* impossible for things to be otherwise than they actually were. God, being a free agent, he claimed, could have created a different world if he had so desired. He could very well have chosen any one from an infinite number of options available to him. There was thus no *logical* necessity why the actual world should be as it is, and hence no logical necessity for anyone in such a world to act as they do. The possibility of contingent facts, and hence of non-necessary truths, he claimed, flowed from the *non-necessity* of God's own original choice of the world as a whole.

[10] Leibniz: *Philosophical Papers and Letters*, p. 691.

But this is a bad argument, and is moreover one that is disqualified on Leibniz's own premises. For it is only by choosing to create the best of all possible worlds (and hence such as does not require constant repair work be done to it) that God acts *rationally*. Theoretically, of course, God could have made a different choice. But if he had, then he would have acted without a sufficient reason, and since the principle of sufficient reason is the highest principle of rationality, this is virtually impossible, for it would imply that God behaved in an arbitrary and irrational fashion, which is contrary to his nature. In short, God *could not* have created a different world without, in effect, ceasing to be what he is, which is impossible; hence the real possibility of an alternative actual world does not exist.

It follows that Clarke's criticism *was* justified after all. For, stripped of the theological language, what Leibniz's argument amounts to, in the final analysis, is that if the world were in any way different to what it actually is, then, strictly speaking, it would *not* be rationally transparent; in other words, the rational transparency and hence the intelligibility of reality is made dependent upon the events necessarily occurring as they do. But, as we have seen, there is no justification whatever for such an assumption.

Necessary conditions and sufficient reasons

To sum up, there are two main conclusions that follow from our discussion. First, the philosophical interest in truth dictates that we should explore the necessary as well as the sufficient conditions of truth claims. Newton's explanations were couched, in effect, in terms of sufficient conditions, and were accordingly consonant with the provisions of the D-N model. But explanations in terms of sufficient conditions tell us nothing about the conditions without which the explanandum event *could not* take place. They only show what inferences follow from what premises, leaving the possibility of alternative inferential accounts open.

In insisting, as against this, on the need for an exploration of both the necessary and the sufficient conditions Leibniz was defending the interests of truth. But — this is the other main conclusion — his defence of the interests of truth against the mere scientific expediency embodied a misconception of what a demand for the necessary conditions actually entailed. Thus, as we saw earlier, while a philosophical explanation of a claim that p demands a statement of the necessary as well as the sufficient conditions of the truth of p, this cannot be reasonably construed as entailing the 'ontological necessity' of the state of affairs reported by p. An explanation in terms of the necessary and sufficient conditions does not demand that we view the world as a 'system of necessity', such that all its properties qualify as its *defining* properties. That this does not follow has been shown sufficiently by our analysis of actions. The necessary conditions needed to explain an action as an action do not make such an action a necessary event.

Leibniz, by contrast, had some difficulty explaining how on his premises free action was possible at all. In the end, he had no option but to accept that acting freely, in the true sense of the term, could only mean acting in accordance with the 'principle of sufficient reason'; and since, on his view, everything that occurred in the world, in as much as it was part of God's original design, occurred with a sufficient reason, virtually all distinction disappeared between natural events and actions, both of which were constituent elements of this design. Indeed if things were in any respect different to how they are in actual fact, they would not be explicable in accordance with the principle of sufficient reason, and hence not rationally accountable at all; with the consequence that the world would be inferior in perfection, which would offend against what Leibniz called 'moral necessity', for God would not be choosing the best available option.

So the inevitable verdict is that Leibniz misinterpreted the nature of philosophical explanation. The reason for this must be sought in his persistent tendency to confuse the necessary conditions with what he called 'sufficient reasons'. An account in terms of 'sufficient reasons' does not leave room for a genuinely free choice. This, however, does not apply to an account couched in terms of the necessary and sufficient conditions. It is entirely possible to provide an explanation in terms of the necessary and sufficient conditions *without* jeopardising either the notion of freewill or the idea of one world. As we saw earlier, an explanation of 'A tries to do x' requires as a necessary condition that if A is sufficiently motivated to do x he can actually translate his motivation into the actual effort. But it does not follow that if he does, then, in the best of all possible worlds, it is necessary that he should.

8 Truth as event

To provide an explanation of a truth claim that p is to provide an explanation of the necessary and sufficient conditions under which p 'hooks' onto the world, or exhibits a fact. At the same time, as our discussion in the preceding chapter shows, extreme vigilance is required against fallacious inferences that are sometimes derived from this. Thus an account in terms of the necessary and sufficient conditions does not require that the world be conceived as a logical mechanism in which ultimately everything can be derived from first principles. The root error of classical metaphysics was to assume that the world could not be made *rationally transparent* unless it was possible, in principle, to show why things in it necessarily occurred thus and not otherwise. Even that arch-enemy of metaphysics Hume seems to have subscribed to this fallacious premise — only to conclude that, as there could be no epistemic evidence to prove the existence of any necessary links between natural phenomena, the rational transparency of the world was itself open to doubt.

The blood ties between classical metaphysics and the incipient natural science ensured that for a long time this view permeated scientific thinking too. The world was conceived as a deterministic system, organised in accordance with strict causal laws. Yet, as we saw, Newton already made liberal use of hypotheses which substantially deviated from this model, and in so doing unwittingly prepared the ground for a pragmatist change of course, which was eventually to lead to a severance of the umbilical cord that held science and metaphysics together. The conviction that natural science, via a steady accretion of knowledge, provided an increasingly accurate picture of what the world *in itself* was like has largely yielded to the view that the essence of the scientific enterprise consists in constructing theoretical models with a view to resolving specific problems thrown up by the available data; the principal — though not the sole — objective being to make more successful *predictions* possible.

One of the consequences of this sea change has been a progressive weakening of the link between *scientific explanation* and *truth*; with the latter concept being effectively replaced by the contextually defined pragmatic notions of utility and success. But while this has been a natural, one might even say inevitable, development, what it has helped to bring home above all, as our inquiry has shown, is not that the concept of truth can be satisfactorily interpreted in terms of such pragmatic notions, but that on the contrary the concept of truth is *not a concept for science*. Natural science has virtually nothing to say about truth. The topic of truth transcends the horizon of its problems, and typically falls within the province of philosophy.

Truth predicates and the content of truth claims

Philosophically, however, truth has proved hard to handle, and the traditional attempts at a definition — from the 'correspondence' to 'coherence' to 'pragmatist' — have in fact generated so much obscurity and conundrum that the tendency, understandably perhaps, has been to focus on the linguistic function of truth predicates, with the aim of showing that the 'problem of truth' (if there be such a problem) could be dealt with satisfactorily by relying on the resources of logic alone. Typical of this approach is that any considerations of the content of truth claims, other than those concerned with logical consistency, are normally left in abeyance. The central guiding notion is that to ascribe the predicate 'true' to a proposition is to execute a metalinguistic manoeuvre whereby the relevant item of the object language is singled out for the specific purpose of emphasising its (normal) object language function, which is to report a particular state of affairs. The predicate is thus seen as a metalinguistic device which enables us to highlight what a specific piece of language (a proposition), in an ordinary context, is meant to convey.

Inevitably this induces reductionist reflections. If the predicate 'true' has no other function than that described above, one is left wondering if it might be dispensable in the long run. A useful inter-linguistic expedient though it certainly is, surely it is not logically essential. It does not after all add to, or modify, the content of the relevant proposition in any way. It as little conveys a genuine property of propositions as 'exists' conveys a property of objects; and just as 'Socrates exists' reduces to 'Someone is uniquely Socrates-like', so 'p is true' reduces to 'It is true that p' or 'Things are such that p', or simply 'Indeed p' or 'p!'. But if 'true', therefore, does not qualify as a 'genuine' property word, and does not convey anything of substance that is not conveyed by asserting the proposition, then there is no need for any large theory of truth. Truth turns out to be a simple logical notion, which does not lend itself to an analytic dissection in terms of other ideas. This, in essence, is the main principle behind what I have called the 'strategy of austerity'. That this is not a tenable position I have shown in chapter 2.

If, however, this approach does not work, then there seems to be no alternative but to refocus attention on the content of the truth claim, and re-examine some of the traditional arguments with a view to finding a more workable theory. A sentence as a vehicle of such a claim, in the first instance, has to satisfy certain formal rules of syntax, but not every syntactically well-formed sentence qualifies as a valid vehicle of a truth claim. As well as satisfying the rules of syntax, a sentence has to comply with certain semantic proprieties. Notoriously syntactically impeccable sentences, on closer inspection, sometimes turn out to be muddled or even downright incoherent. But then the question is, exactly what features of the content are, and what are not, truth-relevant? What conditions must the content satisfy if it is to be capable of 'expressing' a truth? Or, to put it in another way, under what conditions can a proposition significantly be claimed to be true?

There are, as we saw, essentially three different types of approach to an analysis of such conditions — the *naturalistic*, the *phenomenological* and the *socio-historical* approach, respectively — and whilst all of them individually are defective in a number of ways, they nevertheless seem contrapunctually to balance out each other's deficiencies, and their underlying premises, if closely inspected, can be seen to be structurally interlinked.

Structural interdependence of the three types of approach to truth conditions

The naturalistic approach involves an attempt to specify the truth conditions in terms of *structure* and *reference*, the underlying assumption being that if two propositions coincide in their logical structure, and if their constituent terms refer to the same things or classes of things, then — the differences in their 'mode of presentation' or surface syntax notwithstanding — their truth conditions are the same.

The immediate difficulty here, as we saw, is one of providing a sufficiently precise definition of structure and reference. Thus the access to logical structure leads, and can only lead, via meaning. But if structure can only be accessed, and made intelligible, through the meaning content, how can the former serve as a basis for providing an account of the latter? It is the meaning that determines the structure, not vice versa. But, then, a consideration of the meaning content *in all its aspects* surely must take priority.

If this is granted, however, then the naturalistic policy of paring down of the content to its 'truth-relevant' essentials becomes hard to defend. For how do we decide which aspects of the meaning content are, and which are not relevant to truth? Any aspect, however trivial, may in the given context turn out to be important. And since the 'deep' structure can be accessed only via meaning, how do we decide when, if at all, two sentences which differ in meaning nevertheless have the same 'deep' structure? Perhaps no non-synonymous sentences ever do. But if that is the case, how can any two such sentences be said to express the same state of affairs?

The naturalistic account of *reference* is similarly defective, and for similar reasons. There is of course no question that the objective truth-relevant content of a truth claim depends upon what the terms used actually designate, or upon what the actual topic 'talked about' (which may or may not coincide with the *intended* topic) in the given instance happens to be. The problem rather is whether there is a case for supposing that such topics are logically independent of any descriptive references that might be made to them. The naturalistic approach implies that this indeed is the case. The idea is that what is really being 'talked about', i.e. the logical subject of utterance, in the final analysis, is located outside thought, and moreover cannot be pinned down in an entirely unequivocal fashion by any descriptive referential expression. No description of what actually exists is such that it cannot as a matter of logic fit more than one individual specimen. From this it is concluded that the actual world is not only external to thought, but is independent of, and pre-exists thought. *And that does not follow.*

To begin with, the externality of reference does not mean that the object referred to can never be uniquely descriptively determined. As we saw, in the case of abstract individuals (e.g. numbers) the reference can be fixed unequivocally via description. 'The smallest even positive integer' cannot refer to more than one mathematical object. Indeed the description in question is part of that object's *definition.* But even where this is not the case, a description remains a logically indispensable vehicle of reference. 'The teacher of Plato' provides a convenient way of referring to Socrates, although the phrase as such is not necessarily individuative of anyone. There may well have existed more than one such person, or there may have been none. There is no certainty, therefore, that any such description will hit a unique target, or that it will hit anything at all. Nevertheless this does not mean that reference fixing in respect of external objects can in the final analysis be effected only non-descriptively, by 'pure ostension'. There is no such thing as 'pure ostension'. The fixing of reference presupposes a point of view, and hence a specific descriptive context; and this means that whilst the targeted object, or objects, may be *external* to thought, there can be no valid grounds for saying that they are *logically independent* of thought.

The *phenomenological* approach (chapter 4) helps to drive home this very point, whilst at the same time allowing a much broader view of facts. The naturalistic approach is inherently reductionist, in that it seeks to explain the truth-relevant content of all truth claims in terms of certain basic states of affairs, from which all reflexive indexical elements and negation are specifically banned. By contrast, the phenomenological approach recognises that *both* these features can form part of basic facts. So far from attempting to separate the truth-relevant content from the 'mode of presentation', it treats the former as a sub-species of the latter. The argument now is that the access to structure and reference leads via the meaning content, and that the latter, in turn, demands an analysis in terms of the intentions and projects of *language users.*

In short, the idea is that the content cannot be divorced from the relevant acts of representation, and should not be treated as some kind of independent ideal entity inhabiting a logical library of 'possible worlds'. Accordingly, an explanation of the 'hook-up' of thought with reality is now sought not in terms of 'agreement with', or 'portrayal of', certain states of affairs supposedly existing independently out there but in terms of what cannot be coherently disbelieved. The general thesis is that a truth claim in the final analysis can be made sense of only with a reference to what can be known for *certain*.

A single-minded pursuit of this approach, however, is similarly apt to lead to disaster. For although the aspect of certainty, or of 'what cannot be coherently disbelieved', must play a role in any account of truth, it cannot serve as a basis for a comprehensive theory of truth. In the end, as we saw, the phenomenological approach fails by its own chosen criteria. It purports to reverse the reductionist policy of naturalism, in particular by providing a *rationale* for a rehabilitation of the indexical features of the meaning content, which, in naturalistic accounts, are treated with suspicion as a source of imprecision and ambiguity, and are generally dismissed as irrelevant to truth. It fails, however, to achieve its own objective, in as much as it proves incapable of accommodating within its own premises the indexical features of time determinations. Tensed indexical propositions about past or future events by their very nature preclude the possibility of certainty in respect of the epistemic evidence, and hence by definition cannot satisfy the phenomenological criteria of what qualifies as a candidate for a valid truth claim. And since they equally resist a naturalistic paraphrase, clearly an entirely different kind of analysis will be needed to account for their 'truth-relevant content'.

In point of fact, what such indexical propositions help to highlight is a more general problem, which both the naturalistic and the phenomenological approach have to confront, but are essentially incapable of resolving, viz. the problem of *objectivity*; and it is this very problem that the *socio-historical* approach attempts to address (chapter 5). But once again we end up with an incomplete and unbalanced account of truth conditions. The excessive emphasis placed upon the conditions of objectivity leads to the role and the importance of the other truth conditions being obscured or underplayed. Indeed, not only do we end up with an inadequate account of truth conditions but find ourselves in an additional predicament of having to choose between two different explanatory accounts: one relativistic, the other evolutionary, both of which are fraught with problems.

The relativistic option, as we saw, involves treating objectivity criteria as strictly context-dependent and variable, with no universal parameters operating across contextual boundaries. The evolutionary option, by contrast, is based on the idea of a universal progress, and involves the idea of history as a steady, if frequently tortuous, process of convergence to a universal standard. Neither option immediately commends itself. The evolutionary option, quite apart from its unpalatable political implications, is difficult to defend not simply because there can be no definitive proof of any 'convergence' to a universal standard, but because any theory of such convergence lays claim to a universality of its own criteria for evaluating the objective content of truth claims, which by definition it cannot redeem until the evolutionary historical process has run its course. The metaphysical fantasies of the 'end of history', which derive essentially from the biblical myth of salvation, and which have gained a measure of philosophical currency mainly through the philosophy of Hegel and its Marxist scholiasts and annotators, have played a significant part in keeping alive this idea of 'convergence'.

As for the *relativistic* option, this option involves an acquiescence in a permanent variability of the objectivity criteria, which are seen as being irretrievably context-based. The difficulty with this option, however, is that the notion of context, as a rule, is not specified, and perhaps cannot be specified with anything like sufficient precision, without a high degree of arbitrariness and artificiality. As a result, there is always a degree of uncertainty over what criteria are properly applicable, or should be applied, in what case. The problem is not only that different societies, or the same society across its history, often apply different institutionalised criteria of significance, but that within one and the same society, however homogeneous or tightly-knit it might appear on the surface, there is always a multitude of substructures and levels of discourse, where different criteria operate and different views compete for influence and attention. Individual religious or political groups, business interests and professional bodies, in varying measure all tend to evolve their own interpretative models of the social, and not infrequently also natural, phenomena that concern them; sometimes moreover in a deliberate opposition to the established, or officially sanctioned standard.

So the conclusion is that neither model can serve as a basis for a comprehensive account of truth conditions, although their respective adherents have often assumed that they can. The evolutionary model fails to justify the universalist claims it makes in respect of its own objectivity criteria, whereas the relativistic model in effect does away with the notion of truth in favour of a pragmatic notion of contextual — institutionalised or semi-institutionalised — *utility*. We are offered certain clues as to where to look for the conditions of objectivity but hardly a secure basis for a rounded up account of what constitutes a significant truth claim.

Nevertheless the socio-historical approach, whilst defective in both its versions, highlights an important aspect of truth claims which is largely ignored or neglected by the other two types of approach, and indirectly helps to complete the logical jig-saw of truth conditions. What finally emerges is a picture of a structural interdependence of the leading ideas that guide and inspire these three types of approach, respectively; viz. the idea of a *world external to propositional thought*, the idea of *certainty of what cannot be coherently disbelieved*, and the idea of *objectivity*. The aim of the diverse arguments that I have been advancing in the preceding pages has been to show that all these ideas enter into the conditions of truth.

Truth claims, existential presuppositions and asymmetry between content and extension

Indeed they form part of the semantic luggage of every truth *claim*. In order to make this a little clearer, consider, first, what I shall call the asymmetry between the content of the claim that p and its extension.

Truth claims are targeted at certain states of affairs, and whilst such states of affairs are reported in propositions, and moreover cannot be communicated in any other way, they are nevertheless not identical with propositions. As we saw earlier (chapters 3 and 7), the relationship between them is not one-one but rather one-many, viz. the same state of affairs can be addressed in propositions which are both semantically and, to a considerable extent, syntactically different.

In claiming that p, then (except, ostensibly, when p is analytic; see later) we are implicitly positing a target which can be addressed from different perspectives. If this were not possible, then no two truth claims could be said to have the same hook-up points unless they were literally synonymous and sooner or later the communication would break down. Furthermore, there is no logical limit to the number of propositions which can be 'extensionally isomorphic' in the given case. The targeted state of affairs thus remains 'transcendent' relative to any perspective, or series of perspectives, from which it might be addressed. It is primarily in this sense that in making an assertion that p we are subscribing to the notion of an extra-propositional world.

At the same time, this inevitably casts a shadow over the notion of truth as a 'correspondence' between thought and extra-linguistic fact: for if the asymmetry between content and extension is ultimate and unavoidable, then the question arises, exactly what does 'correspond' to what? The world is a room with many mirrors — why should any image be 'closer' to the facts than any of the others? It seems that we shall either have to devise a different account of how thought 'hooks' onto reality, enabling us to accommodate the diverse — albeit extensionally isomorphic — contents under the umbrella of truth, or alternatively pursue a reductionist path in the hope of sifting out those features of the content which remain constant throughout, and act as 'bearers' of truth value.

The naturalistic approach, as we saw, involves the choice of the latter option. Its underlying premise is that in any given instance the symmetry between thought and extra-linguistic fact can in principle be restored by bracketing out those elements of the content which are not relevant to truth, and concentrating on those which are. If it is possible for two different propositions to be extensionally isomorphic, i.e. target the same state of affairs, it is argued, then not all their semantical and syntactical features can be equally important: some will be of a superficial nature, and will have no effect on the truth value, whereas others, which do have a bearing on the truth value, will have to be the *same* in both cases; and the question is simply one of identifying these latter features and bringing them to light. In short, the problem could be overcome by applying a reductionist analysis to the propositional content, with a view to extracting that which 'matters' to truth.

Such a strategy, however, superficially attractive though it may seem, does not work in the long run (chapter 3). Two propositions may be extensionally isomorphic, in the strict sense of conveying the same state of affairs, while nevertheless carrying different messages, and hence expressing different — albeit logically interlinked — *truths*. Passivisation provides a good illustration of this. Thus an ostensibly innocuous transposition from active into passive (or vice versa) may sometimes result in significant shifts of truth-relevant meaning, even though the 'external' state of affairs remains unaltered. In point of fact, two semantically different propositions can never express literally the same truth. They carry different messages, and by definition have different truth conditions. But, then, there is strictly no room for a distinction between what is 'truth-relevant' and what is not 'truth-relevant'. Truth encompasses *all features of content*, even though it has to be accepted that propositions with different contents can aim at the same extra-propositional targets; just like different singular terms can be designative of the same individual objects.

Paradoxically, a reductionist strategy by seeking to minimise, or even eliminate altogether, the asymmetry between content and extension from the truth-relevant content threatens to obscure the very notion of an extra-propositional reality; thereby undermining one of the cardinal articles of faith enshrined in its canon. For how else could the latter notion be made precise except by appealing to just such an asymmetry? Indeed an analysis of truth claims shows that neither of these notions can be given up without in effect sacrificing both. That 'Galileo was born in Pisa' and 'The author of *Sidereal Messenger* was born in Pisa' both report the same state of affairs. This evidently cannot be decided by simply inspecting their respective contents, which are different. If they do convey the same state of affairs, then it is because 'Galileo' and 'the author of *Sidereal Messenger*' both refer to the same entity. But this assumption makes sense only on condition that both truth claims posit an external object which can be addressed from different perspectives. It is this assumption that creates a 'hook-up' point for the two different contents, without, however, in any way diminishing, let alone obliterating their differences.

What applies to singular propositions, applies equally to general propositions, which target *classes* of objects. Thus the state of affairs conveyed by 'All humans are mortal' arguably is the same as that conveyed by 'All rational animals are mortal', and of course there might be any number of other non-synonymous propositions, which are extensionally isomorphic with both. Clearly the possibilities of substitution of coextensional terms (and hence of manufacturing extensionally isomorphic propositions) are limitless. What is important to note is that it is precisely the asymmetry between content and extension which makes the isomorphism of such propositions possible.

An obvious exception to the rule seems to be analytic propositions. 'All bodies are extended', 'Two sides of a triangle put together are greater than the third', or simple identities like 'Socrates is (i.e. is none other than) Socrates', surely belong in a different category. The propositional content in such cases marks off the relevant state of affairs in such a fashion that any 'asymmetry' seems to dwindle to nought, and the distinction between content and extension becomes otiose. Yet this is not quite true, even here. For such propositions ultimately say something about ourselves (or beings *like* ourselves). They embody certain rules of consistent thought, but only in the sense of representing that which cannot be coherently thought or conceived to be otherwise by us, and are thereby implicitly anchored in an 'extra-propositional' reality.

But, in addition, where names of individuals or classes are involved there is an automatic presumption of the possibility of multiple referencing. Thus with regard in particular to 'Socrates is Socrates', the two sign tokens flanking the 'is' sign both name the same individual, and to know what it is for them to be co-referential in this sense is at the same time to understand that one of them could be replaced with a different, *non*-synonymous, but none the less *equi*-referential expression, resulting in an extensionally isomorphic proposition, though of course no longer a tautology. (I shall revert to this shortly.)

Another, seemingly more credible, exception represents propositions about properties of abstract individuals, like numbers. In such cases, if two propositions are extensionally isomorphic, they are *necessarily* isomorphic. Thus 'The number immediately following the number 6 in the series of integers is a prime' and 'The positive square root of 49 is a prime' are extensionally isomorphic, not just as a matter of fact but as a matter of necessity. But, then, surely there can be no question of any asymmetry between content and extension, for the two descriptive referential expressions, respectively — viz. 'The number immediately following the number 6 in the series of integers' and 'The positive square root of 49' — both form part of the *definition* of the number concerned. Indeed it might be argued that numbers literally unravel into sets of such descriptions, which, in turn, merely refer, synoptically, to certain types of mathematical operations rather than designating some ontological items existing in their own right. But if that is the case (which, of course, is not an entirely uncontroversial view), then all that it shows is that numbers cannot be treated as extra-conceptual entities.

Notice, however, that the situation changes radically if a descriptive reference, or references, are made to certain *specified* pluralities of things rather than to numbers *tout court*. Thus 'The number of mortal sins is a prime' and 'The positive square root of 49 is a prime' both report the same state of affairs even though they differ as regards to content; but although extensionally isomorphic as a matter of fact they are not *necessarily* extensionally isomorphic. The reason for this is obvious: whereas 'The positive square root of 49' cannot hit more than one individual target, 'The number of mortal sins' (given alternative theologies) conceivably might.

So the general conclusion is that, in asserting that p, one is inevitably committing oneself to the notion of an extra-propositional world. When a truth claim is made, the existence of such a world is implicitly posited. Moreover such a world must *actually exist* if what is asserted is to be true.

The idea of certainty

But this is just one ingredient of the semantic luggage of a truth claim. Another (as indicated earlier) is the tacit supposition of certain *unerring beliefs*. There are of course many things that one cannot coherently believe, and just as many things that one cannot coherently doubt. I cannot coherently believe that A is not A, that I have never existed, that I am always mistaken. Such beliefs are incoherent because their opposites cannot be coherently *disbelieved*. But the point is not only that there are certain beliefs which are impervious to doubt, but that *every truth claim involves such beliefs*.

Nor, it should be added at once, are such beliefs confined to certain general logical beliefs (e.g. that two contradictory beliefs cannot both be true at the same time). On the contrary, every truth claim presupposes a very specific 'incorrigible' belief, in this sense: that if I assert p, then, provided I understand what I am saying, I cannot at the same time coherently disbelieve or doubt that that is how I claim things are. Of course, it is possible to assert p without believing that p. To say 'It is raining but I don't believe it is' is odd but not incoherent. What one cannot coherently assert, whilst being fully aware of what one is saying, is 'It is raining but that is not what my statement is intended to convey'; or, if p is the object of my belief, 'I believe that p but I am not sure *what* I believe'.

What is more, as was shown earlier (chapter 4), in some cases one can be certain about the *evidence* required to make p true. This applies in particular to first-person experience reports. Thus I cannot coherently claim that I am hungry if I can never be certain if what I say is true. Speaking generally, if I am in principle unable to decide with certainty whether or not I am in the mental state F, then I cannot meaningfully claim that I am in that mental state. It is incoherent to suppose that one could have a clear grasp of a concept of a mental state without being able to know with certainty whether a specific experience qualifies as its exemplifying instance.

Of course this does not apply to *all* concepts. Thus it is not a condition of my having the concept of a table that in any given instance I should be in a position to decide with certainty if a table is actually there. Whilst I cannot have the concept of a table without holding at least some correct beliefs about tables, it is not inconceivable, however unlikely, that I might make the wrong identification on every single occasion. Evidently one can have a clear grasp of a concept of a physical object without necessarily succeeding in identifying any particular specimen. Indeed one can make significant truth claims in respect of such objects *irrespective* of the availability or otherwise of certainty in respect of the verifying evidence. In contrast to concepts of mental states, the possession of a concept of a physical object does not demand that its application should yield a truth sometimes.

Nevertheless this does not mean that any mention of certainty in such cases is inappropriate. For, as I have shown earlier, in making truth claims about anything at all one is implicitly making certain assumptions about what cannot be coherently disbelieved. Thus I cannot coherently claim that x is a table, without being able, in principle, to know with certainty that that is what I purport to convey, or that the belief I happen to entertain is *of the relevant sort*, or that things appear to me as such and such. I cannot be certain that what I perceive is indeed a table, but I can at least be certain about the *perceptual belief* I hold. In a sense, I must be able to know my 'mind' with certainty in order to be able to make a meaningful truth claim about anything at all.

Secondly, even if one does not happen to entertain the relevant belief oneself, one has to be in a position to know what it means to hold such a belief; and this, among other things, involves knowing what it is to be *certain* in respect of having such a belief. In short, one cannot understand what it means to make a truth claim that p without understanding what it is to believe that p; and to understand what it is to believe that p is to understand what it is to be certain about the kind of belief one entertains. Moreover it is to understand what it is to be certain about the kind of perceptual experience that accompanies such a belief. To take again the above example, I cannot coherently believe that what I perceive is a table without at the same time being able to decide with certainty whether I am in fact having a table-perceiving experience (irrespective of whether a table is actually there).

The certainty, then, to which I am entitled is *twofold*, viz. a) the certainty (barring verbal error) as to how I experience the world from my own point of view, and b) the certainty as to what anyone who makes truth claims, myself included, cannot coherently disbelieve. This may not seem a great deal, but it is important none the less. That a notion of certainty as here specified enters into the concept of truth can I think hardly be disputed. The possibility of such certainty is implicit in any assertion we make. A different question entirely is of course whether such a notion alone is robust enough to shoulder a comprehensive theory of truth.

The doctrine of Protagoras

The philosopher who seems to have thought that it can — if, that is, what Plato says in the *Theaetetus* can be relied upon — was Protagoras. Protagoras' starting premise in his treatise on truth, it appears, was that no coherent notion could be formed of truth 'in itself'. If there was truth, then it was only relative to an observer or cognitive agent, who knows something to be true; and one can know something to be true only in the sense of having an unerring perception of how at any given time the world looks from one's own point of view. In other words, 'I am the judge of what is for me, that it is, and of what is not, that it is not.'[1] And since my point of view is subject to variation and change, inevitably my view of what is true will change too.

In his own critical comments Plato was anxious to point out what seemed to him to be an obvious similarity between this doctrine and the Heraclitean thesis that the world was in a state of continuous flux. The view common to both Protagoras and Heraclitus, Plato claimed, was that there was nothing fixed or permanent 'out there'; nothing, in fact, that could be meaningfully said to be such and such *by itself*. Rather all things were merely 'in the process of *becoming for someone*' [my italics — E.P.].[2] The world to all intents and purposes remains an impenetrable shapeless mass unless and until it acquires a specific character for a perceiver or a cognitive agent, who sees it thus from the point of view he happens to occupy. Independently of any perceiver it cannot meaningfully be attributed any definitive features at all. From which it follows automatically that there is no truth 'in itself'; only *perceived* truth.

But if that is indeed so, Plato objected irritably, how can we make sense of the distinction between how things seem to me and how they *objectively* are? After all, we do accept that we are sometimes wrong. If truth reduced to knowledge as perception, as Protagoras claimed, what right did he, Protagoras, have to set himself up as a teacher of others, and moreover expect to be handsomely rewarded for his pains?

It is difficult to believe, however, that Protagoras would have left himself open to such ridicule, and Plato's ill-tempered and rather shallow jibe may well have been occasioned by a misapprehension of what Protagoras was really intending to say. For if Protagoras' arguments concerning truth as perception are seen, as probably in large part they ought to be, not simply as a more sophisticated restatement of the Heraclitean doctrine of flux, but on the contrary as an attempt at a *reductio ad absurdum* of the kind of naturalistic metaphysics, as exemplified, among others, by Heraclitus' own theory, then a more

[1] *Theaetetus*, 160c.

[2] Ib. 157a.

sympathetic evaluation of his doctrine becomes possible.[3] His arguments in such a case can no longer be dismissed as a simple-minded effort to defend an absurdly relativistic position which lacked any coherent notion of objectivity, but should on the contrary be seen as an attempt to highlight the need for a new theory of objectivity — a theory which so far from being subtractive of, or 'reductionist' in respect of the subject-related, indexical features of truth claims recognises their irreducibility and importance, and is sufficiently flexible and ecumenical to embrace them within its orbit; in short, the kind of theory which neither the Heraclitean metaphysics, nor, for that matter, Plato's own brand of metaphysics, within their own respective frames of reference, were capable of accommodating.

Truth claims and objectivity

The merit of Protagoras' arguments is thus to have shown that the issue of objectivity cannot be 'resolved' at the price of sacrificing the indexical features of truth claims. Any reductionist manoeuvre designed to remove such features from the truth-relevant content can only result in a corruption of truth, and is doomed to fail in the long run. But, then, how should the problem of objectivity be addressed? What does confer objectivity upon truth claims?

The answer to this, as we saw earlier, is that it is in the social world that we have to look for clues. In articulating a truth claim one is engaging in a public act and is implicitly giving a hostage to fortune. The employment of specific concepts on such occasions may or may not be judged appropriate; it may deviate from some established rule, or indeed be out of line with what one purports to express in the first instance. The criteria in terms of which such things may be decided will of necessity be operable in principle by others as well as by the speaker himself. It follows that one can never be the sole arbiter as to whether an error, be it linguistic or factual, has occurred in the given instance.

[3] In my book *Change and Selves* (chapter 1) I have argued that Zeno's paradoxes of motion *mutatis mutandis* can be interpreted in a similar fashion, viz. as an attempt at a *reductio ad absurdum* of naturalistic metaphysics. The Sophists were more subtle thinkers than they are generally given credit for.

At first glance, this directly contradicts the requirement of certainty. We said earlier that the use of concepts (in truth claims) presupposes the possibility of certainty in respect of certain beliefs concerning exemplifying instances of such concepts. But what kind might such certainty be if no sooner the belief is specified than it becomes susceptible to error? If certainty is possible at all, then surely it cannot flow from anything that is capable of being brought under a concept and expressed in words; and this means that it cannot have much to do with truth.

In chapter 5 I have argued that this is a misconception. Consider again what is involved in having concepts of mental states. Suppose I wish to broadcast the fact that I have a toothache. Evidently there is always the possibility that for one reason or another I might misreport my experience. Once uttered, my statement becomes a public property, and can be scanned for error by other language users. But although I cannot be certain about the accuracy of what I say, I can nevertheless be certain about my own *intention*: I cannot both have the concept of a toothache and not be certain about what I intend to report when I utter my statement. Moreover it is incoherent to suppose that one can have the *concept* of a toothache without being capable of being certain as to whether the experience in question is in fact taking place. To understand the concept of a toothache is to be able to decide whether the experience is, or is not, of the relevant sort, notwithstanding the fact that one can never know for sure whether one has committed an error in *reporting* the experience on a particular occasion.

The distinction has thus to be made between what one *intends* to convey and what one actually *succeeds* in conveying. If what I say corresponds to what I intend to convey, then I can be certain that my statement accurately reports my experience. This still leaves plenty of scope for error, for my achievement may well fall short of my intention. What I actually succeed in communicating will not be only for me to judge. Nevertheless I do have the right to be certain as to whether that which I am judged to have succeeded in communicating does or does not correspond to what I wanted to say in the first instance.

A particular problem of reconciling certainty with objectivity, as we saw, arises in connection with temporal placing. If I understand the concept of a toothache, and if the words I utter mean what I think they do, then I can say with certainty that that is the experience I have. But

I cannot say with certainty that I had a toothache yesterday, or even two minutes ago. The relevant evidence in such cases is expressly located out of reach on a temporal scale. At the same time, it would be futile to try to paraphrase such statements into a 'neutral' idiom, devoid of tense and indexical expressions, on the grounds that certainty was available when the experience actually took place. The indexical temporal placing ('yesterday') is a constitutive part of the truth-relevant content of what I say, and cannot be written out of my statement without altering its substance; and if so, the certainty is by definition *not* available.

In point of fact, the problem posed by the use of tensed verbs in temporal placing is more severe than it might appear, for we heavily depend on tense in reporting public events as well as personal experiences. Nor is this simply a matter of expediency or personal preference. For although superficially it may seem that tense can be axed out of such reports, a closer inspection soon reveals that this cannot be achieved without creating an ambiguity as to what message exactly is being conveyed.

Consider the following example. 'The train left the station at 8 a.m.' Contrary to what might appear, this is not equivalent in respect of its truth-relevant content with 'The train (tenselessly) leaves the station when the clock (tenselessly) shows 8 o'clock'. The reason for this is not simply that the former statement, unlike its tenseless paraphrase, places the event within the context of the speaker's own time, but because the paraphrase in question does not necessarily express a temporal relation at all. A brief reflection is sufficient to see why that is so. The word 'when' in the paraphrase plays the role of a *conjunction*, not a temporal adverb — the word 'while', for example, would have served just as well. In so far as the paraphrase contextually may be taken to convey a temporal relation, then it is only provided it is interpreted in a way that involves a recourse to the ideas of past, present and future. Taken purely on its own, the paraphrase conveys nothing intrinsically temporal, and, for all we know, might be describing a scene in a painting. Or conceivably it might be saying merely that the two events in question are contextually connected by virtue of forming part of a larger event — the 'station event', say — which embraces them both; in which case, a reference to my waving of a handkerchief would be just as appropriate as a reference to the clock. But being a feature of a complex event (which may have any number of constituent features) does not necessarily have anything to do with time.[4]

In short, truth claims about temporal relations depend for their intelligibility upon a clear grasp of tense; and in so far as tensed temporal determinations ultimately point back to an experienced form of 'presentness', they, in turn, depend for their intelligibility upon the experienced 'indexical' time. None the less, they all carry *objectivity claims*, and the conditions of objectivity in such cases, as we saw earlier (chapter 5), can only be explained with a reference to an institutionalised chronology of the socially constructed time.

But, of course, all truth claims without exception, those which do as well as those which do not involve the use of tense, are subject to the objectivity conditions. These conditions have to do not only with the general rules of syntax, but with a variety of semantical and general categorial proprieties that a truth claim, in the context in which it is made, must satisfy before it can qualify as a valid truth candidate; and such conditions, as has been shown, demand an exploration of the way language is used within the historical institutional framework of social life.

The structural approach and its implications

This concludes my discussion of truth conditions, which was begun as an exploratory critique of three fundamental models of explanation in chapters 2-5. The defended thesis throughout has been that an account of truth required an examination of the semantic structure of *truth claims*, and that what this structure revealed was the interconnectedness of three fundamental ideas, viz. the idea of an extra-propositional world, the idea of certainty in respect of what cannot be coherently disbelieved, and the idea of objectivity.

This has substantial philosophical implications, and in particular calls into question some of our most cherished common sense beliefs about truth. In the remainder of the present chapter I propose to round off my discussion by commenting briefly on three specific propositions which are entailed by the general view of truth that I have been

[4] See chapter 5.

advancing, viz. (i) *that truth claims are essential to truth*, (ii) *that truth and falsehood are not logically on a par*, and (iii) *that truth does not exist until it occurs*.

(i) Necessity of truth claims

All these propositions go against the grain and sound improbable at first sight. Why, to begin with, should truth claims be relevant to an understanding of what truth is? What conceivable relevance might my, or anyone else's, for that matter, claim, or the ability to claim, that things are such and such have to things actually being such and such? That a proposition has a truth value, if it does, surely is independent of what anyone asserts or believes, or might assert or believe. That there are other forms of intelligent life elsewhere in the universe might or might not be true: either alternative can be intelligibly contemplated without the need to assert, or assent to either. Nor does the *possibility* of such a hypothesis being asserted or denied have any bearing on the consideration of its truth or falsity.

This seems patently obvious. Yet on closer inspection it becomes hazy. Undeniably we can, and do, intelligibly speak of propositions being *possibly* true or *possibly* false without wishing to assert anything. Possibly, very probably even, there is intelligent life elsewhere in the universe, but I do not wish to commit myself one way or the other. There can hardly be any doubt about what this means. Nevertheless if such talk makes clear sense, then it is only with an eye to a possible truth claim. The reason for this is simple: a proposition can be significantly described as possibly true or false only in as much as an extra-propositional reality is presupposed which the proposition is meant to be 'about'; and the targeting of such an extra-propositional reality takes place precisely within the context of *truth claims*.

The point is that the concept of truth and the concept of an extra-propositional reality necessarily go together; that they are logically interlinked. At the same time, the question of truth (or falsity) does not arise *automatically*; i.e. merely in virtue of what the proposition 'means'. A proposition lends itself to a variety of different uses. It may occur in a fairy tale, or it might be employed rhetorically, or possibly uttered in jest. We can, and often do, tell ourselves all manner of amusing stories about 'possible worlds', without concerning ourselves about truth. It is only when truth claims are made or posited that truth becomes an issue.

But does this, it will be asked, necessarily apply in all cases? Take tautologies again. Surely that everything is identical with itself ranges over all possible worlds, and is true even if nothing existed outside thought, irrespective of whether any truth claims are made by anyone, or are even possible. A distinction between the proposition and the extra-propositional reality which the proposition is supposed to be 'about' surely cannot be sensibly drawn in this case. A truth claim here, if it should be made at all, does not involve any extra-propositional existential commitment. No reality external to propositional thought need be posited or presupposed.

The answer to this, as I indicated earlier, is that such propositions are not 'truths', strictly speaking, but represent rather consistency rules, spelling out the conditions of coherent thought. If they can be treated as 'truths', then it is only in so far as they can be said to articulate certain features peculiar to the kind of beings that we are, viz. how, as a matter of fact, our own (coherent) thought functions; and to that extent they are implicitly targeted at an extra-propositional reality.

Another possible exception seems to be *self-referential* propositions. These propositions, on the face of it, present more of a problem, in as much as they — unlike tautologies — carry factual information. Thus the expression 'This is a sentence' manifestly is not trivial. At the same time, what the sentence says, it seems, is neither more nor less than *what it aims at*. But then a truth claim in such a case — should it be made at all — does not require a distinction between the propositional content and the extra-propositional target. This impression is mistaken, however, for this distinction is implicit in the use of the inverted commas, which act as a nominalizing, and hence a targeting device, whereby the expression in question is converted, in effect, into an analogue of a *second-level assertion*.

Nevertheless doubts might still persist about the need for truth claims. Consider examples of propositions where there is no target to be hit. Suppose that relying on past experience I claim in all innocence that the entire cash in my wallet is in Pounds Sterling, and it turns out that the wallet is empty. Whilst there is no ground for impugning my sincerity, my truth claim will nevertheless be disqualified in the light of a matter of fact which is *independent* of what I say, namely that the wallet contains no cash. Sometimes, moreover, a truth claim, whilst ostensibly well formed, will on closer inspection turn out to be disqualified as a *matter of logic*. Thus no assertion of 'The greatest natural number is even' will yield a truth value, for the simple reason that such a number cannot exist. But then, what conceivable relevance might truth claims have to the truth value in such cases?

Suppose that, employing the familiar strategy, all such doubtful propositions are presented in an 'existential' form[5]; then, surely, they would automatically acquire a truth value regardless of any assertion. The first of the two examples above would then read 'There is money in my wallet, and all of it is Sterling', and the second 'There is a number which has the property of being the greatest natural number, and is even', both of which could be meaningfully denied. Such paraphrases have the merit of being free from any ambiguity, and are true or false by virtue of their logical form alone, irrespective of whether they are, or possibly might be, objects of truth claims.

What reply might be given to this? Take the second example first, viz. 'There is a number which has the property of being the greatest natural number, and is even'. The central issue here turns out to be one of *coherence* rather than of truth value. The point is that in this case the existential proposition is merely a fancy way of talking about certain logical inferences. What is said, in effect, reduces to the claim that the series of natural numbers can be brought to an end, such that its last member has the property of being even; and this is incompatible with the *definition* of natural number. In other words, the proposition is *incoherent* rather than 'false'.

Admittedly this does not apply to the first example, which evidently does not involve any incoherence. What is more, the majority of existential propositions that we come across in the ordinary course of events seem to fall in this category, and hence cannot be reduced to logical inferences along the above lines. But, then, neither are such propositions true or false of the actual world *simply in virtue of being existential*. An existential proposition might feature as part of reported speech, or it might be uttered by a fictional character in a story, or it might be the subject of a 'mock assertion' within a game of make-

[5] See chapter 1, p. 5.

believe, and consequently lack what Frege termed the 'usual force' (cf. chapters 2 and 4). In such cases, the normal considerations of truth and falsity will not apply.

Truth claims, therefore — at any rate, such as are, or might be, made under normal conditions — have a key role to play. But in what sense exactly do they involve a reference to a reality external to thought? Suppose that a claim is made to the effect that certain entities do not exist, or that the existence is explicitly asserted of something which turns out to be fictional. In such cases what exactly is 'talked about', if anything? Certainly not 'nothingness'. There is precious little that can be said about 'nothingness' at the best of times. That nothing is a unicorn is a claim about everything that exists in the world. What is more, without the assumption of an extra-propositional reality such a claim would be void of meaning. On the other hand, that there are nine Muses and that Muses are fictional, in a sense, are both true. But notice that the first proposition is true only in as much as it is intended as a shorthand for 'There are nine Muses in Greek mythology', or 'according to Homer'. Taken as it stands, it is of course an error, a falsehood, because the world 'out there' does not contain Muses — which, in turn, makes the second claim (which, like 'Nothing is a unicorn', is about everything that exists) true. In other words, in either case there is a presumption of an 'external' reality.

(ii) Truth and falsehood are not logically on a par

Consider now the second of the three propositions I said earlier are entailed by the view of truth that I have been advancing, viz. that truth and falsehood are not logically on a par.

What has been established so far is that it is only in respect of possible truth claims that propositions can be meaningfully said to be about anything external to themselves at all. In this regard, a proposition is much like an anchor lying on deck; it can neither hook nor fail to hook onto anything until it is cast. At the same time, this does not mean that truth reduces to a property of truth claims. Truth and falsehood, I have argued, have no 'bearers' of which they might be predicated, in the way in which sweetness or acerbity might be predicated of an apple. A truth claim that p purports to address a state of affairs external to p, and is 'true' provided the conditions for the occurrence of truth are satisfied; the existence of the relevant state of affairs being one such condition. If the conditions for the occurrence of truth are not satisfied in respect of the claim that p, then they are satisfied in respect of the claim that not-p. But that they are necessarily satisfied in one of the two cases does not mean that truth, therefore, is a property of truth claims.

The view that truth is in the nature of a property, or rather a relational property, is implicit in all versions of the so-called 'correspondence theory'. The central idea is that propositions are 'made' true or false by virtue of agreeing or failing to agree with, or 'map', certain extra-propositional facts. Sometimes, as we saw earlier (chapter 6), this thesis is significantly qualified, by making the 'agreement' in question dependent upon certain conditions, to do specifically with the manner in which we contextually tend to refer to, and describe, what we observe. But although this qualification is significant, in as much as it signals the abandonment of the naive view of agreement with, or picturing, facts which are supposed to exist 'out there' exactly as, but *prior to*, being depicted, it nevertheless retains the general notion of 'agreement with', and being 'made true' by something extra-propositional. This is misleading. For although truth claims target 'external' states of affairs, they are not 'made true' *tout court* by virtue of 'agreeing' with such states of affairs. Rather, as I have tried to show, such states of affairs *enter* into truth events via the relevant propositions under certain specific conditions, namely those pertaining a) to the evidence of what cannot be coherently disbelieved and b) to the objectivity of what is uttered.

The thesis that propositions are 'made' true by virtue of 'agreement with' external states of affairs runs into trouble no sooner than *negative* propositions are taken into consideration. To take again an example I gave earlier, if 'This sheet of paper is not green' is true, what exactly is it that 'makes' this proposition true? The fact that the paper is white? Clearly the proposition would be true even if the paper were blue, or any other colour except green. So what extra-propositional fact does the proposition 'map' or 'agree' with? Evidently there is no 'agreement' with anything, and the proposition is true precisely *because* there is none.

Now it might seem that the difficulty presented by negative propositions might be obviated by excluding negation from the relation of 'agreement' (with external fact). After all, it might be said, to assert a negative proposition is just another way of characterising the corresponding positive proposition as *false*. To assert that 'This sheet of paper is not green' is equivalent to claiming that it is false to say that it is green. In other words, rather than implying 'agreement' of the proposition with a 'negative fact' out there, what is being said is simply that *there is no fact for the proposition to agree with*. Negation can thus be eliminated altogether from the 'mapping' relationship between propositions and facts. It follows that there won't be, indeed cannot be, logically basic negative propositions; only *positive* propositions which are either true or false.

This won't work, for the problem has been merely shifted from negation to *falsehood*. Thus the key question for the correspondence theory continues to be: If this piece of paper is not green is false, what 'makes' it false? Certainly not the fact that it is white, for, as we have seen, the paper could be any other colour, or no colour at all; i.e. it is not any specific colour attribute that 'makes' the proposition false, but rather the absence of one. But then clearly there is no alternative but to accept that 'This piece of paper is green' is false for the simple reason that it is *not* green; and this, of course, will bring back the problem of negative propositions — which is precisely what we have been trying to avoid.

Now the reply to this is likely to be that the notion of falsehood is logically ultimate, and is neither capable of, nor does it require a 'definition' in terms of negation. Truth and falsehood, it will be said, are both logically primitive concepts, end of story. But if that is the case, then the correspondence theory is again in trouble, for it is difficult to see how we could avoid having to postulate *false facts* in order to explain what 'makes' a proposition false. In the place of 'negative facts' we would have 'false facts', and nothing much would have been gained in consequence.

The only reasonable option, therefore, seems to be to accept that negation is more fundamental than falsehood, and that it is falsehood that we should try to explain in terms of negation rather than *vice versa*. Falsehood is not a primitive notion; nor can it be treated as logically on a par with truth. The falsehood of p is the truth of not-p. At the same time, the use of negation in an account of falsehood does not necessarily commit us to accepting the existence of 'negative facts'. For on the theory that I have been advancing, negation enters into truth not as part of a state of affairs 'out there' but as part of how we ourselves see things, viz. *as a mode of presentation*. The external states of affairs targeted in truth claims, taken by themselves, are neither 'positive' nor 'negative'. They are *propositionally represented* as positive or negative. If not-p is true, it means that there is a state of affairs such that it forms part of truth just as represented by not-p (with not-p, in addition, being subject to certain objectivity conditions; in accordance with the provisions set out in chapter 5); it does not mean that such a state of affairs exists in the way it is propositionally represented *prior* to, and *independently* of its propositional representation. Propositional representations are not likenesses of certain 'pre-existent' facts; rather they are *interpretations* of certain segments of the extra-propositional world.

(iii) Truth does not exist until it occurs

Finally, a few words must be said about the last of the three propositions mentioned earlier, viz. that truth *does not exist until it occurs*.

Truth, I have argued, is not explicable as a property, either of propositions or of truth claims. To call p 'true' is to say that there exists a state of affairs such that under certain specified conditions it forms part of truth as represented by p. Truth takes place when all the conditions for its occurrence are fulfilled. If the conditions are not fulfilled, then to call p 'true' is an error. But error here is just that: an aberration, an oversight, a blunder — it does not indicate the existence of an 'irreducible' falsehood. For falsehood, in the strict sense, does not exist, only truth does. To describe p as 'false', or claim that the conditions for the occurrence of truth in respect of p are not fulfilled, is merely another way of saying that they are fulfilled in respect of *not*-p.

If this is granted, however, then it is clear that what I called earlier the 'strategy of austerity' (chapter 2) is doomed to failure. One of the main aims of this strategy was to overcome the difficulties which bedevilled the property view of truth by showing that truth predicates were in principle dispensable, and that truth is a logically primitive, simple notion. This entailed dispensing with the misleading idea of 'correspondence', which was an altogether positive result; unhappily it also meant doing away with the distinction between propositions and (extra-propositional) states of affairs, which was anything but helpful.

We saw in the preceding chapter that accounts of *actions* in particular presuppose such a distinction. What is more such a distinction is of fundamental importance to the grasp of truth claims generally. For propositions taken on their own are neither true nor false; rather the question of their truth or falsity arises, and can only arise, in respect of possible truth claims, in which the actual existence is posited of certain states of affairs at which the proposition, or propositions, in question are targeted.

But in addition to this, the 'strategy of austerity' has nothing of any interest to say about the problem of *negative* propositions. Rather the view is that there really is no problem, for — it is argued — the truth of not-p (if not-p is true) reduces to p being false, and since falsehood is a primitive concept, there is nothing further to add. But, as we saw earlier, this is manifestly unsatisfactory, since the converse holds too, viz. the falsehood of p reduces to the truth of not-p, and, as has been shown, it is *negation* that is more fundamental, in as much as it enters directly into the content of truth claims through our 'mode of presentation', whereas falsehood is just a form of error.[6]

It seems, therefore, that the only sensible course of action is to focus on truth claims and explore their semantic structure, with a view to elucidating the conditions of the *occurrence* of truth. If this approach is adopted, however, then it soon becomes evident that there can be no truth without a cognitive agent, and moreover that truth does not, indeed cannot, exist until it occurs. Thus if it is true that this paper is not green, it is true not in virtue of some pre-existent extra-propositional fact 'out there' of its being not green, or in virtue of an irreducible falsehood of the proposition that it is green. Rather it is true because a certain state of affairs 'out there' *enters* into truth, under certain objectivity conditions, through the relevant 'negative' mode of presentation by a cognitive agent, or agents.

The easiest way to illustrate this is with the help of propositions which contain indexical elements, or are directly dependent for their intelligibility upon those which do. Thus that the table is to the left of the book-case qualifies as a candidate for truth provided it can be spelt out as: a) The table is to the left of the book-case from where *I now stand*; or b) If anyone — i.e. any observer or cognitive agent endowed

[6] On the concept of error see my book *The Concept of Reality*, chapters 9 & 14.

with the faculty of spatial discrimination similar to my own — occupied the position x (which may or may not coincide with the position I happen to be at), *they would be able to see* the table to the left of the book-case. Notice that although (b) is a general proposition it nevertheless presupposes an indexical relation between a potential observer and the object observed. Moreover this indexical relation is derived by analogy with my own case. If the table is to the left of the book-case, it is because that is where it is, or would be, relative to myself were I to occupy the relevant position.

But although indexical propositions provide particularly telling examples, the same conditions ultimately apply to all propositions regardless. There is no difference in this respect between 'The book is to the left of the book-case', 'The Earth moves around the Sun' or 'All men are mortal'. No such propositions are true *tout court*; rather they *become* true, or *enter* into truth via respective truth claims, in relation to an observer, or observers, who occupy a specific frame of reference. A reference to an observer, or a potential observer, who is cognitively equipped similarly to ourselves, whether made explicit or not, is a condition of significance of what is being uttered. Independently of any observers no such proposition can be attached any determinate meaning.

The question of truth or falsity arises only on the assumption that it is the *actual world* that is being 'talked about'; and this means only with regard to possible truth claims, in particular those that carry with them — to use the Fregean term again — the 'usual force'. In a sense, any propositional candidate for truth has to be treated as being tacitly prefaced with 'The actual world is such that . . .' or 'is so arranged that . . .' This already hints at the complexity of truth. For a proposition, if true, is not true unconditionally, but becomes true when certain extra-propositional circumstances (under certain objectivity conditions) appear to an observer or cognitive agent exactly as *propositionally articulated* in the relevant judgement. When I claim that the table is to the left of the book-case from where I stand, I am saying that the world being what it is, that is how things are relative to the position I happen to occupy. Similarly when I make a general claim, viz. that if anyone were to occupy position x, they would be able to see the table to the left of the book-case, I am making a second-order claim to the effect that the world is such that were the appropriate truth claim to be made it would yield truth, or would result in an *occurrence* of truth.

Now, of course, the stock riposte to this is that if a truth claim in respect of p results in an 'occurrence' of truth, it is because p is true, not the other way round. Truth does not come 'on and off', depending upon whether someone posits something as true. If the vase on my desk is empty, it does not cease being empty if no-one expresses the relevant thought, let alone makes an actual truth claim to that effect. The table being to the left of the book-case for an observer at position x, does not depend on anyone actually making the claim. If it is true that the Earth moves round the Sun — even if it does so only in respect of an observer occupying a particular frame of reference — this does not cease to be true when no-one believes it does. If p is true, it is true regardless.

But this is a metaphysical bias masquerading as sound sense. The only justification offered for it is that we can understand the *possibility* of p being true even if no-one ever claimed or imagined it to be so. But just what does this mean? Consider the following analogy. A film, as everyone knows, can be stored on a video tape; but to say that a video tape 'contains' a film is to say merely that *if* the tape were to be inserted into the video machine, an observer (with the cognitive faculties similar to our own) would see a film appear on the screen. The tape does not contain pictures *tout court.* It carries certain invisible traces, which *yield* pictures when the tape is run through the machine. Similarly to say that p is true is to say that p *yields* truth in the context of a *truth claim.* Or, to take again our earlier example, to conceive of the possibility of this sheet of paper not being green is to conceive of the possibility of the truth occurring in the context of the relevant judgement. To say that this sheet of paper is not green when no-one makes the relevant judgement is to say that the world is such that *if* somebody (with appropriate cognitive faculties) made the relevant judgement, they would be instrumental in the relevant truth event taking place. It is to make a judgement about how the world (*our* world) works, and such a judgement is *itself subject to the same conditions.* The point is that in the absence of any judgements, the conditions for the occurrence of truth cannot be fulfilled. The idea that the truth of p pre-dates or, for that matter, survives its actual occurrence cannot be given any intelligible meaning.

Theory of truth and philosophical explanation

To sum up, the salient points of my argument may be stated as follows. To provide an account of truth is to provide an account of the conditions that make its occurrence possible. The method of identifying these conditions is through an exploration of the logical structure of truth claims. This yields us a structure of three inter-twining strands; with each strand being a *necessary*, and all of them jointly providing a *sufficient* condition of the occurrence of truth. Thus to make a claim that p is to claim, in the first instance, the existence of a state of affairs external to the relevant act of thought. Next, it is to imply the possibility of unerring knowledge about the *kind* of claim one is making: one cannot coherently make a truth claim that p in the full knowledge of what one is doing while at the same time disbelieve that that is what one intends to assert; or, to put it in another way, if the world appears to me in a particular manner, then I can be *certain* about the manner of its appearance. Finally, what I assert is subject to certain objectivity conditions, which determine the content of what on any given occasion I actually succeed in expressing.

What this shows is that whereas there can be no truth without propositional thought, truth is not 'propositional' in the sense of propositions being its sole vehicles. Truth is an event of which propositions are a feature. To call p 'true' is to claim that there is a state of affairs such that it forms part of the structure of truth as represented by p. If 'true' indicates a property, then it is only in the sense of *being part* of truth; not part of a thing or entity of some sort, but part of an *event*. Truth is neither an entity nor part of an entity. Rather it occurs when all the constituent elements of its structure are in place, and does not exist *until* it occurs.

The immediate reaction to this, as we saw, is to dismiss it on the grounds that it presupposes what it purports to explain. What is being offered, the inevitable objection runs, is an account of the conditions that must be satisfied before truth can take place, not what it means to say, in a given instance, that such conditions are as a matter of fact satisfied. For suppose it is the latter claim that we wish to make. Then it still makes sense to ask: *true* or *false*? And if so, then the tripartite account of truth sketched out above, whilst possibly providing a *criterion* of truth, does not give a full account of its *meaning*.

This objection is misplaced, for this reason. To say that the truth conditions are satisfied in the given instance is just another way of saying that the relevant truth event takes place; or, to express it differently, that the propositional thought p hooks onto reality, or exhibits what is the case. Conversely, if the relevant truth event takes place, then the tripartite truth conditions are satisfied. They are not always satisfied — error is a common enough occurrence — but truth cannot occur unless they are, even if the truth in the given case happens to be that they are not. In short, if the tripartite conditions in respect of a truth claim that p are not satisfied, then a second order truth claim to that effect will have to satisfy the tripartite truth conditions. Hence they are *always* satisfied where truth is concerned, and necessarily so; for that is what being true means. Any attempt to define the 'meaning' of truth beyond this can only lead to a vicious regress.

An account of truth is thus intrinsically reflexive and self-validating, although its reflexivity makes it neither trivial nor unnecessary. It is *not* trivial because the ordinary notion of truth as things being as they are said to be, which we all believe to grasp so readily, turns out to have a complex substructure. Things are as they are said to be only under certain conditions, and it is only by clarifying those conditions that a truth claim can be given substance. At the same time, the demand for such a substantive account is implicit in every truth claim that we make. To bow to this demand is to discharge a fundamental moral imperative. It is also to engage in an exercise in truth, whereby the intricate lacework of fibres is brought to light which hold the world together, and our own role is highlighted in the scheme of things.

Index